The Mass Media and Environmental Issues

Studies in Communication and Society

Series editors: **Ralph Negrine and Anders Hansen**
University of Leicester

Published in this series so far:

The Mass Media and Environmental Issues
Edited by Anders Hansen
TV News, Urban Conflict and the Inner City
Simon Cottle

The Mass Media and Environmental Issues

edited by

Anders Hansen

Leicester University Press
Leicester, London, New York

Distributed exclusively in the USA and Canada by St. Martin's Press

Leicester University Press
(a division of Pinter Publishers Ltd)
25 Floral Street, London, WC2E 9DS

First published in Great Britain 1993
Paperback edition first published 1994

Distributed exclusively in the USA and Canada by St. Martin's Press, Inc.,
Room 400, 175 Fifth Avenue, New York, NY 10010, USA

British Library Cataloguing in Publication Data

A CIP catalogue record for this book is available fromThe British Library

ISBN 0 7185 1444 0 (Hardback)
     0 7185 2053 X (Paperback)

Library of Congress Cataloging-in-Publication Data

The mass media and environmental issues / edited by Anders Hansen.
    p. cm. - (Studies in communication and society)
    Includes bibliographical references and index.
    ISBN 0-7185-1444-0
    1. Mass media and the environment. I. Anders Hansen, 1957-
    II. Series: Studies in communication and society (Leicester, England)
    P96.E57M37 1993
    363.7-dc20   93-3392
                                                                    CIP

Typeset by Saxon Graphic Ltd, Derby
Printed and bound in Great Britain Biddles Ltd of Guildford & King's Lynn

For

Debbie

Contents

Part 2: Messages, meanings and media coverage   105

Part 3: Making sense of mediated environmental meanings   179

List of figures

List of tables

List of contributors

Alison Anderson is a Lecturer at the University of Plymouth. She is particularly interested in the relationship between news sources and media practitioners and has recently completed a doctorate on the production of environmental news. Prior to this, Dr Anderson was a research assistant at Thames Polytechnic and assisted Professor Philip Schlesinger with an ESRC funded project on 'Crime, law and justice and the mass media'.

Jacquelin Burgess is a cultural geographer working in University College London with particular interest in environmental and landscape meanings, mass media and qualitative research. She is writing a book for the UCL Press Social Research Today series, edited by Martin Bulmer, which will be published in 1994. Jacquie Burgess and Carolyn Harrison are currently conducting research funded by the Economic and Social Research Council to explore cross cultural dimensions of public understanding of Global Environmental Change. Dr Burgess has worked as a consultant on projects associated with place marketing, and landscape documentaries for BBC1 and Channel 4.

John Corner is Senior Lecturer in Communication Studies at the University of Liverpool. He has written widely on media topics and on aspects of cultural analysis. Together with Jeremy Hawthorn he edited *Communication Studies: An Introductory Reader* (Arnold, 4th Edition, 1993) and his other publications include the edited collections *Documentary and the Mass Media* (Arnold, 1986) and *Popular Television in Britain* (BFI, 1991), as well as many book chapters and journal articles. With Kay Richardson and Natalie Fenton he wrote a study of television treatments of nuclear energy, *Nuclear Reactions* (John Libbey 1990) and he is currently working on a book about television and changes in political, ethical and aesthetic values. He is an editor of the journal *Media, Culture and Society*.

Simon Cottle is a Lecturer in sociology and mass communications at Bath College of Higher Education. His research interests include the sociology of journalism and news production with particular reference to the portrayal of social problems. His study *TV News, Urban Conflict and the Inner City* is also published this year by Leicester University Press. He is currently writing an undergraduate mass media text, and designing Masters courses on 'Media and the "Troubles" in Northern Ireland' and 'Media and Health Promotion'.

Eileen Coughlan has a BA in Psychology and is completing her Master's degree in the Graduate Program in Communications at the University of Calgary. Her research interests focus on the use of humour in the communication of sensitive topics.

Jon Cracknell read Social and Political Science at the University of Cambridge before following the MA in Mass Communications at the Centre for Mass Communication Research, University of Leicester in 1990–91. He now works for Bryceson Goodhart, a London-based political consultancy which works on both environmental and non-environmental issues.

Sharon Dunwoody is Evjue-Bascom Professor of Journalism and Mass Communication and is on the instructional staff of the Institute of Environmental Studies at the University of Wisconsin-Madison. She is also head of the Center for Environmental Communications and Education Studies, which conducts research on various aspects of communicating science to the public. Her research interests include understanding all aspects of mass media communication of scientific and technological information, from the behaviours of sources and journalists through to the coping strategies of information consumers. She also does research more generally on the sociology of journalists. Her most recent studies have focused on various dimensions of risk communication. In 1986 she coedited a book (with Sharon M. Friedman and Carol L. Rogers) titled *Scientists and Journalists*, dealing with relationships between reporters and sources. Her work has appeared in *Journalism Quarterly, Journal of Communication, Newspaper Research Journal* and in science-and-society journals such as *Science, Technology & Human Values*.

Edna Einsiedel is a Professor of Communication Studies in the Faculty of General Studies, University of Calgary, where she also serves as Director of the Graduate Program in Communications. Her research interests are in the area of science literacy and science communications. She has conducted studies in the areas of health and environmental communications in North American and third world contexts. Her studies have been supported by the Social Science and Humanities Research Council of Canada, Industry Science and Technology Canada.

Robert J. Griffin is Associate Professor in the College of Communication, Journalism and Performing Arts at Marquette University in Milwaukee, Wisconsin USA. He is Director of the school's Center for Mass Media Research and former Director of the Graduate Program in Journalism. He earned his PhD in Mass Communications (specializing in theory and behavioural scientific research methodology) and his MA in Journalism (with emphasis in environmental communications) from the University of Wisconsin-Madison. With Sharon Dunwoody, he has been conducting research into various aspects of press coverage of health risks from local environmental contamination, funded by a grant from the United States Environmental Protection Agency. He has also done research and published articles concerning other aspects of environmental and energy communication. He recently co-authored chapters on news coverage of environment, science and energy issues in Griffin, Molen, Schoenfeld and Scotton (eds), *Interpreting Public Issues* (Iowa State University Press, 1991), a textbook for advanced reporting courses.

Anders Hansen is a Lecturer in mass communications at the Centre for Mass Communication Research, University of Leicester. His main research interests include science communication, journalistic practices and media roles in relation to science and environmental issues. His work in these areas has been supported by the Economic and Social Research Council. He is currently conducting a study, funded by the European Commission, of press coverage of the Human Genome Project. He is the convenor of an international working group on environmental issues and the mass media, which has met during the last three biennial Conferences of the International Association for Mass Communication Research.

Carolyn Harrison is a biogeographer in the Department of Geography, University College London. She has extensive research experience, consultancies and publications in biogeography, ecology, nature conservation and countryside recreation. Her most recent book *Countryside Recreation in a Changing Society* (London: TMS Partnership) was published in 1991. Dr Harrison is a member of the MAB/UK Urban Forum; Chair of Growth Unlimited, a voluntary environmental group based in Camden, and a board member of the London Ecology Centre.

Olga Linné is Senior Lecturer at the Centre for Mass Communication Research, University of Leicester. She has recently completed (with Anders Hansen) an international project on environmental issues and the broadcast media. This continues to be one of her main interests. She is a Vice-President of the International Association for Mass Communication Research (IAMCR).

Stig Arne Nohrstedt, PhD, is director of the Communication and Public Relations Programme, University of Örebro, Sweden. He has published extensively on communication processes and media roles during the radioactive fallout in Sweden following the Chernobyl accident. His main research interests are crisis communication, news journalism and war reporting.

Kay Richardson is a Lecturer in the School of Politics and Communication Studies at the University of Liverpool. She is co-author of *Researching Language: issues of power and method*, and of *Nuclear Reactions – form and response in public issue television*. She is currently working towards a book dealing with representations of poverty on British television. Her research is in the area of political discourse and its mediation in the press and on television, as well as the field of television audience research with specific reference to documentary programming.

James Shanahan received his PhD from the University of Massachusetts in 1991. He is currently an assistant professor in the College of Communication at Boston University. In addition to research interests in the environmental area, he has published about media effects on democracy, media in Latin America, and health issues.

Introduction

Anders Hansen

In the relatively short history of 'the environment' as a social problem, public and political concern has gone up and down in cycles. Roughly sketched the trend started with a tremendous acceleration in the 1960s, continuing into the very early part of the 1970s, and then declining and settling for a period into the 1980s. This was followed by a considerable surge again in the mid-to-late 1980s, followed by what looks to be a downward trend in the beginning of the 1990s, as concern about the environment has given way to concerns about economic recession, unemployment, the Maastricht treaty, and major political developments around the world, including the break up of the communist bloc, the war in the Gulf, and the civil war in the former Yugoslavia.

Although the environment occasionally and spectacularly draws attention to itself in the form of major disasters and accidents, environmental problems by and large depend for their public visibility on complex processes of claims-making activity. The ups and downs of public and political concern about the environment are a poor indicator of the state and nature of environmental degradation. What they tell us instead is something about the political processes which facilitate, accommodate and enable the temporary prominence of certain concerns in what Hilgartner and Bosk (1988) have called the public arenas. Following a constructivist approach, the prominence of certain social issues, at certain times, is relatively (although not exclusively) independent of the severity of such issues (as measured for example by science). Nor does their fall from prominence in these arenas necessarily signal that the issues have been successfully resolved. It may simply be that they have been overtaken, and perhaps squeezed out altogether, by other, newer, issues – in public arenas which are all characterised principally by 'limited carrying capacities', be they the mass media, the courts, or the parliamentary political process.

It is one thing to observe and trace the ups and downs in public concern about the environment, in political attention to environmental issues, or in media coverage of the environment. This gives us some clues to and insight into 'environmental issues' *vis à vis* other significant issue areas, such as poverty (although many would argue that 'poverty' is, or should be, considered as an environmental issue), homelessness, education, the health service, AIDS, etc.

It is another and perhaps more instructive thing to consider the significant changes over time in the range, type, and nature of the issues which, as an aggregate, constitute public and political discourse on 'the environment'. That the environment and environmental issues should mean different things to different publics is not in itself particularly surprising – that would probably be the case regardless of issue area, although, clearly, some issue-areas allow a much greater discursive diversity than others. What is significant, however, is to understand the processes which – relatively independently of the nature and severity of environmental problems – lead to certain environmental issues becoming the 'dominant' issues at certain times, issues which in turn become short-hand referents, icons, or even allegorical representations of the environment.

The reason why the changes in distribution over time of individual environmental problems, as discussed in public arenas, is a useful quarry for research is not simply, or even primarily, to do with their relationship with 'real' (as opposed to discursive) environmental problems. Rather, it is to do with the way in which their elaboration and maintenance in public arenas offer insights into the power of different groupings in society to define what should be the focus of public concern, action, and, ultimately, resource-allocation.

It is noticeable for instance how 'the environment' has for some considerable time been defined in the public sphere largely in terms of anything nuclear (nuclear power, nuclear radiation, nuclear waste, and nuclear weapons), in terms of 'pollution', and in terms of conservation/protection of endangered species. Geographically, the public arenas discourse on the environment has been very Western oriented – with little or no emphasis on the enormity of environmental problems facing Third World countries. But the geographic orientation of the environmental debate has been changing significantly during the recent years and has veered toward more global issues, such as Global Warming, the hole in the ozone layer, the Greenhouse Effect etc. In Britain, a shift toward focusing on global aspects of environmental issues, has served as a politically expedient way of deflecting attention away from the pressing environmental problems on Britain's doorstep (most significantly, in relation to fellow members of the European Community and neighbouring European countries attacking Britain for its slow response to problems of sulphur-emissions from British coal-fired power plants contributing to acid rain and associated problems in Scandinavia and other parts of Northern Europe, and in relation to pollution of the North Sea and the Irish Sea).

Notably absent, or very low-profile, in the public discourse on environmental issues have been environmental dimensions of the North-South divide and of the dependency-relationship between the industrialised West and the developing countries of the Third World. Equally surprising has been the virtual absence from environmental issues discussion of the rapid development in bio-genetics with its dual potential for spectacular progress (in terms of diagnosing, preventing, and curing many genetically inherited diseases) and spectacular disaster. As Plein (1991), Nelkin (1987) and others have demonstrated, the problematisation of biotechnology and genetic engineering in the mid-1970s – problematisation which, characteristically for so many issues with an environmental dimension, arose from within the scientific community itself (see for example Strodthoff, Hawkins and Schoenfeld, 1985) – had, by the early 1980s, given way to a largely economic discourse on biotechnology, focusing on the great scientific promise and economic potential of such technology. A debate about the potentially considerable dangers of biotechnology and the release of genetically modified organisms into the environment has remained very low-profile throughout the 1980s and into the beginning of the 1990s. While 'disaster' researchers predict (see Quarantelli, 1989) that the next major disaster/catastrophe is more likely to happen in the area of genetic engineering than in relation to nuclear power or accidents involving nuclear weapons, the major environmental pressure groups have kept a conspicuously low profile on issues of biotechnology and genetically modified organisms. One reason for this may well, as Eyerman and Jamison (1989) have suggested, be the inherent complexity and considerable scientific uncertainty associated with these issues.

The aim of this book is to show how communication research has contributed to our understanding of the wider social role played by the mass media and related communication processes in the elaboration of the environment as a problem for public and political concern. How far has the rise of the environment on the political agenda been brought about by the mass media? To what extent are the mass media an important or significant agent in the general political process? How far is mass media coverage of the environment structured by the economic context of the media, by the professional norms and practices of journalists, by news values, and by the strategies of information management adopted by the major actors on the environmental stage? Who gets to define what environmental issues are about? How do the mass media contribute to policing the boundaries of public debate about the environment? How do mediated images contribute to the formation of public opinion? In what ways do different publics draw on media representations for making sense of environmental issues? These are among the key questions addressed by the contributors. The contributions are structured around the three main domains of inquiry into communication processes: the *production* of environmental coverage, the *content* of media coverage, and the *audiences* for media coverage of environmental issues.

In the first chapter, Jon Cracknell discusses the role played by the mass media, environmental pressure groups and the civil service in the elaboration of environmental issues. Taking his point of departure in Hilgartner and Bosk's analysis of public arenas and in Solesbury's classic analysis of the process of environmental policy-making, Cracknell examines the differentiated nature of interactions between the mass media and the civil service, and the symbiotic, yet problematic, relationship between environmental groups and the mass media. His analysis points to the need to differentiate meticulously between different types of issues as well as between different types of environmental groups ('insider' and 'outsider' groups). Drawing on insights into the theorising of 'the social construction of the environment' as well as on the practical experiences of environmental campaigners and groups, Cracknell presents a strong argument for the targeting of multiple arenas combined with a clear sense of political 'timing' in the process of environmental issues campaigning.

Sharon Dunwoody and Robert Griffin offer a detailed analysis of journalistic strategies and press coverage of long-term environmental issues. Unusually for studies of media coverage of environmental issues, they are able to examine the wider contexts which circumscribe and influence such reporting. Through three carefully executed case-studies they are able to show how the coverage of long-term environmental problems can be understood through: the mental maps or frames which journalists routinely deploy as interpretative filters, through the occupational norms of journalists, and through an understanding of the type of community in which the newspapers operate. Dunwoody and Griffin show how the reporting of environmental problems in regional/local newspapers is framed by official bureaucracies and influenced by the prevailing power structure in the communities served by such papers, but perhaps most significant is their finding that environmental risk stories tend to be reported, not in terms of risk, but as stories about how community problems are solved.

Several of the points raised in Chapter 1 are followed up in detail in subsequent chapters. The concept and role of 'primary definers' – those individuals and institutional representatives who are accessed in media coverage and who help frame and define not only what the issues are but also, and more importantly, the terms of reference for their discussion – is a prominent focus for several chapters. In her chapter, Alison Anderson critically examines the conventional notion of primary definers in media coverage. She argues that this concept, with its focus on the voices which actually appear in media content, is too limited because it ignores the complex process of negotiation and conflict which often precedes the appearance of primary definers in the media. Drawing on her study of the publicity practices of major environmental groups as well as government departments she demonstrates the complex and very different approaches adopted even within groups of primary definers which might otherwise have been viewed as part of the same camp.

Olga Linné discusses the differences between Danish and British television journalists in their coverage of environmental issues, and, more specifically, in their perception of the environmental pressure group Greenpeace as a news source. Like Alison Anderson in the preceding chapter, she takes issue with Stuart Hall's classic definition of primary definers and argues for a view of primary definition which is sensitive to historical changes as well as to cultural differences. The differences between Danish and British journalists in their attitude to Greenpeace – as a source of environmental news and comment – must, she argues, be seen as one of change over time and in the context of the different cultural climate *vis à vis* environmental issues in Denmark and Britain.

Drawing on the influential work of Jürgen Habermas, Stig Arne Nohrstedt offers an insightful examination of the legitimation and communication problems associated with the communication of environmental information, and with the management of disaster and risk information in the modern 'risk society'. His extensive studies of communication processes, legitimation crises, and risk management in Sweden following the radioactive contamination from the Chernobyl accident form the anchoring point for his discussion of the construction and handling of risk information. The problematic and conflict-laden interaction of those institutions and centres of 'expert' knowledge who are charged with the production and management of risk information, and their interplay with media and various publics, are mapped out and discussed against the background of both public relations theory and Habermas's theory of communicative action.

While the chapters in Part 1 are primarily concerned with the production-side of the communication process, the chapters in Part 2 focus on actual media coverage – on the content-side of mass media communication of environmental issues. Simon Cottle, in his chapter on the modalities of television news, offers a rare – in communication research generally, as well as in research on media coverage of environmental issues more specifically – comparison of regional and national television news coverage. From a careful analysis of not just the broad types of environmental issues covered in national and regional television news, but also of the actors accessed and the televisual formats deployed, Cottle unpacks the considerable differences which exist across different forms of television news programming. While Nohrstedt draws on Habermas's theory of communicative action, it is to Habermas's work on 'the public sphere' that Cottle turns for a framework for understanding the mediation of the environment in television news programming. Working his way from a general content-analytic mapping through to a more qualitative examination of narrative and televisual formats, Cottle demonstrates how news coverage of the environment is not merely a question of the provision of environmental 'information' but that it works also at a deeper cultural level which engages deep-seated popular beliefs about nature and the environment.

In the following chapter, the focus shifts from television to the press. Edna Einsiedel and Eileen Coughlan position themselves firmly within a constructivist framework which sees press coverage of the environment as the product of the complex interactions of organisational constraints, professional practices and norms, news-values, cultural resonances, and claims-making activity. Combining an analysis of press coverage of environmental issues with an analysis of environmental reporters, Einsiedel and Coughlan outline some of the mixture of organisational constraints and more subjective characteristics of reporters which circumscribe and influence the nature of environmental press coverage. They complement this analysis with a longitudinal study of headline-references to environmental topics to show not only the significant shifts which have taken place since the 1970s in environmental topic-emphases, but also in the headline-language deployed in environmental coverage. This, they argue, reveals an increasing emphasis on the global nature of environmental problems and on a more holistic view of the environment, both paralleled by an increasing emphasis on the environment as a social problem of some urgency.

In the next chapter, Hansen offers a longitudinal analysis of British press coverage of an environmental pressure group whose name has become a cultural short-hand for anything 'green' or 'environmental', namely Greenpeace. Charting the press coverage of Greenpeace and other environmental groups over a five-year period, he focuses on the agenda-building strategies and power of Greenpeace – the extent to which this highly successful pressure group has been able to influence both the amount of coverage and the frames of debate. The analysis reveals the closely parallel 'ups' and 'downs' of coverage across different newspapers – a finding which itself points to the ability to influence media attention – but it also shows that the degree of prominence which Greenpeace is capable of securing across different environmental topics is highly variable. Drawing on theories of news production and of the media and social movements, this chapter further shows that while the agenda-building potential and power of Greenpeace may be variable, the group has been remarkably successful both in terms of deflecting scrutiny away from itself as an organisation and in terms of increasingly securing and maintaining its position as a legitimate and authoritative primary definer in environmental debate. It is argued that this has been achieved principally through an 'alliance with science' and through astutely engaging with developments in news fora which already enjoy routine media-attention.

In Part 3, the focus shifts to the third major dimension of the classic communication process model: the audience. In Chapter 9, James Shanahan addresses the role of television in the development, maintenance and change of public attitudes and beliefs with regard to the environment. Drawing on the well-established 'cultivation-approach' developed by George Gerbner and his colleagues at the University of Pennsylvania, Shanahan explores the relationship between television viewing and environmental concern. He argues that while the mass media are often seen as a potentially major factor in increasing people's awareness of environmental problems, there is good reason from research on related topics to believe that the cumulative influence of television viewing may hamper rather than encourage environmental concern. In his longitudinal study of television viewing and environmental concern, Shanahan does indeed find some confirmation for this suggestion: despite overall increasing levels of environmental concern, viewers who are more heavily exposed to television consistently express lower levels of concern about the environment.

The macro-level analysis of cultivation research is complemented in the following chapter, by Jacquelin Burgess and Carolyn Harrison, by a rather different approach to analysing and understanding the construction of environmental meanings. Starting from a review of developments in the conceptualisation of media audiences, and the turn to ethnographic and qualitative approaches to the study of media audiences and meaning construction, Burgess and Harrison offer a detailed case-study of the claims-making process in relation to plans for a commercial development (theme park, film studios, housing etc.) of a marshland area officially designated as a nature conserva-tion area. Through their detailed analysis of the claims-making and motives of the major actors involved, Burgess and Harrison demon-strate the central role of the local media in particular as an arena for the circulation and inflection of claims relating to the proposed development. Resonating with arguments in some of the earlier chapters (Dunwoody and Griffin; Cottle), the important differences between national and local media are shown. Burgess and Harrison proceed with an examination of how local people in the area affected by the proposed development make sense of and interpret the issues. The study confirms the overwhelming dominance of contextually defined and locally anchored knowledge, rather than media images and messages, as the framework within which sense is made of the claims circulated by different sets of actors.

The problems of researching the role of the mass media in relation to environmental claims-making and, more generally, in relation to the construction of meanings around environmental issues are the focus of the last chapter by John Corner and Kay Richardson. Using examples from their research on how viewers make sense of and interpret nuclear power issues from their representation on television, Corner and Richardson outline a number of key dimensions which, they argue, are important for the mediation of nuclear power and environmental issues more generally. These include: the role of expert/scientific knowledge and discourse; the symbolic resonances invoked in much environmental coverage (activating deep-seated cultural classifications such as 'nature', 'growth', 'dirt' and 'death'); and the varied interpretative frames (personal, political, evidential, civic, etc.) which are brought into play by viewers at different points of the interpretative process.

Methodologically Corner and Richardson are strong advocates of detailed micro-level analysis which pays careful attention to both textual analysis (the construction of meaning in media content) and 'qualitative' audience research (the audience construction of meaning from or in relation to, or in the context of, media texts), but they also caution against the type of 'qualitative' audience research which does little more than read respondents' remarks at face value. While making a case for detailed micro-level analysis as the key to uncovering how viewers construct meaning from media texts, they also recognise the need for such analysis to be anchored within the wider context of factors influencing the production of environmental media content. Corner and Richardson thus offer a number of suggestions about, not only the conceptualisation of audience and media in what Burgess and Harrison in the previous chapter call 'the circulation of claims' and environmental meanings, but also for the specific dimensions which may help develop the study of mass mediated images and their contribution to the social construction of environmental meanings.

References

Eyerman, R., & Jamison, A. (1989), 'Environmental knowledge as an organizational weapon: the case of Greenpeace', *Social Science Information*, *28*(1), 99-119.

Hilgartner, S., & Bosk, C. L. (1988), 'The rise and fall of social problems: a public arenas model', *American Journal of Sociology*, 94(1), 53-78.

Nelkin, D. (1987), '*Selling science: how the press covers science and technology.*', New York: W H Freeman & Company.

Plein, L. C. (1991), 'Popularising biotechnology: The influence of issue definition', *Science, Technology, & Human Values*, 16(4), 474-90.

Quarantelli, E. L. (1989), 'The social science study of disasters and mass communication', in L. M. Walters, L. Wilkins, & T. Walters (Eds.), *Bad tidings: communication and catastrophe* Hillsdale, New Jersey: Lawrence Erlbaum Associates.

Strodthoff, G. G., Hawkins, R. P., & Schoenfeld, A. C. (1985), 'Media roles in a social movement', *Journal of Communication*, 35(2), 134-53.

Part 1:

Building the environmental agenda

1
Issue arenas, pressure groups and environmental agendas

Jon Cracknell

The emphasis in this chapter is on the impact of environmental media coverage. The approach taken is perhaps more political and less media-centred than that adopted by some of the other contributors. My concern is with the following kinds of questions. Do 'environment pages' in the quality press precipitate significant changes in environmental policy? Have features in women's magazines led to less environmentally damaging behaviour on the part of consumers? Do environmental pressure groups devote too much time to media-related campaigning? Is media coverage always a blessing for environmentalists, or can it have adverse effects too? In short, does environmental media coverage achieve very much in terms of mitigating environmental damage?

I cannot pretend that this chapter can answer any of these questions in a conclusive way, indeed it is likely that this can never be achieved. Instead what I hope to do is to illuminate some of the issues which those seeking to influence political decision-making on the environment encounter. These are relevant issues for communications researchers working in the environmental field, as they lie in the crucial interstice between theoretical analysis and practical application.

Much of what is said here will necessarily be conditional, for while there are effective and ineffective ways to campaign on environmental and other social issues it is not possible to describe one standard strategy that will fit all issues. Successful campaigning requires lateral thinking and flexibility. Ultimately, however, preserving our environment means changing behaviour, whether this is by means of changed government policy, public education or any other route. The mass media has a potentially important role to play here, as do mass communications researchers. One way in which the latter can contribute is by trying to articulate theory (which has the benefit of 'distance') with practice (which refuses to fit into neat models or frameworks). It is with this kind of endeavour in mind that this chapter has been written. In what follows I have concentrated exclusively on the United Kingdom, partly for reasons of space, but also because a culturally specific approach is necessary if one is going to consider the role of the media in the policy-making process, a point made clearly by Hansen and Linné (1986).

Theoretical concepts

In order to explore the links between environmental media coverage and environmental policy-making I intend to draw loosely on Stephen Hilgartner and Charles Bosk's (1988) 'public arenas model' and on Solesbury's (1976) study of environmental pressure. These two pieces of research provide a number of concepts which are useful when considering the impact of environmental media coverage.

Hilgartner and Bosk's model concentrates, as its name implies, on the 'arenas' through which social problems become defined and are brought to society's attention. A brief list of arenas relevant to the environmental movement in the United Kingdom might include: the mass media; the civil service; both Houses of Parliament; institutions of the European Community; the courts and public enquiries; industry; the high street; the research and scientific community; the education system; political parties; and the Trades Unions. The sponsors of social problems ('issue entrepreneurs') make use of these arenas in order to establish visibility for the issues with which they are concerned. In doing so they compete against the sponsors of other issues, for the total size of the social and political agenda at any one time is limited by the 'carrying capacities' of the arenas from which it is composed. They also compete with those in the same policy field who may have different interpretations of the issues. Issue entrepreneurs hope that by propelling their problems up the agenda of relevant arenas they may invoke the action which is required to ameliorate them.

This description of the context in which social problems are discussed resonates well with reality, where arenas do have 'principles of selection', 'carrying capacities', marked cultural and temporal characteristics, etc. It is limited, however, by the fact that Hilgartner and Bosk concentrate, quite consciously, on the processes which lead to the 'collective definition' of social problems, rather than those which account for the 'collective action' that might ameliorate them. Their focus lies with arenas in which the primary goal is attracting attention, and their framework is consequently most valuable when applied to the mass media. Although they identify the importance of the interactions between different arenas, they do not attempt to unpack these connections.

One also has to be careful about treating 'the mass media' as one arena. The media is perhaps more accurately thought of as a set of arenas, each of which has distinct differences in terms of the audience it can reach, the selection principles which govern it, its political significance, etc. Thus environmental documentaries on television may select very different topics, and perform a very different role, from quality press coverage of a specific dispute. The media is also different from other arenas in that we come to know what happens in many societal arenas via the media. In many senses the media and politics merge, and effective use of the media has become a requirement of political success in many societies.

A further drawback to the Hilgartner and Bosk model is that it fails to resolve the problem of the temporal development of issues. The authors are quite right to criticize models of social problem development which employ rigid 'natural history' formulations, whereby issues are perceived as going through a common cycle of birth, maturation and death, etc. Such models fail to reflect the diversity of temporal development of social issues as well as the crucial importance of interactions between different problems.

Against this, however, one has to recognize that at different times in an issue's life different strategies are required in order to take it forward. This recognition is well made by Solesbury (1976), who identifies three tasks with which issue entrepreneurs must engage in order to achieve a satisfactory resolution of their concerns. These tasks are 'commanding attention', 'claiming legitimacy', and 'invoking action'. Solesbury correctly points out that the tasks need not be pursued in any particular order, indeed issue entrepreneurs may be engaged in two or more of them simultaneously. Each may require the use of different arenas, or alternatively of different tactics within the same arena (see Blumer, 1971). Much of the skill of successful issue entrepreneurship lies in identifying which arenas one should be employing and how their effect can be maximized (Jordan, 1989). Multi-arena activity and a flexibility of approach is as essential in environmental campaigning as with any other type of campaign. This is dealt with in more detail later on.

Using mass media arenas

Environmental organizations have traditionally been heavy users of the media and this is reflected in the considerable amount of communications research dedicated to environmental coverage. Major environmental pressure groups tend to have staff who are experienced in the production of stories and in supplying information to journalists. The issues on which the groups choose to campaign are undoubtedly influenced by considerations of likely coverage. This is important as it can mean that 'non-sexy' and unmediagenic subjects are targeted less than those with instant media appeal, regardless of the intrinsic importance of the issues in question.

Some explanations for the symbiosis between environmentalists and the mass media

To follow are some of the factors which account for the media-orientation of environmental groups.

Environmental issues are often mediagenic, the stories they provide frequently have good pictures and can be conveniently symbolized, for example, seabirds stranded in oilslicks, the menacing shape of a nuclear power plant (see Gamson and Modigliani, 1989 or Corner, Richardson & Fenton, 1990). In addition to the televisuality of the natural world environmental journalists can take advantage both of audience fear and of the attraction of local conflict (for example, residents oppose a new development proposal). All of these aspects of environmental campaigning conform well with the selection principles of mass media arenas.

Environmental problems quite often become visible through disasters, which tend to conform to the news value criteria that are an important selection principle in the media arena.

Environmental campaigning often has a surface consensuality which is attractive to media practitioners, it can appear to be less overtly threatening in political terms than the claims of other social problems groupings, as for example the poverty lobby. The differing experiences of Des Wilson[1] at SHELTER[2] and Friends of the Earth testify to the impact which the presence of an issue in one arena has on its treatment in another: the fact that homelessness was conspicuously political in both party and ideological terms counted against those trying to command attention for it, whereas the 'apple-pie' nature of environmentalism did not present this threat.

Early environmentalists lacked the contacts which might have made low-profile campaigning effective and thus felt they had little option but to resort to publicity-seeking. This trend was allied to an anti-establishment and 'alternative' orientation within the environment movement, and to a fondness for visually amusing and eye-catching 'stunts'.

These explanations for the symbiosis between the environment movement and the practitioners of mass media arenas are by no means exhaustive. However, they do help to indicate why there is often a sympathy for environmentalism on the part of the media, with a concurrent media-consciousness on the part of environment groups.

But what effect does it have?

The remainder of this chapter is taken up with consideration of the effects of environmental media coverage. First the situation is considered in relation to the three tasks identified by Solesbury (1976), 'commanding attention', 'claiming legitimacy', and 'invoking action'.

Commanding attention

Many social problem sponsors spend a good deal of their time trying to command attention. In looking for publicity, campaigners may be trying to achieve a number of things. They may be hoping to draw attention to issues which might otherwise be ignored, they may be offering alternative interpretations of particular situations, and they will be attempting to establish a profile and an image for the organization they represent. All these activities are worthwhile and essential parts of most campaigns, with a key rationale for the last goal being that of financial support.

It is important to remember that groups are competing to have their names mentioned in media reports not only because this provides them with credibility in the eyes of policy-makers but also because visibility leads to new members. In the UK a reduction in the level of environmental coverage following a burst of interest in green issues (between 1988 and 1990) has resulted in a marked decline in the funding of some of the larger environmental groups. The fact that campaigning organizations are competing for supporters leads to attempts at differentiation within the environmental movement so that varied markets can be effectively tapped. It can also lead to a lack of cooperation on joint projects as different organizations can become jealously protective of what they see as their territory or approach. Some consequences of this are discussed further below.

Claiming legitimacy

The very act of achieving media coverage can result in credibility for the organization concerned, although this is likely to be dependent in part on the media format. If an environmental group's research is taken as credible by a journalist and is actively compared with that produced by government or industry then this tends to help legitimize the environmental group's findings. What is happening is that the journalist is conferring a degree of their own legitimacy, which they hold by virtue of position or reputation, onto the sponsors of the issue in question.

In a similar way a cumulative build-up of media coverage on a set of related social problems can act both to stimulate and to reflect shifts in public opinion. In the United Kingdom a seminal speech by Prime Minister Margaret Thatcher in September 1988 helped to trigger a wave of media interest in green issues. The Thatcher speech conferred a new degree of political legitimacy on the environment movement (via a political arena) and this was diffused through many other arenas with the assistance of the mass media. In other situations environmental (or frequently 'man-made') disasters have had a similar trigger effect, with the result being a snowballing of column inches and airtime. Legitimization of the kind just referred to can play a very important role in moving environmental issues from the fringe of political arenas to a more central position. Policy options that were once considered politically unacceptable, as for example carbon taxing, road pricing, etc., have thus achieved a new credibility.

But while the mass media can play a crucial role in conferring legitimacy they can also act as very powerful delegitimizing agents. One of the key problems for environmental organizations stems from a conflict between the need to command attention and the need to claim legitimacy. This problem is clearly described by Greenberg (1985) and it is returned to later on.

Invoking action

Most campaigns are undertaken in the hope that action will be invoked, although the structure of the campaign is likely to differ radically depending on the action being sought. Indeed the selection of appropriate arenas and tactics must be made on the basis of a sensitive understanding of the benefits and drawbacks of the various possibilities. The audience at whom the campaign is targeted will also play a crucial and determining role with regard to strategy.

Consumer oriented campaigning

There is no doubt that mass media coverage can lead to changes in consumer behaviour. The rise of green consumerism in the UK in response to the wave of media interest mentioned earlier provides a clear indication of the mass media acting as a channel between the arena of the high street and various others. Changes in shopping habits undoubtedly have a part to play in halting environmental degradation, both via knock-on effects spreading out from the high street into other parts of society and by providing a first step on the road to changes in individual behaviour.

Having said this, the change in behaviour required is arguably of negligible cost to the consumer. 'Environmentally sound' products may cost more at the till but they offer benefits in terms of self-esteem and peer approval, thus the balance is redressed and the overall cost is low. Persuading consumers that they should not just switch from one brand to another, but that they should consciously consume less is another matter altogether. Here the political ramifications are considerably more significant, both for producers and consumers. Non-demanding changes of behaviour may result in peer approval but more radical actions can quickly lead to peer rejection. For example, if one gives up one's car and insists on always cycling then one may become vulnerable to negative rather than positive stereo-typing, the same is not likely to be true if one chooses to purchase a car running on unleaded fuel.

While the mass media may play a seminal role in inspiring superficial changes in consumer behaviour there is less evidence to show that more active environmentalism can be engendered. Authors such as Wiebe (1971), Sandman (1974), Draper (1987), McMillan (1988), and Stearn (1988) all cast doubt on the media's power to provoke significant lifestyle changes without the help of other agencies. Wiebe points to the danger of 'well-informed futility' as a consequence of environmental coverage, and Draper makes similar points about the passivity-reinforcing qualities of television. Stearn comments that 'mass education via the media falls short of what is needed to change people's habits; viewing a programme does not lead to action to get a car retuned to run on unleaded petrol. The television producers know it and the environmental organisations know it' (1988, p. 20).

Not only is there the suspicion that mass media coverage is limited in terms of the degree of empowerment it can engender. In addition the cyclical nature of media interest in social issues can contribute to a transiency in terms of behaviour change. To some degree each wave of media interest breaks higher up the shore, with a residual and cumulative effect in terms of the development of awareness. But it is also the case that changed behaviour can rapidly revert to prior behaviour once the media spotlight is diverted elsewhere, with the most costly changes being those that are most vulnerable to such transience.

Government oriented campaigning

The legitimizing effect of mass media interest on social problems has already been mentioned. By alerting governmental institutions to public interest in environmental issues the mass media undoubtedly helps to push environmental concerns up the political agenda. But there is a significant difference between simply commanding atten-tion and the politicization of specific policy decisions which have environmental consequences. One of the difficulties which has been faced by environmental pressure groups has been to manage these different tasks.

The most effective use of the media as a campaigning tool is often when the issue in question involves a clear decision. Here the media can help to produce focused rather than diffuse pressure. Focused pressure counts to politicians, as the law of anticipated reaction is a crucial factor in generating political will-power. It is for this reason that environmental media coverage can often be particularly effective at a local level, for example residents demonstrating against a polluting factory. This kind of coverage is very different from that which indicates a general enthusiasm for environmental protection. That this difference between focused and diffuse political pressure matters can be seen if one considers the fate of environmental issues on the national electoral stage. In the UK during the general election in April 1992 there was much lamenting of the fact that the environment failed to appear on the media agenda in any major way, despite the wave of interest which has been described above. This can be explained largely by the fact that no parliamentary seat in the UK was likely to change hands as a result of environmental issues. Diffuse media coverage in the period between the elections indicated that the public was in favour of environmental improvement, but the public is also in favour of better health care, increased employment, improved education, etc. When the competition for attention between competing policy demands is temporarily heightened then interest demonstrated by diffuse media coverage can be easily pushed to one side.

This is not to suggest that all one requires for political success is focused media coverage. As Simon Bryceson[3] put it,

Civil servants would regard media coverage of environmental issues as being emotive rather than informative, so in that sense they're quite hostile to it from the word go. The politicians of some influence in the United Kingdom, i.e. the Conservative politicians, would regard coverage by TV, and indeed the major national newspapers, as being likely to have been produced by people who were hostile to them politically, and overly sympathetic to the environmental groups who had fixed up the photo-opportunity or whatever it was. In addition to which, the Department of the Environment is actively aware, and maintains a watching brief, on what all the environmental groups are doing, so it's very difficult to coordinate or provoke media coverage of an environmental issue without the DoE knowing who provoked it and why. So the chances of them seeing something on the television or reading it in the paper and saying "I say chaps, we ought to do something about this" are virtually zero. (Bryceson, 1991)

It is to suggest, however, that targeted media coverage which respects the political dimensions of a particular situation is qualitatively different from more diffuse awareness-raising. The next section is concerned with the civil service as an arena, and looks at some of the consequences of executive action for media coverage of the environment.

The civil service as an arena

Inertia

Bureaucracies in general are characterized by inertia. They tend to seek continuity, and as a result pressure is required in order to make them act. Hilgartner and Bosk rightly point out that government departments are faced with requests for attention and resources from many competing social problems. As Miller (1987, p. 98) puts it, 'pressure groups are called just that because officials prefer to maintain the status quo rather than involve their Department – and possibly a number of others – in the time, expense, and disruption of revising policy unless absolutely necessary.'

Consensus and secrecy

If the inertia and continuity identified above are features of the majority of bureaucracies, then consensus and secrecy can be seen as particularly strong British attributes, as O'Riordan points out when describing the style of British policy-making,

This can be characterized as consensus-seeking on the basis of selective consultation. One of the great traditions of conflict resolution in British political affairs is to keep all discussions as far as possible confidential from the public at large and to encourage co-operation among all interested parties on the basis of protracted discussion. The outcome of this is that the assumptions and principles upon which policy is based and which determine the decision in individual cases are not published, so few people have any means of challenging directly the policy-making process. A corollary is that if any group wants to know how government are thinking they have to become participants. This means that they require a degree of political respectability *and* the ability to produce information or research that public officials need to know or cannot afford to ignore. (O'Riordan, 1979, p. 418).

The fact that the policy-making process becomes increasingly secretive as issues go through it (Solesbury, 1976, p. 392), has obvious implications for the ability of journalists to get information back to the public. While this may be offset by the pressure groups involved offering briefings, it has to be said that most of the routine meetings that constitute government business fail to meet the criteria of news, important though their cumulative effect may be.

This idea that activists tend to lose control of their issues as they go through the policy-making process is supported by Spector and Kitsuse:

While official response may give the protest group its finest hour, it may also represent the beginning of the end of its control over the claims it raises . . . Although the group may be called to testify before the committee, it often finds itself cast in the role of providing information, rather than defining and negotiating the nature of the problem . . . The committee may seek out other and opposing views on the topic, reducing the original group to simply one voice among many. When the hearings are over, the members of the committee will be the new experts and authorities on the subject. While the original group may comment on the report of the committee, it is that report that will define the issues. (Spector and Kitsuse, 1977, p. 149).

This might not be a problem if the news media were willing and able to follow the intricate twists and turns of the policy-making process, but this is rarely the case for general audience formats. The result is that the clarity of the groups' original positions are likely to be lost, and that the leverage provided by public opinion may be dissipated.

The above quotes give some indication of the lack of public understanding of the policy-making process. In the case of the environment this is exacerbated by the technicality of the issues which are being debated. Indeed, as Grant points out (1989, p. 114), there is actually very little public opinion in relation to the majority of issues which pressure groups and government discuss, and the effectiveness of this weapon is consequently reduced.

A loss of clarity and lack of public interest/understanding of the policy-making process obviously present problems for organizations who thrive on dramatic and symbolic media coverage. It becomes more and more difficult for such groups to encapsulate the issues in eye-catching slogans the further into the bureaucracy that they proceed. There are a number of reasons why this is so.

Suppression

The civil service is well aware of the public's desire for 'news', and takes advantage of the media's short attention span by employing the tactic of 'suppression' in order to avoid decisions. When suppressing an issue, the aim is to delay its resolution for as long as possible, thereby exhausting its sponsors, and reducing their chances of maintaining public interest. The sponsors of environmental issues are particularly vulnerable in this respect, as the technicality of their claims often leads to a drawn-out policy-making process.

Not only is there the chance that public or parliamentary opinion will become distracted by other social problems, there is also the possibility that external factors may intervene, such as recessions, elections, wars, etc.

Partial responses

Even if an issue's sponsors are able to force their claim through to the point of decision, there is still no guarantee that they will achieve a satisfactory outcome. Instead, a range of partial responses may be employed, such as reassurances, tokenism and organizational change (Solesbury, 1976 p. 394). These may give the appearance that the problem has been tackled, but in practice fall short of an adequate response.

Such partial responses link clearly to a further consequence of 'news values'. This is the marked decrease in the value of media coverage once a battle over principle has been won. Conflict is of course a prime news value, with one result of this being that public attention is likely to be directed elsewhere once it has been offset. This means that news coverage tends to be far less effective a weapon in the defence of victories than in campaigning for initial change. This trend is recognized by Parlour and Schatzow (1978), who argue that one of the consequences of institutionalization for environmental issues is that they are likely to receive reduced media coverage, as it will be widely perceived that solutions are in hand. (The corollary to this, as identified by Downs (1972), is that institutionalization confers longevity on issues, by increasing the number of arenas in which they compete and thus providing plentiful 'news pegs'.)

Access and legitimacy

A further difficulty for groups who are trying to deal with the executive is that it has greater access to the media than they do, and is in a much stronger position to frame the issues with which it is involved (as was mentioned earlier). The fact that the government has become more pro-active in its news management strategies over the past decade or so, as Hansen (1991, p. 5) points out, is of undoubted significance where environmental campaigners are concerned. The government tends to have a clear advantage over those presenting alternative explanations of social problems, in that journalists see it as a natural source of information and tend to accord it automatic access (Einsiedel, 1988; Gamson and Modigliani, 1989; Hansen, 1991).

This is despite findings by MORI (1991) which show that British environmental journalists are both highly critical of the government's record and also sceptical of their news-management ability. The *Sunday Telegraph*'s Environment Correspondent, Greg Neale, described the situation as follows. 'Government has access to enormous amounts of information and is therefore a very good source, but can be cagey about releasing all of it, and frequently you must be prepared to make your way through a lot of information, much of it extraneous. You also have to be aware that Government is in the business of news management as much as news release'. Government departments not only incur journalistic criticism in relation to the quality of their information. In addition Richard North of *The Independent* points out (in Warren, 1990, p. 48) that, 'a lot of time government is not sitting on information because the news is bad, they often sit on news that does them favours. They are just bad communicators.'

Given the evident reservations of journalists when dealing with the government, and the fact that the larger environmental pressure groups are often considered to be reliable sources of information, the findings that while major environmental pressure groups may act as important initiators of coverage, they do not generally figure prominently as primary definers in actual coverage (see Hansen, 1990; also Einsiedel, 1988) are somewhat worrying. While environment groups, then, may be playing an important agenda-setting role, their ability to shape the resulting coverage may be limited. This is crucially important, as getting coverage is only half the battle, getting the coverage to say what you want it to is another battle altogether. The fact that issue entrepreneurs must compete with regard to the definition or framing of their concerns was mentioned at the start of this chapter. It links directly to Solesbury's second task, that of 'claiming legitimacy'. Environmentalists must not only have the resources to be able to produce their claims and to command attention for them, they must also render their concerns in such a way that their case appears credible through the media. This can be much more difficult than simply creating coverage in the first place, and the ways in which environmental meaning is constructed have been considered by researchers such as Molotch and Lester (1975), Luke (1987), Gamson and Modigliani (1989), Burgess (1990) and Hansen (1990), all of whom have contributed to our understanding of the politics of meaning within environmental coverage. Gamson and Modigliani's work is particularly interesting in this respect, as they attempt to define the interpretive 'packages' that constitute US media coverage of nuclear power, relating shifts in this media discourse to changes in public opinion. In doing so they highlight the importance of ongoing news routines to this fundamentally competitive process, as well as indicating the advantage held by 'official' sponsors over social movement organizations contesting dominant interpretations. Not only do they consider the impact of different media formats on the way that this discourse is constructed, they also look at the conditions of access which govern who gets to shape the news, and at how these relate to 'legitimacy' and the journalistic concept of 'balance'.

Fragmentation

One final complication for those trying to influence environmental policy (and those trying to comment on it) is that policy-making is spread between many governmental departments. This is partly a consequence of the diversity of environmental concerns, but also a feature of British policy-making in general. Not only does this create difficulties for journalists trying to cover the issues, it can also lead to those seeking change being directed towards departments with nominal responsibility for the issues but little practical power (see Lowe and Goyder, 1983 on this point).

Against this, one has to recognize that the ability to exploit interdepartmental wrangling and rivalry can be crucial to groups who want to exert pressure on the executive (Porritt and Winner, 1988, p. 85) and it is to the question of lobbying approaches that I now want to turn.

Varied approaches

Writers on pressure politics have generally adopted a two-fold typology when commenting on the ways in which campaigning organizations generate pressure. This dichotomy casts groups as either 'insiders' or 'outsiders' depending on the resources and strategies which they are able to use. While it usefully points to the existence of different lobbying strategies any rigid insider/outsider typology is limited in applicability. Thinking in terms of a spectrum of approaches is more appropriate, flexibility being at a premium for successful lobbying organizations. Where the designations insider and outsider are used in the following discussion it is merely to signify that differences of approach do exist.

Insider strategies

Insider groups are those which have regular access to, and dialogue with, the bureaucracy, and who belong to policy communities. They may be 'expert' organizations who are invited to contribute to governmental committees because their knowledgeability is recognized. Alternatively they may be groups whose personal political contacts guarantee that their case is heard. In order to qualify for such status a group's values will have to show some congruence with those of the government department concerned and the group must also be willing to play by the rules the bureaucracy sets down (Rose, 1974; Solesbury, 1976). Hilgartner and Bosk recognize this when they speak of the 'cultures' of different arenas.

In addition to this cultural congruence an issue's sponsors must be seen to have something to offer in exchange for their status. This usually falls into one of three categories:

(a) Expertise. The group may have produced research which bears on a policy decision, and which the government is eager to have access to.

(b) Cooperation. The cooperation of the group may be necessary in order for the government to implement policy. (Many farming organizations would fall into this category along with some from industry, in marked contrast to most environmental groups.)

(c) Silence. Groups may be invited into consultative frameworks in the hope that this will discourage them from exerting pressure through more public arenas such as the media. Civil servants are eager to prevent both their department and their minister from being embarrassed by pressure groups (Wilson, 1984, p. 129). UK government departments tend to respond to pressure either by discrediting those making the claim, or alternatively by offering them access in exchange for less confrontational tactics.

Insider strategies can be summarized as attempts to work from within the system, rather than to rail at it from the outside. There is a danger, however, that such a blanket description hides the varying degrees of 'insiderness', or legitimacy, possessed by different groups. Those that have always had close links with the bureaucracy, i.e. 'ultra-insiders' or establishment bodies, can exert far greater leverage than those which are sporadically given access to dissuade them from using other tactics. Insider status can have distinct advantages (see Lowe and Goyder, 1983; Grant, 1989) but environmental groups must be wary of accepting a token insider position which emasculates them while failing to offer real rewards.

The traditional reliance on the media of environmental groups makes them particularly vulnerable in this respect, for they use media coverage as a way of demonstrating public support and thus generating political pressure. This is clearly not the case for ultra-insiders, who are usually reluctant to draw attention to their activities, and are only likely to become active in the media when put on the defensive.

Outsider strategies

If insider groups base their strategies on influence through information, then outsider organizations place an emphasis on unpredictability. By generating public concern or outrage through the media they hope to force the hand of the government, and thus get a rapid commitment to action. Traditionally theorists have seen this as a last resort, but in response to my suggestion that confrontational strategies are ineffectual Chris Rose[4] replied,

No. If that was the case Greenpeace wouldn't be the most feared environmental group with the government. They hate Greenpeace, and the reason they hate them is that you can't deal with them. If you've got somebody who's nice, and willing to have lots of dialogue, and go along and sit on lots of committees then you've co-opted them . . . You need people with insider status, but to think that this is an alternative is completely naive. You've got to be out there putting the boot in, any politician will tell you that. (Rose, 1991)

That this is how Greenpeace views the situation was confirmed by Sue Adams,[5] who felt that part of the role of pressure groups was to remain outsider bodies. As she put it, 'if you're getting on too well with the government then you ought to be worried' (Adams, 1991).

There are problems with confrontational media strategies, however, and central to these is the conflict between the goals of 'commanding attention' and 'claiming legitimacy' (as mentioned above). The problem is a straightforward one, which is that attempts to command attention through the media by direct action or stunts may provide civil servants and politicians with an opportunity to portray the claims-makers as irrational, and thus undeserving of serious attention (see Greenberg (1985) on this point). There is a danger that the debate will become focused on activists' means and not their ends, as is the case with the paramilitary animal liberation organizations. The risk of losing public sympathy by employing semi-legitimate or illegitimate tactics needs to be carefully considered when campaigns are planned, and Greenpeace has paid a penalty in this respect, as Draper (1987) shows. It is no good trying to campaign behind the scenes for environmental change if those you are trying to influence will not speak to you because of your organization's public image. Renegotiation of a public profile can be a very difficult thing to achieve, which means that environmental groups need to consider the face that they present to the media with great care. Whiteley and Winyard (1987, p. 120) make the contrast between 'responsible' and 'irresponsible' publicity, and suggest that while the former can be extremely effective, the latter (for example, attacks on the character and motives of ministers and officials) can permanently damage a group's chances of exerting influence. A further and in some ways separate problem for organizations using stunt-like tactics in order to generate media coverage is that their novelty has worn off over time. News editors are now less likely to cover such actions than they were five or ten years ago, with the result that these organizations must seek new ways of ensuring that their message is heard.

Strength through diversity?

That publicity on its own is rarely sufficient to achieve success is recognized by Des Wilson (1984) and there are a number of examples of environmental groups dominating the media debate on an issue, yet failing to have their claims taken up. Chris Rose describes the power of the farming lobby in this respect:

despite winning the press debate almost hands down, it came as no surprise when the conservation lobby failed to make much impact on the Wildlife and Countryside Bill which became an Act very much in line with the wishes of the National Farmers' Union and the Country Landowners' Association. Environmentalists were up against a political and propaganda machine which has been described by one ex-minister as "the most powerful lobby in Britain, probably in Europe", and was credited as long ago as 1962 as having a relationship with government "unique in its range and intensity". (Rose, quoted in Wilson, 1984, p. 6)

At the same time, the relative lack of other sanctions where environmental groups are concerned means that they must be careful when entering arenas which may restrict their ability to evoke public concern. The retention of a capability to 'command attention' through dramatic action is important, for some of the groups which are achieving a degree of insider status are in danger of being co-opted while failing to reap the desired benefits. It is relatively rare for an environmental group to be consulted before policy is conceived or drafted, at the point at which real influence can best be exercised. Given this fact, it is important that the environmental movement does not lose its capacity for generating public awareness through bold action. At the same time, however, environmental groups need to become much more aware of the political context of the issues with which they are concerned, such that their enthusiasm for media-related activities does not result in damage to their cause.

The need for a balance is clearly made by Eric Draper in his article on the Greenpeace media machine (1987). He points to the trade-off between short-term 'mediagenic' actions (which may influence specific disputes), and long-term movement building. He argues that while the politics of symbols and their manipulation may be an appealing tactic to the powerless, the environmental movement is not weak and isolated, and that 'high on the Green agenda should be translating popular support into radical policy changes before it is placated with measures that mitigate, but don't stop environmental destruction' (1987, p. 9).

Clearly a combination of insider and outsider lobbying is desirable, and this is linked to the idea that one should employ as many arenas as is practicable in order to exert pressure. This is the case both within single organizations but perhaps even more so across the environmental movement in general. Here the ecological principle of strength through diversity is perhaps relevant. As Julie Hill[6] of the Green Alliance put it:

I personally believe that you need a sort of spectrum of approaches. For instance, Greenpeace put forward what are often seen as 'radical' positions; since many will be reluctant to take these ideas up in entirety, this can help to create a receptive climate for the somewhat more 'mainstream' or incremental approaches of groups like the Green Alliance. There's a productivity in this kind of diversity. (Hill, 1991)

This would be fine if it worked in practice, but against it one has to bear in mind Des Wilson's comment that 'one of the worst aspects of voluntary activity in Britain is the lack of co-operation and sometimes downright hostility between different groups. Wasted energy and emotion in rivalries between organizations and wasted resources in duplication of effort and lack of co-operation, are unforgivable.' (Wilson 1984, p. 37). The territoriality which is bred by the need to compete for financial support in a limited market has been mentioned earlier in this chapter. Its ramifications are clear when one considers the opportunities for coordinated campaigning activity.

Conclusions

My concern has been to look at some of the interactions between the arenas of the mass media and the civil service where environmental policy-making is concerned. Unpacking the connections between these arenas is difficult, indeed it may be impossible to achieve any conclusive results. However, this lack of firm conclusions should not be used as a reason for avoiding the exercise.

What I hope to have shown is that while environmental organizations tend to make heavy use of the media there can be distinct limitations in a media-based approach. Some of these limitations are created by the inherent nature of different mass media arenas, and these have been well recognized in other mass communications research (see Cracknell, 1991, Appendix B, for more detail on this). In addition, however, the use of certain arenas at certain stages during the development of an issue can in itself be counter-productive. As issue entrepreneurs seek to 'command attention', 'claim legitimacy', and 'invoke action' they commonly need to employ a variety of tactics and a range of different arenas. This can create conflicts within the organizations concerned, as they compete with other social claims-makers for a limited pool of resources. As has been shown above, it is all too easy for pursuit of one of the tasks identified by Solesbury to result in setbacks with regard to another.

I would contend that if mass communications research on the environment is to be really useful to those campaigning to save it then it needs to consider the networks of feedback which exist between the media and other social arenas. We come to know the world around us largely through the mass media, and their role in constructing our 'environment' is crucial. At the same time it is easy to forget that there are many non-media influences on policy-making and that many of the most effective pressure groups (regardless of their causes) choose to have negligible public profiles.

For a number of reasons environmental pressure groups have tended to orient their campaigning towards the media. This is not necessarily misguided, but there is a danger that such organizations will start to see column inches, rather than political effectiveness, as a measure of success. Communications researchers should be careful to guard against making a similar error and should perhaps spend more time looking at the impact of coverage in specific situations, than at its cumulative level or mode of production.

In some senses the UK environmental movement is in transition along the spectrum of insider and outsider lobbying identified above. Scientific credibility was the first step towards claiming legitimacy and what is required for further progress is greater economic and political sophistication. Mass media research which articulates the real-world experiences of environmentalists with the benefits of the 'overview' provided by academia can help in this process.

Notes

1 Des Wilson is widely regarded as the UK's leading authority on pressure group politics. During his career he has founded SHELTER, CLEAR (the Campaign for Lead Free Air), The Campaign for the Freedom of Information and a number of other organizations, as well as having been the Chairman of Friends of the Earth UK. In the 1992 general election he was campaign director for the Liberal Democrats.

2 SHELTER, The National Campaign for the Homeless, was launched in December 1966 and continues to lobby on behalf of the homeless.

3 Simon Bryceson started his career at Friends of the Earth and has been a political lobbyist for over ten years. He now runs his own consultancy, Bryceson Goodhart, which provides advice to leading environmental pressure groups as well as commercial clients.

4 Chris Rose was the first Director of Media Natura, the UK's environmental media charity. He is now the Programme Director of Greenpeace UK.

5 Sue Adams is Media Director of Greenpeace UK.

6 Julie Hill is the Director of the Green Alliance, a non-profit making body working on environmental policy and politics. The Green Alliance concentrates on building networks between environmental groups, policy-makers and politicians.

References

Adams, S. (1991), Interview conducted by the author, 5 June.

Blumer, H. (1971), 'Social problems as collective behaviour', *Social Problems*, 18, pp. 298–306.

Bryceson, S. (1991), Interview conducted by the author, 9 May.

Burgess, J. (1990), 'The production and consumption of environmental meanings in the mass media: a research agenda for the 1990s', *Transactions of the Institute of British Geographers*, New Series, 15 (2), pp. 139–61.

Corner, J., Richardson, K., Fenton, N. (1990), *Nuclear reactions: form and response in public issue television*, London: John Libbey.

Cracknell, J. (1991), *Environmental pressure groups and the media in Britain*, unpublished MA thesis, University of Leicester.

Downs, A. (1972), 'Up and down with ecology – the issue attention cycle', *The Public Interest* 28, pp. 38–50.

Draper, E. (1987), 'The Greenpeace media machine', *New Internationalist*, May, pp. 8–9.

Einsiedel, E. (1988), *The Canadian press and the environment*, paper given at the International Association for Mass Communication Research conference, 1988.

Gamson, W., Modigliani, A. (1989), 'Media discourse and public opinion on nuclear power: A constructionist approach', *American Journal of Sociology*, 95 (1); pp. 1–37.

Grant, W. (1989), *Pressure groups, politics and democracy in Britain*, Hemel Hempstead: Philip Allan.

Greenberg, D. (1985), 'Staging media events to achieve legitimacy: A case study of Britain's Friends of the Earth', *Political Communication and Persuasion*, 2 (4), pp. 347–62.

Hansen, A. (1990), 'Socio-political values underlying media coverage of the environment', *Media Development*, 37 (2), pp. 4–6.

Hansen, A. (1991), *Television news coverage of environmental issues*, paper given at the Seminar on 'Environment and Development Issues: What sort of television?', University of Sussex, Falmer.

Hansen, A., Linné, O. (1986), 'Problemas ambientales y medios de comunicacion colectiva (Environmental issues and the mass media)', *Cuadernos de Comunicacion*, 96, pp. 47–55.

Hilgartner, S., Bosk, C. (1988), 'The rise and fall of social problems: A public arenas model', *American Journal of Sociology*, 94 (1), pp. 53–78.

Hill, J. (1991), Interview conducted by the author, 9 May.

Jordan, G. (1991), 'The professional persuaders', in G. Jordan (ed.), *The commercial lobbyists*, Aberdeen: Aberdeen University Press.

Lowe, P., Goyder, J. (1983), *Environmental groups in politics*, London: George Allen & Unwin.

Luke, T. (1987), 'Chernobyl: The packaging of transnational ecological disaster', *Critical Studies in Mass Communication*, 4, pp. 351–75.

McMillan, S. (1988), *Broadcasting and conservation – The 'new era' in environmental television*, unpublished MSc thesis, University College London.

Miller, C. (1987), *Lobbying government*, Oxford: Basil Blackwell.

Molotch, H., Lester, M. (1975), 'Accidental news: the great oil spill as local occurrence and national event', *American Journal of Sociology*, 81 (2), pp. 235–60.

MORI (1991), *Survey of Britain's environment journalists*, London: Market Opinion Research International.

O'Riordan, T. (1979), 'Public interest environmental groups in the United States and Britain', *Journal of American Studies*, 13 (3), pp. 409–38.

Parlour, J., Schatzow, S. (1978), 'The mass media and public concern for environmental issues in Canada 1960–1972', *International Journal of Environmental Studies*, 13 (1), pp. 9–17.

Porritt, J., Winner, D. (1988), *The coming of the greens*, London: Fontana.

Rose, C. (1991), Interview conducted by the author, 9 May.

Rose, R. (1974), *Politics in England today*, London: Faber & Faber.

Sandman, P. (1974), 'Mass environmental education: Can the media do the job?', in J. Swann (ed.) *Environmental Education*, Chichester: John Wiley.

Solesbury, W. (1976), 'The environmental agenda: an illustration of how situations may become political issues and issues may demand responses from government: or how they may not', *Public Administration*, 54, pp. 379–97.

Spector, M., Kitsuse, J. (1977), *Constructing social problems*, Menlo Park, California: Cummings.

Stearn, J. (1988), 'Whatever is environmental education coming to?', *Urban Wildlife*, 1 (2), pp. 19–21.

Warren, S. (1990), *Aspects of British press coverage of environmental issues in the 1980s*, unpublished MSc thesis, University of Wales, Cardiff.

Whiteley, P., Winyard, S. (1987), *Pressure for the poor*, London: Methuen.

Wiebe, G. (1971), 'Mass media and man's relationship to his environment', *Journalism Quarterly*, 50, pp. 426–32.

Wilson, D. (1984), *Pressure: the a to z of campaigning in Britain*, London: Heinemann.

2
Journalistic strategies for reporting long-term environmental issues: a case study of three Superfund sites[*]

Sharon Dunwoody and Robert J. Griffin

Reporting on environmental contamination presents journalists with enormous challenges. For one, pollutants usually confront audiences with hazards to their health, saddling reporters with the task of explaining the extent and nature of those risks. For another, pollution problems often come wrapped in highly technical language, making explanation of even the simplest phenomenon difficult indeed. For yet another, environmental contamination, like other environmental issues, is awash in ambiguities (Griffin et al., 1991). Experts rarely seem to know what *that* particular chemical does in *that* particular situation, and even when they claim to know, they may disagree. And finally, this kind of environmental issue can go on for years without resolution, a disconcerting dimension for an occupation such as journalism that wants to limit itself to what happened today.

In this chapter we characterize some of the ways journalists cope with coverage of a specific class of long-term environmental risks: Superfund sites in the United States. These are extensively contaminated sites that constitute risks to health but are difficult to clean up. Their designation as Superfund sites makes them newsworthy, yet they take years, perhaps decades, to restore.

This study explores the processes by which newspapers covered three contaminated sites in Wisconsin from their designation as Superfund sites to the present. We interpret our data through the lenses of three conceptual frameworks. The first is the concept of schema or frame, an individual-level cognitive structure that guides

[*] This chapter is based on research funded by the Risk Communication Research Program of the US Environmental Protection Agency

a journalist's process of 'making sense' of a story. The other two concepts are factors that could strongly govern the construction of journalistic frames: occupational norms and community structures.

Media coverage of environmental risks

Research into media coverage of environmental risks has looked more intensively at the journalistic products – risk stories – than at the processes that affect story construction. With few exceptions, such studies attempt to explain how coverage comes about by inference rather than by direct observation or measurement.

These analyses of media coverage seem to yield two large patterns of findings. One is that media coverage of risks does not mirror 'reality', as defined by the researcher. For example, Greenberg et al. (1989) found that the television networks in the United States focused disproportionately on sudden violent environmental risks such as large chemical spills or airplane crashes. These disasters make compelling TV footage but, cautioned the researchers, cause fewer deaths than other, more chronic environmental risks such as smoking and asbestos exposure. In a slightly different vein, Singer examined the goodness of fit between media accounts of a variety of risks and the original scientific reports and found the news stories made 'a substantial number of errors' (Singer, 1990, p. 105). In both these studies, media stories were compared to a particular reality, one defined operationally by the researchers, and were found wanting.

A second pattern of findings from this body of research is that risk stories contain very little risk information, as defined by science. For example, Sandman, Sachsman, Greenberg and Gochfeld (1987), in a study of newspaper coverage of environmental risks, reported finding scant 'explicit risk information in articles that are ostensibly about environmental risk' (p. 52). In fact, they found that about two-thirds of the paragraphs analyzed dealt with other dimensions of environmental issues, such as assigning blame or calculating the cost of the environmental damage. Of the third of the paragraphs that did discuss risk, only 17.4 per cent addressed the basic risk issue: 'How dangerous is this substance or situation?' (p. 11).

Singer and Endreny (1987) reached a similar conclusion in their study of hazards coverage in fifteen media outlets. For example, they reported that of 624 stories published or aired in these outlets in 1984, only 5 per cent contained any information about the annual mortality associated with the particular hazard being addressed.

Unfortunately, most of the available studies of media coverage of environmental risk are descriptive. The authors speculate about why the patterns found in their stories exist, but they rarely bring data to bear on that very important issue. In the next section, we first establish what we contend is the guiding principle for story selection and organization, the 'frame'. We then posit two predictors of frames and, in the case studies that follow, explore the explanatory power of those two predictors.

Theoretical framework

Frames

All individuals interpret their world by calling on knowledge structures that are acquired through shared social learning, individual experiences and personal reasoning (Graber, 1988). If, on encountering workers toppling a large aged tree in their neighbourhood, two individuals react differently, they may do so in part because that event has activated two very different interpretive schemata, or frames. One person may view the scenario with relief because she defines the tree as a potential hazard that strong winds may send crashing onto nearby homes. The other, conversely, may react to the process with sadness since he views the tree as a grand old survivor of pre-settlement days. 'Humans', says Mendelsohn (1990, p. 38), 'act according to what they know and understand (or misunderstand), and not necessarily according to what they simply see or hear.'

These mental maps come in wildly varying levels of sophistication across individuals and, for any one person, will vary greatly in level of detail across topics. The important point is that they play a crucial role in sense-making. Things in our world have meaning only to the extent that they get incorporated into these customized frames.

Journalists, too, make sense of their world by incorporating stimuli into their available cognitive maps (Gitlin, 1980; Stocking and Gross, 1989). However, they employ frames not only to interpret phenomena for themselves but also to construct the stories that we encounter in our daily newspaper or TV news report. 'A frame', say Tankard et al. (1991, p. 5), 'is a central organizing idea for news that supplies a context and suggests what the issue is through the use of selection, emphasis, exclusion, and elaboration.'

These frames are essential for journalistic work because reporters and editors must make speedy decisions about what in their environment is worth their attention. A journalist with thirty minutes to write a story does not spend that time contemplating 'what the story is about'. That particular decision is made in seconds, and the reporter then uses the bulk of her thirty minutes to select and order information in ways that are consonant with the chosen meaning framework.

Considerable evidence suggests that frames utilized by journalists for story construction are not idiosyncratic (see for example Rachlin, 1988; van Dijk, 1988). Rather, journalists across a wide range of media seem to employ similar mental maps and, thus, produce stories that reconstitute the world in similar ways. Evidence is growing that those frames influence the ways in which stories about science and environment are constructed for public consumption. For example, when a nuclear power plant at Three Mile Island (TMI) sprang a leak in 1979, many media organizations defined the event initially as 'an accident' and sent general reporters – individuals adept at covering fast-breaking news – to the scene. It was not until many of these journalists began floundering in a sea of technical terms and frankly terrifying images – for example, the ominous hydrogen bubble that was hypothesized to be growing inside the damaged reactor – that these organizations redefined the event and sent in their science reporters. Rubin, who headed a subsequent investigation of media coverage of TMI, reported that journalists' information-gathering efforts were so accident-oriented during the crisis that 'science writers had little opportunity to ask sophisticated questions of knowledgeable sources' (Rubin, 1980).

A study of journalists' coverage of social science research topics by Weiss and Singer (1988) found that reporters rarely defined the topics they dealt with as belonging to the domain of science or of scientific disciplines but, instead, framed them as 'crime stories' or 'poll stories'. The absence of a 'science' frame, then, made the use of scientific information rare in these accounts. For example, if a journalist decided to write a story about the homeless, he might very well frame it as a 'first-person feature story' without ever considering that social scientists have not only tried systematically to count the number of homeless but also have sought explanations for their presence on urban streets around the world. A feature story frame may send our journalist out on the streets overnight to talk with homeless individuals, but it will not prompt him to seek out the kind of scholarship that might help his audience understand the homeless as a social phenomenon.

In a more recent study, Ryan, Dunwoody and Tankard (1991) examined newspaper and magazine coverage of two risks – a nuclear power plant accident and publication of a study positing a relationship between coffee-drinking and pancreatic cancer – and concluded that coverage differences were more closely related to the employment of different frames than to other predictors. The cancer story was immediately defined as a 'risk' story, while the nuclear power plant story was defined as an 'accident' story. As a result, stories about the former concentrated on explaining the risk while stories about the latter focused on 'what happened' in the course of the accident. Although small amounts of radioactive steam did escape from the power plant during the accident, journalists paid little attention to questions of risk in their stories.

Do either occupational or societal factors contribute to this homogeneity of frames? We ask those questions next.

Occupational norms

Nearly all the authors of the media-coverage-of-risk literature cited attribute coverage patterns to journalistic occupational practices. For example, Greenberg et al. (1989) argue that topic choices by network TV news journalists in their study were associated more with occupational standards of newsworthiness than with level of risk. Similarly, Singer and Endreny (1987) assert that the poor fit between amount of media coverage and level of risk in the stories they examined could be understood if news judgments are taken into account.

> A rare hazard is more newsworthy than a common one, other things being equal; a new hazard is more newsworthy than an old one; and a dramatic hazard – one that kills many people at once suddenly or mysteriously – is more newsworthy than a long-familiar illness. (p. 13)

The bottom line, say these and other researchers, is that normative practices of the occupation – definitions of news, the presence of deadlines, and equipment constraints, for example – play an over-whelming role in frame construction. A journalist's personal prefer-ences notwithstanding, she will 'see' dimensions of her world as newsworthy only through the prism constructed by those norms. Most likely, the prism is invisible to the reporter. Its impact, however, is substantial.

For example, Dunwoody (1979) studied the behaviours of major US science writers who were covering a large scientific meeting. She found that reporters defined the sprawling, days-long meeting as a series of discrete events (paper presentations) that could be framed for audiences as brief timely accounts of research. Stories culled a small number of presentations from the literally hundreds available at the meeting and presented them as *the* news of the day. The bulk of the meeting's contents were rendered invisible, Dunwoody contended, by a process that highlighted not the most important science information but information that accommodated such con-straints as a reporter's deadlines, the specter of competition from rival science reporters, and the need to select topics that the editor would find worthy.

Phillips (1977) takes this a step further, arguing that occupational norms reward journalists for defining the world in a discrete, fragmented way and effectively bar them from seeing bigger, more conceptual frames:

> Journalists are nontheoretic knowers who depend upon instinctive, concrete, first-hand "acquaintance with" events, not formal, systematic "knowledge about" events . . . Unlike the social scientist or engineer who looks at a discrete event or fact through concepts derived from a theory, the journalist qua bricoleur apprehends "reality" by noting concrete signs. (p. 70)

In their study of New Jersey newspapers' coverage of environmental stories, Sandman et al. (1987) found support for the influence of organizational/occupational norms when they asked reporters to explain why stories were constructed in particular ways. For example, journalists sent to cover environmental emergencies explained that their primary goal was to report what happened, not to delve into the nature and extent of the risk. Noted the authors:

> In large part, the tendency to favor the details of the emergency over the health risk details is journalistic tradition; journalists have typically been trained to cover emergencies, and that is what they feel comfortable doing. (p. 67)

Community structures

The effects of macro social systems, such as communities, on communication is a topic ripe for heightened systematic inquiry (McLeod and Blumler, 1987). Over the years, a number of scholars have argued that powerful influencers of social meaning exist at the societal level. It is the basic structures and ideologies of societies, they say, that control the ways in which individuals, as well as groups, make sense of their world. Journalists – like everyone else – are very much the creatures of prevailing social norms and power structures.

Exploring the role of such structures empirically is very difficult. But one team of mass communication researchers, Phillip Tichenor, Clarice Olien and George Donohue of the University of Minnesota, offers a strategy that we utilize here. They examine the impact of community structure on journalistic decision-making by differentiating communities in terms of community 'pluralism', or structural diversity.

As Tichenor, Donohue and Olien (1980) note, communities that are more pluralistic have a larger and more diversified population, a greater number and variety of interest groups, and a more heterogeneous distribution of power bases. Less pluralistic communities, in contrast, tend to have a smaller and less diversified population and fewer centers of power. While low-pluralism communities tend to work in an atmosphere of consensus, with decision-making commonly based on precedent and tradition, high-pluralism communities tend to work in an atmosphere of greater conflict, and decision-makers are forced to take into account the interests of the various groups that are often at odds with one another.

News media are an integral part of communities and tend to reflect the concerns of the power structure of their particular setting, usually serving as reinforcers of established authority, powerful interests and mainstream values (Olien, Tichenor and Donohue, 1989). Conflicts, of course, can occur in any community. But differences in the ways in which conflict is managed also give the news media different roles to play in more pluralistic as compared to less pluralistic communities.

In less pluralistic communities, as Olien, Donohue and Tichenor

(1968) note, community leaders and interest groups tend to work out conflicts informally, through interpersonal channels. Local news media in these less pluralistic communities play roles as legitimizers of projects, builders of consensus, and instruments for tension management. Such media would treat intracommunity conflict very gingerly, as such conflict could threaten existing power bases. Reporting that would point fingers at individual or institutional members of the community, expose local wrongdoing, or raise sensitive issues would not be consistent with a consensual role. 'A newspaper in a one-industry town is unlikely to report that industry in a critical way', observe Tichenor, Donohue and Olien (1980, p. 220). 'It will reflect community consensus about that industry through reporting socially noncontroversial aspects of that industry and generally avoiding reports that would question it.'

In more pluralistic communities, however, it is difficult for community leaders and interest groups to settle conflicts through interpersonal channels. Conflict is a more routine part of public life in these communities, and negotiations must take place at formal public levels (public hearings, trial balloons, events staged by interest groups to get media attention), resulting in more conflict reporting by the mass media (Olien, Donohue and Tichenor, 1968; Olien, Tichenor and Donohue, 1989; Donohue, Olien and Tichenor, 1985b).

'Such emphasis on conflict is not necessarily disruptive', they explain, 'but is part of the process of resolving conflicts and managing them at tolerable levels' (Olien, Donohue and Tichenor, 1978, p. 446). Community leaders in more pluralistic communities are more likely than those in less pluralistic communities to perceive the local press as taking the initiative in reporting conflict (Donohue, Olien and Tichenor, 1985a), and in general the news media in more pluralistic communities tend to perform more of a 'feedback' role by drawing attention to local problems (Tichenor, Donohue and Olien, 1980).

As Olien, Donohue and Tichenor (1978) observe, community pluralism ultimately affects the configuration of information available to citizens. But how would those effects be manifested in coverage of environmental risks? In one study of newspaper coverage of a high-level nuclear waste repository siting issue, Dunwoody and Rossow (1989) found that newspapers in more pluralistic communities covered the issue more extensively, were more likely to reflect conflicting views, and did more enterprise reporting on the topic than did newspapers in more homogeneous settings. The behaviour of the media in less pluralistic settings suggested they were trying to minimize social disruption by minimizing coverage of the issue itself.

Before turning to the case studies, which explore how these two classes of predictors – organizational/occupational norms and community structure – influence coverage, we first briefly explain Superfund sites.

Superfund sites

In 1980, the US Congress enacted the Comprehensive Environmental Response, Compensation, and Liability Act (CERCLA), now commonly known as 'Superfund'. This Act authorized the US Environmental Protection Agency (EPA) to investigate and respond to releases of hazardous substances that may constitute a risk to human health or to the environment. Congress reauthorized the law in 1986, increasing the funds available for cleanup from $1.6 billion to $8.5 billion.

Sites are inspected and, if they pose serious enough risks, are added to the US EPA's National Priorities List, a roster of the nation's worst hazardous waste sites. All sites on the list are eligible for Superfund money. Once listed, each site undergoes a lengthy set of investigations to determine the type and extent of contaminants present, their likely risk to human health, and the feasibility of various cleanup options. EPA also tries to determine who caused the contamination and actively solicits the help of perpetrators in cleaning it up. These so-called 'potentially responsible parties', if they are still in business, are often reluctant to take responsibility for the problem, inviting protracted legal battles. Throughout the Superfund process, EPA holds public hearings to update citizens in communities surrounding the sites.

As of 1992, the US EPA had placed 1,275 sites on the National Priorities List. Cleanup has been completed at only 80 – a mere 6 per cent – of those sites. The case studies that follow will illustrate the lengthy and complex life spans of cleanup efforts at these locations.

Of the 1,275 sites throughout the country, thirty-nine are in the state of Wisconsin. Three of those thirty-nine sites are the focus of the rest of this chapter. The three sites fit a number of criteria that we considered important to our study of media coverage. None had prompted the widespread – and atypical – publicity of Love Canal in New York, or Times Beach, Missouri, yet each had generated a reasonable amount of local media attention during its life span and was still 'active' at the time of the case study. In each case the Superfund location was served by at least two newspapers of different sizes, usually from different communities, a factor important to the consideration of community structure as a predictor of coverage patterns. Finally, in each case the Wisconsin Division of Health had completed studies of health risks posed by the site and had reported those risks to residents and to journalists. Thus, specific information about the type and extent of health risks was available to interested parties.

Our primary questions were as follows:

• What were the dominant frames within which journalists organized information about the Superfund sites, and how did those frames change over time for any one site?

- What role did information about the level of hazard play in coverage of these sites?
- Did occupational/organizational norms influence coverage?
- Did community structure seem to play a role in the way that newspapers covered a site?

For each case study, we gathered Superfund stories from available newspapers for analysis and then journeyed to the site to interview journalists, editors and sources. We also interviewed the EPA remedial project manager responsible for each site at EPA District 5 offices in Chicago. Given the retrospective nature of the case studies, it was impossible to secure archival tapes from local television or radio stations. So, although those media also covered the sites on a regular basis, we were not able to analyze them.

Each site was sufficiently different that we will report findings separately. But we will devote some time at the end of the chapter to a discussion of commonalities. Although we are hesitant to generalize from an *n* of 3, some of the patterns that these case studies share are suggestive and, we think, worthy of attention.

National Presto Industries site in Eau Claire

History

Situated on land between the communities of Eau Claire and Chippewa Falls on the western edge of Wisconsin, the 325-acre site that eventually became National Presto Industries was originally owned by the federal government and purchased by National Presto in 1948. The company initially produced consumer goods on the site but, in 1954, dedicated the plant to producing metal bodies for projectiles and shells under a contract with the US Department of the Army. The company ceased manufacturing operations on the site in the late 1960s, and the facility is now on Department of Defense standby status. National Presto continues to thrive as a producer of small appliances and maintains its national headquarters in Eau Claire.

Waste water generated at the facility was originally discharged to seven seepage pits on the property. When serious overflow problems developed in 1954, National Presto began pumping the waste water from the pits into a former sand and gravel pit. In the late 1960s, the company built three new waste water lagoons. At one time, up to 2.5 million gallons of waste water per day was being discharged into the pits and lagoons.

National Presto also disposed of spent forging compound on the site. The compound, which contained roughly equal parts of asphalt, graphite and mineral oil, was shuttled to an independent location on the property from 1967 to 1969 but also showed up in some of the lagoons.

In the early 1980s, the Wisconsin Department of Natural Resources (DNR) began to test for the presence of contaminants in the National Presto vicinity. In 1983 the DNR detected traces of six volatile organic compounds (VOCs) and five heavy metals in one of the lagoons and, in 1985, discovered that some private wells on the north side of Eau Claire and in the unincorporated town of Hallie, which is immediately adjacent to the National Presto site, contained levels of volatile organic compounds that exceeded state standards. In 1986, the DNR linked the National Presto wastes to the contamination of Hallie wells.

The National Presto site became a Superfund site in 1984. Subsequent investigations detected the presence of organic and inorganic contaminants in the soil and waste on the site and confirmed the presence of VOCs in nearby wells at levels exceeding Wisconsin standards. In 1986, DNR ordered National Presto Industries to begin furnishing nearby residents with uncontaminated water; National Presto balked.

State officials examined the health risks posed by the site and in 1989 warned that residents in the contaminated area should avoid drinking or using the contaminated water. The VOCs present in the water, health officials explained, cause cancer in laboratory animals, thus raising a concern that they may also cause cancer in humans.

In 1990, the EPA recommended that the Hallie township build its own water system to bypass the contaminated wells. Later that year, National Presto Industries obtained US Department of the Army funding to help ameliorate the problem and announced it would make those funds available to help pay for the new water system.

As of 1992, the Hallie water system is nearing completion. National Presto is apparently working to clean up its own site and is seeking additional funds from the army.

Media coverage

Since the National Presto Superfund site is situated between Chippewa Falls and Eau Claire, the daily newspapers in those two cities both define the contaminated site as local news. The *Chippewa Herald-Telegram*, an afternoon paper, serves a community of more than 12,700 and had a 1992 circulation of 8,479. The Eau Claire *Leader-Telegram*, also an afternoon paper, is the newspaper of record for a community of some 55,000 individuals and, in 1992, reported a circulation of 31,753.

What were the dominant frames in the newspaper coverage and how did they change over time?

The newspaper stories about the National Presto site over an eight-year period (1985–92) do indeed emphasize different dimensions of the issue. And the movement from one focus to another looks logical. Here's a listing of frames as they developed over time:

1985/6	Well testing reveals the presence of contamination.
1986	Are the contaminants harmful?
1986	The federal government steps in via Superfund to administer the cleanup.
1986	Who's responsible for the problem?
From 1986 to present	How can we clean up the problem in a politically acceptable way?

Four patterns are of interest here; we will articulate a fifth in the next section.

First, some frames are represented in more stories than are others. In fact, some frames have extremely short life spans while others remain dominant for years. The theme of the overwhelming majority of stories in this case study was the last one: given a problem, how can we fix it? This 'solution' frame dominated coverage, in all likelihood, because cleaning up a Superfund site takes years. In this case, the first temporary solution – requiring National Presto to furnish clean water to residents whose wells were contaminated – was proposed in 1986. The final solution – construction of an independent water system for the township of Hallie – was just nearing completion in 1992.

Second, the two newspapers seemed to move linearly through frames. They rarely cycled back to pick up old ones. Once National Presto Industries had been identified as the source of the contamination in 1986, for example, we rarely encountered stories subsequently that reiterated that position. That piece of information had become an 'assumed' part of the story.

Third, stories were overwhelmingly event-oriented, suggesting that the story frames were driven as much, if not more, by source actions as by reporter decisions. For example, when EPA held a public hearing to report on the litany of possible solutions to the contaminated water wells in Hallie, stories reflect that 'solution' theme.

Yet, fourth, it is also clear that the issue was interpreted by journalists and, most likely, everyone else within a particular social context extant in the communities at hand. Recall that the unincorporated town of Hallie decided to resolve its water problem by building its own municipal water system, thus abandoning the private contaminated wells upon which residents had historically depended. Driving that very expensive decision was a complex political relationship among Chippewa Falls, Eau Claire and Hallie. Both cities coveted pieces of Hallie and annexed when they had an opportunity. Hallie asserted its independence fiercely. Thus the years-long 'solution' frame was immediately couched as a search for a solution within a very territorial social context.

For example, when asked what the National Presto Superfund story was really about, Janean Marti, Chippewa Falls bureau chief for the Eau Claire *Leader-Telegram,* responded that it was a tale about 'a township trying to preserve its identity'. Another reporter, Bill Gharrity of the Eau Claire *Leader-Telegram*, responded similarly that a large component of the story dealt with 'turf battles'.

How did level of health hazard fare as a story frame?

Hazards to health flared briefly as a theme in 1986 and, again briefly, in 1989. The first flare followed the initial stories about finding contaminants in Hallie wells. The second flare was the direct result of a US EPA public meeting on 5 April at which a state health official discussed the results of a study of possible health impacts from the VOCs found in the water. But those flares were short-lived. More significant, we think, is to note how little newspaper space was devoted to questions of health risk over the life span of this Superfund site. Among the literally hundreds of stories about National Presto, no more than a handful even mention threat to health. We will speculate on reasons for this at the end of the chapter.

Information about level of risk in that handful of stories, for the most part, reproduced the details provided by sources. The uniform message of the stories – that the contaminants presented a small but significant health risk – survived differing perceptions of the risk held by journalists covering the issue.

Eau Claire *Leader-Telegram* reporter Janean Marti, for instance, felt that the risk posed by the contaminants was so small that it bordered on being insignificant, and she became concerned that sources were pushing residents to be more worried than they need be. When she received what she termed an 'alarming' memo from a governmental official that advised Hallie residents to keep their children away from the National Presto site, Marti sought out another source, who 'belittled' the risk, to provide some balance in her story.

By way of contrast, Mark Baker, editor of the *Chippewa Herald-Telegram*, never questioned the message that the risk was a significant one. 'The risk was real', he said. Thus, the only issue that mattered to his newspaper was how to help Hallie residents ameliorate the problem.

Although stories that contained risk information for the most part offered up official risk estimates uncritically, it is not clear that all reporters or editors understood the information they printed. The one instance we found in which a newspaper criticized a risk estimate, in fact, supports an argument on behalf of ignorance. The most commonly cited characterization of risk at the National Presto site was that the levels of VOCs in Hallie well water exceeded Wisconsin's risk standard, which limits the level of risk to no more than one death for every million people who drink the water every day for seventy years. Specifically, the Wisconsin DNR calculated that the level of contaminants in the wells raised the risk to one death in 100,000.

In an editorial on 24 October 1987, the Eau Claire *Leader-Telegram* got the risk estimate wrong. It somehow mistook the level of risk as posing 'a one in one hundred thousand risk of contracting cancer from drinking *70 gallons of water per day* over 70 years' (our emphasis) and devoted the editorial to a critique of government officials who pushed communities to do something about risks that are so small. Concluded the editorial: 'The EPA and DNR should do their part by disseminating realistic information. Warning people not to drink 70 gallons of water a day for 70 years hardly qualifies.' No one at the newspaper apparently knew enough about risk levels to have questioned the original, inaccurate, assertion.

Did occupational/organizational variables make a difference in extent of coverage?

Although the Eau Claire *Leader-Telegram*'s circulation is nearly four times that of the *Chippewa Herald-Telegram*, those resources did not translate into more or significantly different stories. Why didn't resources get reflected in the coverage? Here are two possible reasons:

* Although one newspaper was larger than the other, both are small, relatively speaking. Thus neither could afford to assign an individual full-time to the Superfund site story. Instead, the reporter covering National Presto at any one time had to fit the coverage in with all the other stories for which he or she was responsible. That produced the second reason.
* Both newspapers responded to events and only rarely initiated stories. Such a strategy would produce similar numbers of stories in the two publications as long as the newspapers responded to the same events.

Did the nature of the communities in which these newspapers were embedded influence their coverage?

We saw some patterns in the coverage that suggest that social structure indeed had an impact. Both these communities are relatively small: Chippewa Falls has fewer than 15,000 residents and Eau Claire has fewer than 60,000. In the terminology of Tichenor, Donohue and Olien, such communities are often structurally homo-geneous. One would expect newspapers in such towns to practice consensual journalism. That is, one would expect them to support the social fabric by playing down internal community conflict.

Internal dissension was a distinct possibility here, for the contami-nator was a local company that, at one time, had been the biggest employer in the area. Exacerbating the issue was the company's reaction to the problem: it tried very hard to avoid responsibility for the contaminated ground water and to avoid paying for the cleanup.

How does a newspaper in a homogeneous community reflect reality when the bad guy is a local good corporate citizen who is balking at taking responsibility for a problem? You cannot ignore the issue or the company. But you can play down the company's role. Thus, you don't highlight the company as a central player in the drama. You don't cover the company aggressively. It never becomes the ultimate bad guy in your stories. Those patterns, we argue, characterized treatment of National Presto in the coverage by the Eau Claire *Leader-Telegram* and were also reflected in the early coverage by the *Chippewa Herald-Telegram*.

But what illuminated this pattern most vividly, we felt, were the repercussions that apparently stemmed from a change in coverage of National Presto initiated by the Chippewa Falls newspaper in the late 1980s. Initial coverage of the National Presto issue by the *Chippewa Herald-Telegram* had all the markings of supportive journalism. The newspaper had been running very few stories about the site, and those stories rarely took National Presto to task. But in 1987 a new editor, Mark Baker, came on board. And he took a very different tack. To Baker, National Presto's behavior made the company 'a poor corporate citizen'. And he felt his newspaper's coverage should reflect that. Subsequent stories were so hard on National Presto, said Baker, that the company complained about the new editor to the newspaper's publisher. The publisher subsequently asked Baker for an explanation. Baker, in urging his newspaper to actively serve as a community watchdog, had apparently violated assumptions about the role of that newspaper in that community.

Better Brite chrome and zinc sites in De Pere

History

The Better Brite Superfund site is really two industrial sites within a half mile of each other, both located in a residential area of De Pere, a small community adjacent to the city of Green Bay in eastern Wisconsin. Better Brite operated one of the sites as a chromium plating facility, while the other was devoted to zinc plating.

Trouble dogged the two sites. The Wisconsin Department of Natural Resources issued a number of citations to Better Brite in the late 1970s after detecting substantial contamination. In 1978, for example, the DNR received complaints about frozen yellow water behind the chrome shop. Inspections indicated extensive chromium contamination of soil and water on the site. The chromium plating tanks, situated largely below ground, were apparently leaking 'like sieves', according to one DNR official. The agency estimated that from 20,000 to 60,000 gallons of plating solution may have escaped from the tanks. The situation at the zinc site was not much better. DNR found elevated levels of cyanide, chromium, zinc, cadmium, lead, silver, selenium, copper and nickel in the soil. The site also contained drums of sludge contaminated with cadmium.

The company made some efforts in 1979 to contain the contamination but the state was not satisfied and, in 1980, filed suit to force Better Brite to clean up its two sites. The company apparently did not comply with the order and, in 1986, filed for bankruptcy and halted operations at the chrome site. The zinc site continued operating, however, and, later in 1986, was sold to another owner who continued the business until 1989. Operations at the renamed Zinc Shop ceased in July 1989.

The EPA entered the arena in 1986, when it sent an emergency response team to the sites to initiate cleanup operations. Within the next year, the EPA removed all on-site contaminants contained in drums or vats, as well as approximately 83 tons of contaminated soils.

Still, in 1988, neighbors of the now-defunct chromium plating plant complained that chromium-contaminated water was collecting in their back yards. The sites were placed on the agency's Superfund list in 1990. That same year, EPA installed an on-site water treatment system to treat up to 2,000 gallons of chromium-contaminated water per day; the treated water could then safely be discharged into the De Pere sanitary sewer system.

Also in 1990, the Wisconsin Division of Health began a preliminary assessment of the health risks posed by the two sites. It reported to the community in 1991 that, although cleanup efforts had left some contamination behind, the chromium still present at the sites posed no health risk to neighbors. The Division of Health inspectors did worry, however, that contamination might still reach the De Pere drinking water supply and expressed concern that one report of high levels of lead in the soil near the chrome shop could signal a health hazard.

As of 1992, the Wisconsin Department of Natural Resources had been granted authority to coordinate the remaining cleanup operations and is exploring options for doing so.

Media coverage

De Pere is served by the weekly *De Pere Journal*, which reports a 1992 circulation of 3,502. The present publisher, Paul Creviere, is the second generation of Crevieres to own the *Journal*. Paul's father bought the newspaper earlier in the century and relinquished control to his son in 1964. Paul's wife, Marie, works as editor; they hire one other reporter to round out the staff.

Just north of De Pere, where the Fox River empties into Green Bay, sits the community of Green Bay, a city of more than 96,000. Two daily newspapers serve the city, the morning *News-Chronicle* with a 1992 circulation of 9,830 and the dominant afternoon *Press-Gazette* with a circulation of 59,410.

What were the main frames in the newspaper coverage and how did they change over time?

The theme of coverage throughout the 1970s was very much one of finding contamination at the two Better Brite sites. The focus on the presence of contaminants continued into the 1980s, as agencies continued testing soils and water, finding ever-increasing amounts of chemicals. The 1980s produced a steady stream of stories that focused on what Better Brite is doing or should do about the contamination, as well as on legal efforts to force the company to take more concerted action. By the late 1980s, the dominant coverage frame had turned to EPA efforts to clean up the sites. From then on, the two primary foci of stories appeared to be cleanup activities and continued legal actions to obtain redress from the now-bankrupt Better Brite company.

Coverage by the three newspapers of this Superfund site, particularly coverage in the Green Bay daily newspapers, shows more frame cycling than we discovered in the National Presto case study. The cycling seems to be a function of two things: journalists' reliance on officials to give them a story frame and the unfolding nature of the Better Brite sites.

For example, the nature and extent of contamination at the National Presto site was relatively quickly established, so the 'what are the contaminants and where are they' theme enjoyed an early but brief life span and never emerged as a dominant frame again. In contrast, exploration of the nature and extent of contamination at the Better Brite sites has stretched over a period of years. Each new finding over the years produced a recurrence of the 'what are the contaminants and where are they' theme. Another reason for this recurring theme may be that at least one of the contaminants, chromium, is visible. Neighbors' periodic complaints about pools of yellow water after a good rainfall may also have promoted the recurrence of that theme.

The frames also varied by newspaper. Specifically, the weekly *De Pere Journal* appears to have covered this lengthy issue very differently than did the two daily newspapers in Green Bay. For example, the 'what are the contaminants and where are they' and a focus on Better Brite as a reluctant actor whose civic responsibilities must be wrung out of them by a court are largely missing in the *Journal* coverage. We will return to this difference later, when we discuss differences that might be attributed to community structure.

How did level of health hazard fare as a story frame?

As in the National Presto case, health hazards got some play early in the Better Brite story and again when the Division of Health reported on its preliminary health assessment in 1991. But those were not the only moments when the health theme was front and center. That frame cycles throughout the years of coverage – again predominantly in the Green Bay daily newspapers – in a pattern quite different from our other case studies. In many ways, hazards to health continue to the present in coverage as a recurring and, perhaps, dominant theme.

This pattern seems peculiar when one realizes that, among the three case studies examined here, the Better Brite sites may be the least hazardous. The Wisconsin Division of Health's preliminary assessment in 1990 found that remaining levels of the most ubiquitous contaminant at the sites, chromium, did not present a health risk. Health officials' primary worries were for the future: that investigators might yet detect abnormally high levels of lead on the sites and that contamination from the sites might eventually find its way into the city water wells.

What accounts for the continued media attention to health impacts are the efforts primarily of one family, whose home abuts the chromium plating site, to keep the theme alive. For years, family members have witnessed yellow pools of water in their back yard, yellow-tinged snow, and yellow water flooding into area basements during spring rains. Despite official conclusions that the chromium contamination does not pose a significant threat, family members complain that it has caused a variety of health problems. As one of them told a *Press-Gazette* reporter: 'It's not stretching it to compare this to Love Canal. In our family everyone has some nerve damage. We've had cancer in one of our daughters. And we're all especially susceptible to skin rashes.' Reporters have generally been sympathetic to the concerns of neighbors of the site. Thus, health risks have remained a prominent theme in coverage. Again, the exception to this pattern is the *De Pere Journal*.

Notably, the emphasis within this frame has been to posit the contamination found at these sites as hazardous indeed. For example, although the Division of Health preliminary assessment in 1991 concluded that the health risks were minimal, the lead on a resulting story by one Green Bay newspaper asserted: 'The former Better Brite plating shops in De Pere pose health problems to neighbors, a new study suggests.' Later, the story explained: 'The sites pose a public health hazard because of the potential for ingestion of on-site soil contaminated with lead and exposure through skin absorption to chromium-contaminated surface water or seepage water.' The story contained no information about level of risk.

Did occupational/organizational norms and resources make a difference in coverage?

The answer in this case study is an emphatic yes. Although the journalists at all three newspapers in this study claimed to write Better Brite stories when 'news' occurred, the total amount of coverage varied rather directly by newspaper size, from the largest of the three, the *Green Bay Press-Gazette*, to the smaller of the two dailies, the *Green Bay News-Chronicle*, and finally down to the smallest paper, the *De Pere Journal*. But the *Press-Gazette* stood head and shoulders over the other two not only in amount but also in type of coverage. While the *News-Chronicle* and the *De Pere Journal* stuck pretty closely to events, the *Press-Gazette* intermittently produced more reflective pieces. For example, a story in 1988 focused on the troubles of one family whose house adjoins the chromium plating site. In 1989 the newspaper returned to troubled families in the area for another story and did a historical retrospective on the site in the same issue.

The reasons for such different behavior, we argue, are grounded in occupational and organizational norms. The *Press-Gazette*, a newspaper with a circulation of more than 50,000, can afford to allow some reporters to specialize. One of their specialists is Terry Anderson, an environmental reporter. Better Brite is on his beat. To Anderson, the Better Brite story is not only news but an opportunity to show readers that, to paraphrase him, businesses need not be big to create an environmental hazard. Even small, seemingly innocuous companies can saddle communities with risks. He treats Better Brite as an ongoing story, touching base periodically with the EPA, DNR and with involved residents. He says he does some 'enterprise reporting', covering stories that are not event-based, but that he, like most reporters, has little time for such efforts. Indeed, most of his Better Brite stories are sparked by hearings, meetings, official reports and the like.

The bottom line, however, is that the ability to field a reporter with some environmental expertise, someone who has remained with the Better Brite story over the years, has allowed the *Press-Gazette* to give its readers a much more extensive accounting of the sites. The *Press-Gazette* coverage is by far the best informed and most comprehensive coverage of the site that we examined.

Did the nature of the communities in which these newspapers are embedded influence their coverage?

We think the answer is, again, yes. Here the interesting comparison is between the daily Green Bay newspapers and the weekly *De Pere Journal*.

Recall that Tichenor, Donohue and Olien argue that newspapers in more homogeneous communities have a greater stake in supporting the prevailing power structure, while those that serve more heterogeneous communities are more likely to be critical. In this case study, the homogeneous community is De Pere; the heterogeneous community is Green Bay. And the newspapers in these two communities indeed covered Better Brite in ways that reflect that 'consensual versus conflictive' difference. For example, while the Green Bay newspapers did not hesitate to depict the (now gone) owners of Better Brite as bad guys who balked at cleaning up the contaminated sites and then, by declaring bankruptcy, fled their responsibilities entirely, the De Pere newspaper took a very different tack. The *Journal* stories not only avoid the issue of who is to blame but seem to have ignored the former owners entirely.

The *Journal* also took a different approach to risk. While the Green Bay newspapers seemed occasionally to play up the health risk angle, the *Journal* played it down. For example, recall that the *Green Bay Press-Gazette* began its story about the Wisconsin Division of Health's preliminary health report in 1991 with the following lead: 'The former Better Brite plating shops in De Pere pose health problems to neighbors, a new study suggests.' Contrast that with the *De Pere Journal* lead on the same story: '"We have alleviated the immediate threat to humans and the environment," David Linnear, US Environmental Protection Agency (EPA) Remedial Project Coordinator, said in reference to the initial clean up at the Better Brite chrome and zinc shop sites in west De Pere.'

Behind these very different frames, we think, are important community differences that are reflected in newspaper behavior. The Green Bay newspapers serve a large and varied community that has wrestled with its share of environmental polluters over the years. Reporters and editors don't soft-pedal stories about damage done by local paper mills, and Better Brite looms as just another in the panoply of polluters. The *De Pere Journal*, on the other hand, serves a small, homogeneous community and its staff is proud of the newspaper's ties to the town. The newspaper clearly views itself as part of the support network for the community and, we think, worked to frame the Better Brite issue in ways that downplayed a story that seemed to reflect poorly on the town, on local government, and on long-time city residents who owned the Better Brite company. All three *Journal* staff members whom we interviewed, for example, repeatedly asserted that the Better Brite issue, while a legitimate story, was not that important an issue in De Pere. The residents of De Pere, they said, were largely indifferent to the sites. That indifference was understandable, they noted, because the sites pose no risk to the community at large. Officials have pronounced the contamination harmless, and city residents 'have no reason to doubt what (officials) tell us'. The publisher and editor of the *Journal* also recalled the former Better Brite owners favorably. The family was active in the local chamber of commerce and would give generously to civic endeavors, they noted. Better Brite was a good, well-run company, they said, whose owners knew nothing about pollution at the time.

The bottom line for the *De Pere Journal*, it seemed, was to attend to the news dimensions of the Better Brite issue when they occurred but to define the larger story as a success story, as a tale about a relatively benign environmental problem that is being handily solved.

Sheboygan River Harbor site

History

About 50 miles north of Milwaukee on the eastern border of Wisconsin, the Sheboygan River empties into Lake Michigan. The harbor there has long been a prominent feature of the city of Sheboygan and has served as a mecca for both commercial fishermen and recreational anglers; the latter have long enjoyed fishing for Great Lakes trout and salmon in both the river and Lake Michigan.

As far back as 1969, however, periodic tests of sediment samples suggested the presence of pollution. In 1977, the Wisconsin Department of Natural Resources detected significant amounts of polychlorinated biphenyls (PCBs) in fish taken from the river and began issuing health advisories limiting fish consumption. Continued sediment testing confirmed the presence of PCBs and such heavy metals as arsenic, lead, copper, zinc, cadmium, nickel, mercury and chromium. The PCB contamination prompted the US government to place 14 miles of the lower Sheboygan River and the 96-acre harbor on the Superfund list in 1985.

Officials identified at least three companies whose operations might have contributed to the PCB contamination. In 1986, one of those firms, Tecumseh Products Company, signed a consent order with the EPA and DNR, agreeing to cooperate actively in the cleanup. The Diecast Division of Tecumseh is a small engine manufacturer situated on the bank of the Sheboygan River in the community of Sheboygan Falls, a small town a few miles upriver from the harbor. The company at one time used PCBs in hydraulic fluids, and its proximity to the river meant that periodic flooding probably washed PCBs into the river.

Tecumseh hired a firm to investigate the extent of PCB contamination and ultimately located three PCB 'hot spots' in the upper part of the river, where concentrations in the sediments ranged as high as 4,500 parts per million. EPA has dredged these sites and is testing the viability of destroying the PCBs in the soil through biodegradation in a facility built on Tecumseh property. Additionally, in 1990 EPA covered approximately 13,500 square feet of river sediments with layers of fabric and gravel, a process called 'armoring'.

Tecumseh continued dredging contaminated soils from eight sites in the river in 1991 and is storing the sediment in a new 600,000-gallon sediment containment tank on its property. As of late 1992 officials continue to monitor the water, fish and sediments for the presence of PCBs. Results of the efforts to biodegrade the PCBs are imminent. A final cleanup plan for the entire site is yet to be proposed.

The EPA is not the only organization working to restore the river and harbor. In 1985 the Sheboygan County Water Quality Task Force was formed to coordinate local efforts to find solutions to the contamination problem. The Task Force represents commercial anglers, the Sheboygan Yacht Club, the Sheboygan Chamber of Commerce, city and county government, sporting and conservation groups, industry and agriculture.

Another player is the Wisconsin Department of Natural Resources, which has prepared its own remedial action plan for the Sheboygan watershed in concert with the International Joint Commission (an organization established by Canada and the eight Great Lakes states to monitor Great Lakes activities) and the Great Lakes Critical Program Act of 1990.

Media coverage

Sheboygan and Sheboygan Falls each has its own newspaper, albeit of different sizes. The *Sheboygan Press*, an afternoon daily with a circulation of 27,070, is the newspaper of record in Sheboygan, a community of more than 49,600 residents. The *Sheboygan Falls News* is a weekly that circulates 2,104 copies to residents of Sheboygan Falls.

What were the dominant frames in the newspaper coverage and how did they change over time?

From 1985 to the present, coverage of the Sheboygan River and harbor site focused on two main themes. One was 'how to clean up the contaminated river'. The other was 'restoration of commercial and recreational fishing'. Some themes, such as 'who is responsible for the problem?' received only glancing attention early in the coverage while others, such as the health risk theme, were missing entirely.

While the National Presto case study offered a kind of linear march of story themes and the Better Brite coverage seemed to cycle from one theme to another and then back again, the pattern of coverage for the Sheboygan site offers a more steady state picture. The two themes – cleanup efforts and restoration of fishing – remained major interpretive frameworks of the *Sheboygan Press* coverage throughout the seven years for which stories were available. The weekly *Sheboygan Falls News* does not follow this pattern; in fact, it hardly attends to the Superfund site at all.

We found a smaller number of major frames in the *Sheboygan Press* coverage than in coverage of daily newspapers in the other two case studies. One reason is that, although we attended to coverage for an eight-year period in this case study, awareness of the contamination of river and harbor sediments preceded that period by a number of years. Periodic dredging of the harbor for commercial boat traffic during the 1960s and early 1970s had produced evidence of contamination, and both the newspaper and community may have focused on the extent and nature of contamination long before the site was added to the Superfund list. Thus, by 1985, reporters had moved on to what for all three case studies is the longest-lived theme: cleanup.

Another possible reason for the brevity of the theme list in this case study is that one popular theme – 'who is responsible for the problem?' – was quickly answered. While in most Superfund sites the responsible party is either long gone or reluctant to participate, in this case Tecumseh, a local business, quickly stepped forward to accept responsibility and to play a major role in the cleanup. Thus missing from the coverage were the many stories following the legal wrangling that sometimes takes place as EPA and local officials try to force the responsible parties to own up to their deeds. Such a frame was prominent in the Better Brite coverage, for example.

Finally, we argue that the major themes adopted by the *Sheboygan Press* are limited to those that reflect the largely economic context within which the contamination issue was given meaning by the community. When contamination was identified in the 1970s, several factors worked to reconstruct that information as an economic, not a health, problem. Among them:

- Sheboygan Harbor is classified by the Wisconsin Department of Transportation as a diversified cargo port but must be dredged periodically to remain navigable. The presence of contaminated sediments halted dredging in the 1980s.
- Sheboygan Harbor has periodic runs of Great Lake trout and salmon, making sport fishing a nearly year-round enterprise. In fact, says former *Sheboygan Press* outdoor reporter Kurt Mueller, Sheboygan has long considered itself 'the capital of big-lake sport fishing'. The state typically has stocked coho and chinook salmon and rainbow trout in the fall and spring within Sheboygan Harbor. But stocking ceased with the discovery of PCB-laden sediments.
- The area is also a lively commercial fishery. Offshore waters of Lake Michigan provide a spawning area for whitefish, and the Sheboygan Harbor provides a nursery for these fish. Commercial fishing for both whitefish and perch takes place just outside the harbor.
- The Sheboygan community has begun constructing a marina in part of the harbor. Efforts in 1986 to dredge the area were rebuffed because the sediments might be contaminated. More recently, the city was able to persuade authorities that the part of the harbor at issue was not seriously contaminated, and work got under way.

The heavy emphasis on waterways as economic entities is operationalized in a particularly interesting way by the *Sheboygan Press*. That newspaper maintains a full-time outdoor reporter – not an environmental reporter – who is responsible for such environmental topics as Superfund sites. The difference between an outdoor and an environmental reporter can sometimes be subtle, but most American journalists would agree that the outdoor writer focuses more on uses of the environment – recreational outdoor activities such as hunting, fishing, boating, for example – than on describing and understanding the environment and its problems. An outdoor reporter, we contend, buys more readily into the argument that nature is at its most valuable when it is being used by humans. Thus, such a journalist will be more appealing to economic power structures because he or she is more likely to define environmental issues in economic terms.

The goodness of fit between the outdoor writer and the Sheboygan community was illustrated at one point when the *Press's* long-time outdoor reporter, Kurt Mueller, resigned. According to the current outdoor reporter, Barry Ginter, the *Press* initially considered dropping the beat. But members of the numerous outdoor and conservation organizations in the area protested, and the beat was retained.

How did level of hazard fare as a story frame?

Not well. Hazards to health barely make an appearance in the newspaper stories we examined. This is particularly surprising because, although the PCB contamination has not posed a risk to drinking water, it does make the local fish inedible. Wisconsin's fishing advisories warn anglers to avoid eating most of the fish available in the upper part of the Sheboygan River. In fact, the list of inedible fish from this waterway is longer than lists for any other body of water in Wisconsin.

It is possible that media stories attended to the issue of health hazards earlier in the life of the river and harbor saga. Former *Press* reporter Kurt Mueller recalled that his early stories indeed noted that a risk to health was present; he remembers hearing and using phrases such as 'PCBs as suspected carcinogens' and 'PCBs, thought to cause cancer'. But both he and current reporter Barry Ginter now define the health risk theme as 'old news'. Mueller argued that later stories do not have the space to rehash information that has already been presented. He also worried that readers would no longer care about the health dimensions of the issue at some point. Ginter said he and his editor assume that most readers are already aware of the health risks. He admitted that he talks to few general readers but noted that the charter captains with whom he deals seem 'highly knowledgeable' about the risks.

Did occupational/organizational norms and resources make a difference in extent of coverage?

Yes. As in the Better Brite case study, the two newspapers here vary dramatically in the resources they can bring to bear on topics such as a Superfund site. The *Sheboygan Press*, while relatively small for a daily newspaper, still fielded a full-time specialty reporter who covered the Superfund sites for years. Both the former and the current outdoor reporter followed the issues systematically and were occasionally given space for longer stories. A careful reading of *Sheboygan*

Press stories over the years would yield a great deal of information about the disposition of the Superfund sites, as well as detailed stories about efforts to begin restocking the river with sport fish.

The *Sheboygan Falls News*, on the other hand, has a staff of one. Her typical day involves seeking news at the police department and at city hall, taking numerous phone calls from residents with items for the next issue and then spending hours doing typesetting and paste-up. In-depth coverage of any topic is out, says editor/reporter/layout person Sandra Kimball. And given her choice of many possible stories, the Superfund sites do not rank high on her list. For one thing, she says, 'I'm not an environmental reporter'. For another, she feels that Sheboygan Falls residents are not interested in the sites. She recalls getting phone calls from readers upset about other issues, such as the town's recent need to create several temporary one-way streets to accommodate the repair of a bridge. But no one calls about PCBs in the Sheboygan River.

Sandra Kimball is right when she indicates that the *News* pays little attention to the Superfund sites. The newspaper contains remarkably few stories on the topic despite the presence, within the city limits, of the company taking primary responsibility for contaminating the river with PCBs. Kimball writes when she gets press releases or other types of information from Tecumseh or the EPA. But she makes no effort to follow the story or even to see for herself what is going on. For example, Tecumseh and the EPA built a facility on company property to experiment with biological degradation of PCBs. Kimball has never visited it, although it is within walking distance of the newspaper office.

Did community structure influence newspaper coverage?

Again, yes. But while Sheboygan and Sheboygan Falls differ rather dramatically in size, they both seem structurally homogeneous. And that level of homogeneity meant that the newspaper in each community was constrained to operate within certain supportive themes.

Sandra Kimball of the *Sheboygan Falls News*, for example, defined the mission of her newspaper as concentrating on local but support-ive news. Residents 'want their kids' pictures' in the newspaper, she said. They want feature stories, not critical reporting. News is what someone brings to the newspaper office and asks to have placed in the next issue, not something dug out of officials' garbage cans late at night. Such a newspaper finds ignoring Superfund sites not only an easy task but a legitimate one.

While the *Sheboygan Press* did not ignore the Superfund site – on the contrary, it has covered the issue quite systematically – it, too, is constrained by the social structure of the community. In this case, that structure promotes giving meaning to environmental contamination as an economic issue. A focus on how these problems influence the economic well-being of the community allows detailed discussion of PCB-contaminated fish, for example, but primarily as a factor having a negative impact on the sport fishing industry rather than as a health risk produced by local industry.

In conclusion

What factors account for the ways in which these Wisconsin newspapers framed coverage of the Superfund sites in these three case studies? We mention four classes of predictors, saving the most important one for last.

First, the process by which a Superfund site is diagnosed and ultimately fixed drove story frames to some extent. Most bureaucratically defined processes have a structure. Scholars such as Fishman (1982) argue that journalists 'see events by using the same phase structures that beat agency officials use to formulate their own and others' activities as events' (p. 224). That is, reporters simply adopt the frames of reference of the bureaucracies that they cover; a dimension of an issue will be deemed newsworthy because officials have defined that piece of the process as important.

Thus, media coverage across the life span of a Superfund site tended to emphasize points of the process that had been established, a priori, as important by US EPA. Officials would reinforce these points by staging hearings and sending out press releases. Newspaper audiences would learn about the results of remedial investigations, about evaluations of health risks, about the filing of law suits. But this controller of story frames renders the bulk of the Superfund siting and remediation process invisible to the public.

Second, sources were able to exercise substantial control over story frames. Related to the first class of predictors is the finding that sources of all kinds were able to drive story themes. Journalists are highly dependent on sources for information, yet they are counseled by the occupation to exercise some skepticism, to question the validity of information. We found little of that skepticism in these case studies. Instead, the journalists we interviewed regarded their Superfund sources as reasonable, responsible and accurate. That allowed sources to play a major role in establishing story frames, we feel.

For example, the severity of risks to health from chromium contamination became a recurring theme throughout the years of coverage of the Better Brite site near Green Bay principally because residents near the site made an effort to keep the issue on the media's agenda.

Third, occupational/organizational norms and resources influence story frames. In common with the numerous authors cited earlier in this chapter, we also found that news-making practices, grounded firmly in occupational and organizational norms, influenced the ways in which journalists interpreted Superfund stories over time. Any given dimension of a Superfund site became news only when it coincided with the interpretive framework provided by the occupation.

One of the major features of this interpretive framework was the incessant hunt for events on the part of reporters in all three case studies. Events are the principal diet of a journalist, and in this case they accounted for the overwhelming majority of stories written about any one site. Journalists acted when someone held a hearing, when an irate citizen complained about the pace of cleanup at a meeting, when a government body made a decision, when a lawyer filed a lawsuit.

One might argue that attention to such things is no better or worse than randomly picking any subset of occurrences to cover within the lengthy confines of Superfund remediation. But such an event orientation does limit journalistic frames in two ways. For one, it allows sources to control the process and the frames, something discussed briefly above. For another, it absolves journalists from attending to the big picture.

Superfund sites are fascinating social phenomena. They represent extremely complex coping strategies that reveal a great deal about a culture's fears, about its priorities, about the state of the art of technology, and about the concerns of prevailing power structures. But for journalists, these lengthy processes seem to loom instead as featureless plains pockmarked by intermittent 'newsworthy' events. Such amorphous landscapes are problematic for an occupation that concentrates on representing reality as something concrete that happened 'today' or will happen 'tomorrow'. As they work to negotiate that landscape, newspapers and their reporters make little effort to step back and view the bigger picture. Instead, they concentrate on accurately representing the cross-section of reality that a single event such as a hearing offers up.

Another major feature of the occupational framework that influenced story construction were traditional assumptions made by the journalists about the information-ingestion habits of audience members. Journalists rarely have access to information about their readers or viewers and thus rely on longstanding occupational assumptions about them. The occupational definition of audience members characterizes them as regular and faithful. It assumes that they follow the ongoing coverage of a story with some care and, thus, will bridle if fed 'old news'. Old news is information that was defined as worthy of attention earlier in the life span of an issue. Once articulated, such information is then assumed to be part of the information base that readers/viewers will bring to bear on later stories. Thus, a reporter may highlight a discussion of the health risks posed by a Superfund site early in the life span of that issue but may balk at the prospect of including risk information in later stories.

The accuracy of these occupational assumptions is questionable. If anything, research has suggested that, while reporters may understand the science information needs of audiences better than editors

(Johnson, 1963), they still make many incorrect assumptions about their readers or viewers (Tannenbaum, 1963; Crane, 1992). Nonetheless, those assumptions seem to play a major role in decisions about the kind of details that are appropriate in stories over the life span of longer issues such as these Superfund sites.

Finally, and most importantly, frames are driven by community structures and by interpretation championed by the prevailing power structure in town. We saw two ways in which community structure influenced coverage of local Superfund sites. One was the pattern predicted by Tichenor, Donohue and Olien, in which community structure led media embedded in those settings to play either the role of promoter or watchdog. Newspapers in more homogeneous communities in these case studies were more likely to downplay the seriousness of hazards at the Superfund sites, confine their reporting to coverage of events, and frame the sites as problems that were being handily solved by local authorities. Their coverage reflected effort, in other words, to keep the 'controversy' contained within town boundaries and to minimize threats to the prevailing power structure. Newspapers in more heterogeneous settings, conversely, were far more likely to cover Superfund sites extensively, to relegate offending local industries to 'bad guy' status, and to regard the risks inherent in the site as worthy of concern and publicity.

A second way in which community structure acted to influence coverage of these Superfund sites was not anticipated. We found that communities in two of the three case studies seemed to play a major role in establishing the larger framework within which the Superfund site would be discussed. The lengthy and, apparently, contentious relationship among the communities of Eau Claire, Chippewa Falls and the township of Hallie, for example, worked to give meaning to the National Presto site as a territorial issue. Within that interpretive framework, the health hazards present at the site were relevant to the extent that they lent credence to motives ascribed to the actions of any single community as it 'poached' on another.

Similarly, the Sheboygan River and Harbor site quickly became framed as an economic issue for residents of Sheboygan and for the *Sheboygan Press*. Within that context, PCBs in fish became problems for the sport fishing industry rather than potential hazards to the health of readers. Heavy metals embedded in sediments in the Sheboygan Harbor became roadblocks to dredging rather than risk factors for residents.

In fact, one of the most important messages that came out of these three case studies for us was that, for the mass media, Superfund sites are not environmental risk stories. They are not primarily – or even substantively – stories about risks to health, although Superfund sites were created primarily to signal that condition. Rather, these stories are sagas about solving community problems, sagas whose main story lines come courtesy of the prevailing power structure. Long-running environmental problems, thus, seem to be recast by the mass media as situational morality plays whose plot and denouement depend to a considerable degree on the nature of the community in which the drama unfolds.

References

Crane, V. (1992), 'Listening to the audience: producer–audience communication', in B.V. Lewenstein (ed.), *When science meets the public*, Washington, DC: American Association for the Advancement of Science, pp. 21–32.

Donohue, G.A., Olien, C.N., Tichenor, P.J. (1985a), 'Leader and editor views of the role of press in community development', *Journalism Quarterly*, 62 (2), pp. 367–72.

Donohue, G.A., Olien, C.N., Tichenor, P.J. (1985b), 'Reporting conflict by pluralism, newspaper type, and ownership', *Journalism Quarterly*, 62 (3), pp. 489–99, 507.

Dunwoody, S. (1979), 'News-gathering behaviors of specialty reporters: a two-level comparison of mass media decision-making', *Newspaper Research Journal*, 1 (1), pp. 29–39.

Dunwoody, S., Rossow, M. (1989), 'Community pluralism and newspaper coverage of a high-level nuclear waste siting issue', in L.A. Grunig (ed.), *Environmental activism revisited: the changing nature of communication through organizational public relations, special interest groups and the mass media*, Troy, Ohio: The North American Association for Environmental Education, pp. 5–21.

Fishman, M. (1982), 'News and nonevents: making the visible invisible', in J.S. Ettema and D.C. Whitney, (eds) *Individuals in mass media organizations: creativity and constraint*, Newbury Park, Calif.: Sage, pp. 219–40.

Gitlin, T. (1980), *The whole world is watching*, Berkeley: University of California Press.

Graber, D. (1988), *Processing the news: how people tame the information tide*, 2nd edn, New York: Longman.

Greenberg, M.R., Sachsman, D.B., Sandman, P.M., Salomone, K.L. (1989), 'Risk, drama and geography in coverage of environmental risk by network TV', *Journalism Quarterly*, 66 (2), pp. 267–76.

Griffin, R.J., Molen, D.H., Schoenfeld, C., Scotton, J.F. (1991), *Interpreting public issues*, Ames, Iowa: Iowa State University Press.

Johnson, K.G. (1963), 'Dimensions of judgment of science news stories', *Journalism Quarterly*, 49(3), pp. 315–22.

McLeod, J.M., Blumler, J.G. (1987), 'The macrosocial level of communication science', in C.R. Berger and S.H. Chaffee (eds), *Handbook of communication science*, Newbury Park, Calif.: Sage, pp. 271–322.

Mendelsohn, H. (1990), 'Mind, affect, and action: construction theory and the media effects dialectic', in S. Kraus (ed.) *Mass communication and political information processing*, Hillsdale, NJ: Erlbaum, pp. 37–45.

Olien, C.N., Donohue, G.A., Tichenor, P.J. (1968), 'The community editor's power and the reporting of conflict', *Journalism Quarterly*, 45 (2), pp. 243–52.

Olien, C.N., Donohue, G.A., Tichenor, P.J. (1978), 'Community structure and media use', *Journalism Quarterly*, 55 (3), pp. 445–55.

Olien, C.N., Tichenor, P.J., Donohue, G.A. (1989), 'Media coverage and social movements', in C.T. Salmon (ed.), *Information campaigns: balancing social values and social change*, Newbury Park, Calif.: Sage, pp. 139–63.

Phillips, E.B. (1977), 'Approaches to objectivity: journalistic vs. social science perspectives', in P.M. Hirsch, P.V. Miller and F.G. Kline (eds), *Strategies for communication research*, Newbury Park, Calif.: Sage, pp. 63–77.

Rachlin, A. (1988), *News as hegemonic reality: American political culture and the framing of news accounts*, New York: Praeger.

Rubin, D.M. (1980), 'Science writers never had a chance in the Three Mile Island nuclear debacle', *Newsletter of the National Association of Science Writers*, 28, pp. 1–2, 10–13.

Ryan, M., Dunwoody, S., Tankard, J. (1991), 'Risk information for public consumption: print media coverage of two risky situations', *Health Education Quarterly*, 18 (3), pp. 375–90.

Sandman, P.M., Sachsman, D.B., Greenberg, M.R., Gochfeld, M. (1987), *Environmental risk and the press*, New Brunswick, NJ: Transaction Books.

Singer, E. (1990), 'A question of accuracy: how journalists and scientists report research on hazards', *Journal of Communication*, 40 (4), pp. 102–16.

Singer, E., Endreny, P. (1987), 'Reporting hazards: their benefits and costs', *Journal of Communication*, 37 (3), pp. 10–26.

Stocking, S.H., Gross, P.H. (1989), *How do journalists think?*, Bloomington, Indiana: ERIC Clearinghouse on Reading and Communication Skills.

Tankard, J.W. Jr., Hendrickson, L., Silberman, J., Bliss, K., Ghanem, S. (1991), 'Media frames: approaches to conceptualization and measurement', paper presented to the Association for Education in Journalism and Mass Communication annual meeting, Boston, Massachusetts, August.

Tannenbaum, P.H. (1963), 'Communication of science information', *Science*, 140 (10 May), pp. 579–83.

Tichenor, P.J., Donohue, G.A., Olien, C.N. (1980), *Community conflict and the press*, Newbury Park, California: Sage.

van Dijk, T.A. (1988), *News as discourse*, Hillsdale, NJ: Erlbaum.

Weiss, C.H., Singer, E. (1988), *Reporting social science in the national media*, New York: Russell Sage Foundation.

3
Source–media relations: the production of the environmental agenda

Alison Anderson

During the late 1980s environmental issues acquired a new legitimacy within the British political arena. This phenomenon was not just experienced by Britain; environmental groups across Europe witnessed a surge in membership and they welcomed their newly found political influence. British environmental groups, such as Friends of the Earth (FoE) and Greenpeace, gained greater access to the news media, particularly the tabloid press (Love, 1990). By the early 1990s, however, the intense interest among the British public had begun to fade. Public opinion polls indicated that the economic recession and the Gulf War had overtaken the environment as the most important issues facing Britain (MORI 1991).

This chapter focuses on the relationship between environmental groups and the media. Within the mass communications literature source roles have received relatively little attention. Where interest has focused upon sources, researchers have until recently analysed source–media relations from a largely media-centric position (see Schlesinger, 1990). Thus, source roles have been generally deduced from content analyses of media texts, or from interviews with reporters. Yet sources play a key role in constructing the environmental agenda. We know very little about the way in which sources (and here we are specifically concerned with environmental groups) view their relationship with the media, about the media strategies they pursue, or about the major constraints which affect them.

This discussion is based upon some preliminary research findings from a content analysis of national press coverage during 1988, together with data from several in-depth, semi-structured interviews, carried out between January 1989 and January 1991. The interviews were with: broadcasters covering environmental topics; journalists reporting environmental affairs in the national daily press and

Sunday newspapers; press officers at the Department of the Environment (DoE); and representatives of industry, environmental pressure groups and related interest groups. The study focused upon four environmental organizations: Friends of the Earth, Greenpeace, the National Trust, and the National Society for Clean Air and Environmental Protection (NSCA). Also, two case studies were made of the reporting of environmental issues. One analysed national press coverage of the seal virus, a disease which killed large numbers of common seals during the summer of 1988. The other examined the local press coverage of the Hinkley 'C' Inquiry into the building of a second nuclear pressurized water reactor at Hinkley Point in Somerset.

An overview of the literature on source roles and the media

Very few comprehensive analyses of environmental pressure groups and the media have been made. Indeed, the failure to conceptualize relations between journalists and sources constitutes a major lacuna within mass communications research:

My observations on source power suggest that the study of sources deserves far more attention from news researchers than it has so far obtained. To understand the news fully, researchers must study sources as roles and representatives of the organised or unorganised groups for whom they act or speak, and thus also as holders of power. Above all, researchers should determine what groups create or become sources, and with what agendas; what interests they pursue in seeking access to the news and in refusing it. Parallel studies should be made of groups that cannot get into the news, and why this is so. And researchers must ask what effect obtaining or failing to obtain access to the news has on power, the interests and the subsequent activities of groups who become or are represented by sources. (Gans, 1979, p. 360)

Until recently, researchers have largely focused upon how the media make use of sources, rather than upon how sources themselves interact with the media. As Schlesinger observes:

Once one begins to analyse the tactics and strategies pursued by sources seeking media attention, to ask about their perceptions of other, competing actors in the fields over which they operate, to ask about their goals and notions of effectiveness, one rapidly discovers how ignorant we are about such matters and this despite the undoubted importance of the contribution that production studies have made to the field. (1990, p. 62)

The majority of studies concentrate upon official sources, such as government, industry or scientists. They indicate that the media tend to rely most heavily upon official sources of information in a number of institutional areas (for example, Tunstall, 1971; Sigal, 1973;

Chibnall, 1977; Golding and Middleton, 1982; Schlesinger, Murdock and Elliott, 1983; Karpf, 1988). When we consider key news sources for environmental news the pattern is not dissimilar. Indeed, research in a variety of different countries suggests that official sources are cited by print journalists and broadcasters much more often than environmental groups (Gandy, 1980; Einsiedel, 1988; Greenberg et al., 1989; Wang, 1988; Hansen, 1991; Nohrstedt, 1991). However, though the evidence clearly indicates that the agencies of the state tend to enjoy the most privileged access to the media, we should not neglect the role of non-official sources. As Schlesinger recently notes:

Empirical studies . . . have failed to investigate the forms of action taken by non-official sources, such as pressure groups. Although pressure to develop an all-encompassing account is obviously at work in the sociology of journalism, the failure to push research beyond its present limits has resulted in a dearth of sustained investigation into unofficial source competition or into the internal organisation of the media strategies of pressure groups. (1990, p. 76)

A seminal study by Hall et al. (1978) *Policing the crisis: mugging, the state, and law and order* argues that powerful 'accredited' sources, such as government departments or the courts, enjoy privileged access to the media. They command greater access to the media by virtue of their claims to expert knowledge, their powerful position in society, or their representative status. Thus, Hall et al. suggest that powerful sources become over-accessed by the media, and as a result, they become 'primary definers' of key issues:

media statements are, wherever possible, grounded in "objective" and authoritative statements from "accredited" sources. This means constantly turning to accredited social representatives of major social institutions – MPs for political topics, employers and trade union leaders for industrial matters, and so on . . . Ironically, the very rules which grew out of the desires for greater professional neutrality, also serve powerfully to orientate the media in the "definitions of social reality" which their "accredited sources" – the institutional spokesmen – provide. (1978, p. 58)

However, by concentrating upon primary definition in the media, the structuralist model overlooks the process of negotiation and conflict prior to definitions appearing in the media. As Schlesinger (1990) suggests:

The model given by Hall et al. is one in which primary definitions are conceived as commanding the field as producing a dominant ideological effect. While this offers a coherent critique of various forms of pluralism, an uncritical adherence to this model involves paying a price. For the structuralist model is profoundly incurious about the processes whereby sources engage in ideological conflict *prior to or contemporaneous with the appearance of definitions in the media*. It therefore rules out asking questions about

how contestation over definitions takes place *within* institutions and organisations reported by the media as well as the concrete strategies pursued
as they contend for space. (1990, p. 68)

What factors govern environmental pressure groups' success or
failure in attracting media attention? To what extent do they develop
strategies to gain in-depth, favourable media coverage? How far are
their specific concerns reflected on media agendas? What factors
influence the complex linkages between the political domain, public
opinion and media agendas? These questions have rarely been
explored in the literature.

Few studies of environmental organizations have given detailed
attention to the media. The handful of studies which have focused
upon this issue are, with a few exceptions, rather dated (Gandy, 1980;
Lowe and Goyder, 1983; Wilson, 1984; Davies, 1985; Greenberg, 1985;
Warren, 1990). The most comprehensive study of environmental
pressure groups, to date, is Lowe and Goyder's (1983) *Environmental
groups in politics*. The authors surveyed seventy-seven national
voluntary groups concerned with the environment between 1979 and
1980. Lowe and Goyder interviewed senior representatives of these
groups about a variety of issues including: membership; staff; access
to the media; internal democracy; cooperation between environmental groups and relations with government departments. Their evidence, though dated, suggests environmental organizations had
changed considerably since the 1960s. In contrast to the older
environmental organizations such as the National Trust, the new
campaigning pressure groups formed in the 1970s actively sought to
use the mass media to influence the political arena and public
attitudes. They used stunts, such as dressing up as rainforest animals,
to focus media attention on issues and to force them into the political
domain. Des Wilson observes: '[these] were seen to be pioneering
fresh approaches, in particular by combining detailed negotiation
with Whitehall and Westminster with exploitation of the media to
force politicians and civil servants to take them seriously' (1984, p.
16).

A more recent study by McCormick (1991), *British politics and the
environment*, analyses the changing role of environmental groups
within the British political scene. Although McCormick is not
primarily concerned with the media strategies of environmental
organizations, he notes the increased emphasis the environmental
lobby placed upon building up contacts with the media during the
1980s. The way in which the press offices of the major environmental
pressure groups expanded during Mrs Thatcher's administrations
gives some indication of the increased importance placed upon media
relations. By the late 1980s a combination of factors ensured that, in
general terms, environmental pressure groups gained greater access
to the media.

Studies suggest that credibility is a crucial factor governing source–media relations. If environmental groups are to attract favourable media coverage they must be viewed as legitimate and authoritative. Greenberg (1985), in one of the few studies to explore the strategies used by environmental pressure groups, claims that the UK's Friends of the Earth have developed a credible, distinctive, identity:

> What makes FoE so unique is that the organisation combines a strong research commitment with its attention-getting tactics. This decision to combine research and media events was made when the organisation was founded because it was felt in order to have credibility and sustain its image, independent of the publicity it generated, FoE had to show that the issues had been seriously thought through and that viable intelligent options to prevailing policies were available. (1985, p. 356)

Environmental pressure groups, such as Friends of the Earth, have become institutionalized within British political culture and there has been a general trend towards greater conservatism (see McCormick, 1991). Once on the fringes of debate, during the late 1980s environmental pressure groups became established news sources. Indeed, a key difficulty with Hall et al.'s (1978) theory of 'primary definers' is that it fails to take account of shifts in source access to the media (see Schlesinger, 1990). The structure of access fluctuates over time; to some degree this reflects media strategies but also external factors, such as the climate of public opinion and political discussion. Indeed, as Hansen argues:

> That the role of pressure groups in the elaboration for media and wider attention of certain environmental issues may be considerably more complex than is suggested by their low profile in actual media coverage has been indicated both theoretically and empirically in studies of environmental journalists . . . The low profile of pressure groups as primary definers in actual media coverage indicates that, while they may play a key role as claims-makers, drawing the attention of the media to particular environmental problems, it is to the fora of "public authorities", "formal politics" and "science" that journalists turn for validation of such claims. Consequently, both continued media coverage and the wider elaboration of certain environmental problems hinge crucially on the extent to which they become part of, and articulated through, the agendas of these other established "fora". (Hansen, 1991, p. 451)

We need to go beyond the present approach, then, and develop a model which recognizes the complexity of the linkages between source activity, public attitudes, media agendas and the political domain. The process through which environmental news is produced is much more complex than traditional studies suggest. The media are only part, though an important part, of the network of influences upon environmental policy-making. By broadly focusing upon the ways in which the media make use of sources, researchers have overlooked a crucial element of the production process.

Power, resources and credibility: environmental pressure groups and the media

The degree to which environmental groups gain access to the media and to government hinges to a large extent upon resources, whether they be income, organizational factors, skills or knowledge (see Moodie and Studdert-Kennedy, 1970; Gandy, 1980; McCarthy and Zald, 1982). The interviews with representatives of environmental groups indicated that the organization of media relations varies a great deal. For example, while Friends of the Earth develop media contacts mainly at the level of the individual campaigner, Greenpeace channel media relations largely through their centralized press office. Chris Rose, director of Media Natura, argues:

> Now Friends of the Earth are completely different in that they operate a sort of continual seepage or trickle system. They are quite happy to get coverage almost anywhere . . . They don't control their media in the same way as Greenpeace does. With Greenpeace, if Sue Adams says basically you shouldn't do it then it doesn't get done. At Friends of the Earth the last person to get an influence on the proceedings is say, Laura Thomas, who is the nearest you can get to Sue's position . . . so although in the public perception the two things are similar and often confused they're utterly different in the way that they use the media. (Rose, 1990)

A further difference between the two organizations is that Greenpeace are particularly geared towards the visual content of newspapers and television news. Chris Rose argued:

> What Greenpeace are very good at is they've invented, if you like, a sort of morality play . . . that takes Greenpeace straight out of the editorial system of gatekeepers . . . it puts them into that sort of tabloid news and that's what headline news in television is all about because it has to be thirty-second subjects, thirty-second visuals . . . So I mean they're using the media in that way, deliberately restricting most of their input using that one visible bit that you can see, using television news, basically, and newspaper photographs. (Rose, 1990)

During the last decade the income of the majority of British environmental pressure groups has dramatically increased, particularly between 1987 and 1989. For example, Greenpeace's annual income for 1980 was estimated to be £175,000, while in 1989 it was £4,500,000. Friends of the Earth witnessed a similar rise in income; in 1980 its income was estimated to be £200,000, but by 1989 it had risen to £20,760,000. Environmental pressure groups receive their funds mainly through membership subscriptions so the expansion in income reflects their rapidly growing membership. In 1989 Greenpeace had 320,000 members, the vast majority of which had joined since 1985. The membership of Friends of the Earth has also grown at a very large rate since the mid-1980s, so that by 1989 it had 120,000 members (see McCormick, 1991).

However, the income of pressure groups such as Greenpeace and Friends of the Earth differs markedly to that of quasi-official interest groups, such as the National Trust, who attract sizeable government grants. The annual income of the Trust was £55,800,000 in 1989. The provision of government grants to environmental organizations is a relatively new development. This reflects the state's recognition that quasi-official groups can undertake some of the work formerly carried out by government departments, and at the same time they are viewed as independent of the state. However, if the grant is large then it is likely that the government will stipulate how it is to be used. In this way the government is able to exert control over such organizations and they become what Lowe and Goyder term 'agents of government'. Also, if they are critical of government there is the possibility that their grant may be withdrawn (Lowe and Goyder, 1983).

Accompanying the rise in income there has also been a dramatic increase in the number of staff employed by environmental organizations. For example, between 1984 and 1989 there was a 900 per cent increase in the number of staff employed by Friends of the Earth; an increase from eight members of staff to eighty (see McCormick, 1991). There has also been a corresponding increase in the number of experienced staff responsible for lobbying and information services. In the late 1970s Lowe and Goyder found over half the groups they surveyed had staff with journalistic or public relations skills. In 1989 Friends of the Earth employed nineteen people with responsibility for campaigns and another eleven staff worked in the information department. Indeed, environmental pressure groups are increasingly attracting staff with journalistic backgrounds. For example, the photo librarian at Greenpeace was photo editor for *City Limits* magazine and the features writer formerly worked for *Living Magazine* and *Woman Magazine*.

Both Greenpeace and Friends of the Earth are currently undertaking major public relations/outreach strategies. They are targeting certain sections of the media, such as women's magazines and the tabloid press. Lucy Thorp, press officer for Greenpeace, claimed:

The department has changed from being one person to being five people . . . Two years ago what we would probably have done with any information that we'd have is send out a news release. Well we realized that that wasn't the best way of targeting the media . . . We're actually targeting specific media, depending upon what the story is. (Thorp, 1991)

Also, Greenpeace are taking advantage of the recent cutbacks in broadcasting through supplying broadcast format footage to television networks (see Anderson, 1991a). Lucy Thorp suggested:

We're going to be doing more filming especially at the moment when we see the television companies have very little money and they're cutting back on their resources. If we can actually supply them with footage they're more likely to run our stories so we do make freely available all of our television footage. (Thorp, 1991)

Similarly, Friends of the Earth are planning to produce their own exclusive photographs. Jan McHarry, senior information officer at Friends of the Earth maintained:

Last year when we were invited to go to Nigeria, to Coco, the site being used for waste disposal, we were actually one of the few groups with photos so when we came back those photos were in tremendous demand so ... that has given us a taster of where you can get an exclusive photo, and extensively you can market that photograph. (McHarry, 1989)

The increasing professionalism of environmental groups is reflected by the widespread monitoring of media output to assess the frequency and quality of coverage about themselves. However, monitoring of the media is closely related to budgetary constraints. Of the four environmental organizations studied, the National Trust, by far the wealthiest group, carried out the most extensive survey. The National Trust was the only organization to have an external monitoring contract to video television programmes. However all of the organizations studied, except the National Society for Clean Air, clipped all the national daily broadsheet newspapers. In addition, Greenpeace use a local press clippings service, reflecting the importance they place upon regional newspapers.

As one might expect, it is government sources which carry out the most sophisticated survey of media output. The Department of the Environment press office subscribes to a press cuttings service of regional and national newspapers. In addition, all broadcasts with ministers or members of the department are recorded.

Past research suggests that environmental organizations regard the national quality press as the most useful medium for influencing political and public debates. Lowe and Goyder (1983) found that the majority of the environmental organizations included in their survey mostly targeted the national broadsheet newspapers. The authors found that 74 per cent of the groups claimed to have received radio coverage, 59 per cent said they had received television coverage, while only 9 per cent stated they had received no media coverage at all. Chris Rose, director of Media Natura, maintained:

The real importance of getting stuff into newspapers is to influence the politicians because they are the people who actually cut them up. And if you want to get a subject on television there's no point going to talk to the TV researchers and people like that because television is an extremely mobile world ... The best way to influence television content wise is to get something in a national newspaper because they all start off every morning . . . and they're presented with the cuttings from the newspapers and they then proceed to ring up the conservation groups. That's how they do their research basically. They'd deny it but that's what they actually do. (Rose, 1990)

However, if environmental groups are to attract quality coverage and access to the corridors of power they need to be seen as credible and legitimate sources. The interviews with print journalists and broadcasters indicated that they still tend to regard non-official sources, such as Greenpeace, with some suspicion. For example, Richard North of *The Independent*, expressed some concern about the reliability of the information contained in Greenpeace literature: 'In the end I stopped reading it altogether because I thought . . . while a bit of it will be right and it will be for the greater good of mankind, substantially it will be wrong in its science or its evidence or its balance' (North, 1989). Michael McCarthy, Environment Correspondent for *The Times* concurred: 'Greenpeace have got a credibility problem with Environment Correspondents because they put things out which aren't true' (McCarthy, 1991). However, the broadcasters were not so critical of Greenpeace as the print journalists. The television journalists claimed they are sceptical about all their sources and that it is the fault of the journalist if he/she relies too strongly upon Greenpeace information without following it up. A typical comment was that of Ashley Bruce, producer of Channel 4's *Fragile Earth:*

I think it's rather silly of the media to sort of heavily rely on something like Greenpeace, which is what they do, and expect them to be giving them absolutely correct information and expect them to be giving them shock horror stories all at the same time and expect them to be experts . . . It's probably the media that ought to be criticised in that sense. (Bruce, 1989)

Despite the suspicions levelled against Greenpeace, the group still manages to attain a relatively large amount of media coverage. Chris Rose, director of Media Natura, claimed the reason why a number of environment correspondents display this attitude is because news editors tend to accept information from Greenpeace without it being channelled through the correspondent:

They don't like Greenpeace and they don't like Greenpeace because Greenpeace goes past them. It gets straight onto the front page of the newspaper because the news editor will say "I don't care whether you think this is news or not, that they're blocking this ship up the Thames, it looks like news as far as I'm concerned and the public will think it's news." (Rose, 1990)

Over the past few years Greenpeace has taken a number of steps to improve its image, such as setting up a scientific unit at Queen Mary College and employing its own research fellow. However, as Rob Edwards maintains, there is a conflict between those within the organization who want to base a strong image on education and scientific research, and those who favour direct action:

The irony is that over the past few years Greenpeace has been making genuine attempts to beef up its scientific credibility. It has devoted more resources to research, to report-writing and to conventional lobbying techniques. It has also sharpened up its advertising and begun direct mail shots. These changes have in turn annoyed some of the direct action traditionalists, who fear loss of purity and effectiveness. (Edwards, 1988, p. 18)

Friends of the Earth have tried to cultivate a rather different sort of image based upon lobbying and research. Jan McHarry, senior information officer at Friends of the Earth, claimed: 'Friends of the Earth's approach is actually based on doing a lot of research and having a lot of answers before we launch campaigns' (McHarry, 1989).

One of the ways in which Friends of the Earth are indirectly attempting to influence the political agenda is through offering advice and expertise to key individuals within the structures of power. For example, the former director of Friends of the Earth, Jonathan Porritt, advised Prince Charles on his speech concerning the environment. However Lawrence McGinty, Science Editor at ITN, suggested that environmental groups could develop a more sophisticated strategy for manipulating cycles of media attention:

What I think they're not actually quite so good at is picking the turning points in environmental coverage and what people think of the environment and knowing how to manipulate those. Those are very hard to do and they've done it a certain amount behind the scenes but not through the media, like Jonathan Porritt writing Prince Charles' speech, or talking to him about it, offering suggestions, whatever it was . . . Unless you're discriminating I think you're too busy just throwing press release, after press release, after press release, reflecting your activity . . . they're not actually standing back and saying hang on that doesn't really matter. What really matters is how people are going to change their minds about the way we need to approach the greenhouse effect, for instance, in the next twelve months. What's going to be the key event and how are we going to make sure that we are there and we can construct it? (McGinty, 1990)

Over recent decades there has been a general movement towards greater coordination among the environmental lobby. The Green Alliance was formed in 1978 with the aim of developing a political strategy for the environmental movement. Tom Burke, director of the Green Alliance, claimed: 'We want to help groups distinguish between the political process (what many people do at many levels) and the governmental process (what a small number of people do). If you want to change the agenda you have to understand politics' (quoted in McCormick, 1991, p. 38). However, environmental groups experience a fundamental conflict over reaching their membership through the media, upon which they rely for funds, and influencing the political domain. A further difficulty is that need to establish their own identities in order to attract new recruits, but they also need to develop a unified public image. Many of the coalitions which have been formed, such as the Council for Environmental Conservation, have lacked effectiveness due to internal problems and disagreements within the environmental movement.

Environmental groups are competing with one another, as well as with statutory bodies, for media space. One way in which the environmental lobby has tried to deal with the problem of the activities of environmental groups overlapping is to compile a media diary. A group of environmental press officers meets regularly to discuss their plans for future publicity events and to put together a diary. Though environmental groups would generally deny that they are competing with one another for media attention, Chris Rose claimed: 'they're competing but they do co-operate to the extent of trying to avoid each other's dates' (Rose, 1990).

Environmental pressure groups are also playing an increasingly strategic role in seeking to shape political priorities. In 1989 a pamphlet entitled *The Green Gauntlet* set out a collection of proposed environmental measures to government; it was a collaborative venture by the World Wide Fund for Nature, Friends of the Earth and Greenpeace. Environmental pressure groups also worked together to produce *Blueprint for a Green Europe*, which made a number of policy recommendations in the lead up to the 1989 European elections.

There has also been a movement towards greater cooperation between voluntary groups and quasi-official organizations over the last ten years. In the early 1980s many environmental groups openly attacked bodies such as the Nature Conservancy Council, but when the government told of its plans to dissolve the Countryside Commission and the Nature Conservancy Council they were supportive of these quasi-official bodies (McCormick, 1991).

The environmental lobby, then, is generally becoming more professional in targeting information to specific media, extensively monitoring newspaper coverage and cultivating an image based upon research-informed campaigns (see Anderson, 1991b). Although environmental groups are increasingly coordinating their activities they have some way to go towards developing a joint strategy. The mobilization of resources is crucial since non-official sources have to compete with official sources for access to the media (see Anderson, 1991c). It is likely that the success of the environmental lobby will depend, to a large extent, upon whether this general growth in expertise, along with increasing consumer pressure, can be channelled in appropriate directions. Also, it will hinge upon the degree to which the demands are viewed as rational by government, as well as politically desirable.

The role of environmental pressure groups in shaping public attitudes, media agendas and political priorities

To some degree the issues which appear on media agendas have already been defined as legitimate by government (see Solesbury, 1976; Hall et al. 1978). However, environmental pressure groups play a vital role in forcing issues into the public and the political domain. The case study of national press coverage of the seal virus during the summer of 1988 illustrates the way in which environmental pressure groups may, in particular circumstances, act as crucial definers of events through mobilizing public opinion. The content analysis of national press coverage of the seal plague indicates that non-official sources played a crucial 'gatekeeping' role. For example, during August 1988 the *Daily Mail* quoted a total of nineteen representatives of environmental or animal welfare organizations, while only twelve scientists, five government sources and one representative of industry was quoted (up to four main sources could be coded in order of prominence).

Several factors during the summer of 1988 combined to ensure that the large numbers of dying common seals off the coast of Norfolk became a political icon. There was mounting public concern across Europe about pollution in the North Sea; there was increasing political pressure on the British government, particularly from American politicians, to refashion its stance on the environment; and here was an issue which was highly visible and emotive. Furthermore it was an issue which fortuitously erupted during the parliamentary recess, when there was little pressing political or business news with which to compete (see Love, 1990; Anderson 1991c). By October 1988 British virologists had identified a phocine distemper virus (PDV) which is a morbillivirus which is similar to measles in humans. Some scientists believed that pollution had weakened the seals' immunity, while others insisted that it played no major role. The precise cause of the virus is still unknown and the Natural Environment Research Council is currently conducting a five year project to analyse the links between pollution and the seal plague. Bruce Fogle recalled the way in which the seals captured the headlines:

Pictures of dead and dying seals, seen in newspapers and on television over the last few days, sear themselves into our minds. The image of the seal is that of the ultimate innocent. With their prominent large moist brown eyes they look like chararcters out of a Walt Disney film rather than the carnivores they really are. ('The Cruel Sea', *London Evening Standard*, 25 August 1988)

The seal virus received widespread coverage among the tabloid newspapers. The *Daily Mail* launched its own 'Save Our Seals' campaign which drew attention towards the extent of public concern about the environment (Love, 1990; Anderson 1991c). Indeed, it seems that this campaign was one of the factors which influenced the former Prime Minister Mrs Thatcher to make her 'green' speech to the Royal Society in September 1988. *The Independent's* Environment Correspondent, Richard North, claimed: 'She would read the same thing millions of times in the *Guardian*, the *Times* and the *Independent* and say these people are whingers. But when the *Daily Mail* takes it up she realises it must be a genuine popular concern and she is sensible enough a politician to follow their lead' (quoted in the *Daily Mail*, 29 September 1988).

Greenpeace were quick to seize upon the seals issue and to define it as a political issue. Unlike the Dutch virologists, who generally refused to offer any speculations about the cause of the virus until their findings were published, Greenpeace were willing to offer speculations to the press. Greenpeace maintained that the evidence suggested pollution was a factor in the seal deaths. They ran a series of advertisements in the national daily newspapers during August 1988 claiming: 'The scientists confirm the very strong indications that pollution is contributing to the seals' deaths.'

Table 3.1 *Greenpeace 'seals' advertisements in the national press*

Newspaper	N	Positioning
The Guardian	3	Front page
The Independent	3	Leader page (2), front page (1)
The Times	2	Front page
Today	2	Diary/gossip page
Observer	2	Front page
Daily Telegraph	1	Weekend section
Daily Mail	1	Diary/gossip page
Mail on Sunday	1	Leader page
Sunday Times	1	Front page

Table 3.1 indicates that Greenpeace oriented their advertising campaign in the popular newspapers towards *Today*, the *Daily Mail* and the *Mail on Sunday*; newspapers whose readership is largely middle-class, female and conservative. Sue Adams, media director at Greenpeace, suggested:

We advertised knowing we'd get its Tory readers, asking them to phone up the DoE to ask what we were doing about it. They were so inundated they couldn't cope and suddenly realised there were a lot of Tory voters out there who really cared about these issues. This forced them to take on the green mantle. (quoted in Warren, 1990, p. 54)

Greenpeace also directed attention towards the seal deaths through organizing an international conference at the Greenpeace Scientific Unit, University of London, and through carrying out their own investigations into the role which pollution played. While Greenpeace mounted a high profile campaign, the Dutch virologists who held doubts about pollution being a central factor, mostly shunned the media. Dr Oesterhaus and colleagues, at the Dutch Institute for Public Health and Protection, told journalists that they would not display their research findings until they were published by the British science journal *Nature* (which has a policy of not revealing unpublished material to the media). However, in the event, the Dutch government put pressure on the scientists to reveal their findings a few days before they finally appeared in *Nature*.

The suspicious attitude of scientists towards the media, particularly the virologists at the Dutch Institute for Public Health and Protection enabled Greenpeace to act as a principle 'gatekeeper' in the early definition stage. Former Secretary and Under-Secretary of State for the Environment, Nicholas Ridley and Virginia Bottomley, claimed that the deaths were caused by a naturally occurring virus. A press officer at the Department of the Environment suggested the reason why government sources did not receive as much space as environmental organizations was that their views were not as newsworthy:

Well that [pollution] made the headlines . . . you could always find an expert to say that, or someone who could call on an expert, particularly if they happen to be attached to one of the organisations which was putting the pressure on . . . The environmental pressure groups were giving the headlines which they were looking for . . . what we will say will actually kill their stories. So they tend, if they know that's going to be the case, not to come to us, or if they don't they will ignore what we say. (DoE, 1991)

It was clearly in their interests to maintain that we should wait until there was firm evidence before introducing expensive measures to tackle pollution. However, the definition of the problem as political ensured that it continued to be a prominent issue within the political sphere and upon the media agenda. As Lang and Lang observe:

The process is a continuous one involving several feedback loops, most important among which are the way political figures see their own image mirrored in the media, the pooling of information within the press corps, and the various indicators of the public response. We argue that a topic, problem or key issue to which political leaders are, or should be paying attention is not yet an issue. Important as the media may be in focusing attention, neither awareness or perceived importance makes an issue. However, once the above-mentioned links are established, a topic may continue to be an issue even if other topics receive greater emphasis in the media. (1981, p. 446)

The case study of the national press coverage of the seal virus illustrates the way in which Greenpeace was able to frame the debate. Non-official sources do not generally gain privileged access to the media unless there is considerable public pressure or the government views their demands as rational. John Ardill, former Environment Correspondent for *The Guardian* maintained: 'A very large extent of our basic information comes from government or quasi-government sources' (Ardill, 1989). However, in this case Greenpeace obtained a considerable amount of press coverage since official sources, such as the Department of the Environment and scientists linked to government bodies, did not act swiftly enough to 'define' the problem. As responders to issues raised on scientific and political agendas, on occasions, non-official sources are treated as prinicipal definers of the debate.

Concluding remarks

As the environment has moved up the agenda in scientific and political circles during the late 1980s, environmental pressure groups have gained greater legitimacy in the media. While pressure groups such as Friends of the Earth and Greenpeace used to rely heavily upon stunts to draw attention to themselves, increasingly they have adopted a pro-active approach and received greater prominence in the media, often as responders to officially sourced information. As Hansen acknowledges:

There is a difference between the attempts of pressure groups to direct public and political attention to an issue which currently is either not in the public eye at all or one which has a very low profile, and, on the other hand, the role of pressure groups as "responders" to claims made about environmental issues in other key fora (e.g. the political forum or the science forum). In the former situation, pressure groups rely heavily on the forum of "public demonstration or protest action" for media coverage, whilst in the latter case they may be given the mantle of legitimacy normally associated, in media coverage, with the fora of "public authorities", "government" or "science". (1991, p. 451)

A key difficulty, then, with Hall et al.'s (1978) theory of 'primary definers' is that it fails to account for changes in the structure of access to the media. At certain times particular actors gain greater access to the media than others. During the late 1980s Greenpeace and Friends of the Earth attracted considerable media attention. Since then they have not experienced such ease of access because the environment has been overshadowed by other issues such as the recession. Hall et al.'s model of 'primary definers' is too static to take account of these shifts.

A further problem is that Hall et al. deduce patterns of source dependence from content analysis, and assume one can generalize about source-media interactions across the media. An examination based purely upon the content of media coverage paints a rather one-sided picture. This sort of analysis needs to be supplemented by interviews with the news sources themselves, as well as with media practitioners (see Schlesinger, 1990). While content analysis is a useful way of measuring the manifest content of texts, it does not reveal latent meanings or the overall context in which they are placed (see Richardson, Dowhrenwend and Klein, 1965; Schatzman and Strauss, 1973; Patton, 1980; Silverman, 1985; Strauss, 1987). As Burgess argues:

The strengths of qualitative research methods lie in their sensitivity to the contexts of everyday life; their ability to explore the structures of meaning among different groups through discourse analysis; and their importance for both theoretically informed case-studies and the development of new theory through the continual interaction between the formulation of questions, the collection of field data and the development of new concepts. (1990, p. 9)

A comprehensive analysis of environmental reporting clearly needs to take account of the role of news sources, since they play a crucial role in the construction of the environmental agenda. The structuralist account of source dependency needs to be refined. In particular, it overlooks the indirect ways in which environmental pressure groups frame the agenda, and it cannot accommodate general shifts in influence. There is a complex web of linkages between media agendas, public attitudes and the political arena and it is difficult to determine the precise influence of each of these interweaving strands. The evidence suggests research has only begun to unravel the multiplicity of roles environmental groups adopt.

References

Anderson, A. (1991a), 'Television coverage of environmental affairs: internal constraints', paper presented at the seminar Environment and Development Issues: what sort of television?, Education Network for Environment and Development, University of Sussex, 13 February.
Anderson, A. (1991b), 'Television coverage of environmental affairs: a new era', paper presented to the Fourth International Television Studies Conference, London, 24–6 July.
Anderson, A. (1991c), 'Source strategies and the communication of environmental affairs', *Media, Culture and Society*, 13 (4), pp. 459–76.
Ardill, J. (1989), Interviewed by the author, 11 January.
Bruce, A. (1989), Interviewed by the author, 8 December.
Burgess, J. (1990), 'Making sense of environmental issues and landscape representations in the media', *Landscape Research*, 15 (3), pp. 7–11.
Chibnall, S. (1977), *Law-and-order news*, London: Tavistock.
Davies, M. (1985), *The politics of pressure: the art of lobbying*, London: BBC Books.
Dept. of the Environment (1991), Press Officer interviewed by the author, 28 May.
Edwards, R. (1988), 'Spirit of outrage', *New Statesman and Society*, 29 July, pp. 16–18.
Einsiedel, E.F. (1988), 'The Canadian press and the environment', paper presented to the XVIth Conference of the International Association for Mass Communications Research, Barcelona, July.

Gandy, O.H. (1980), 'Information in health: subsidized news?', *Media, Culture and Society*, 2/(2), pp. 103–15.

Gans, H.J. (1979), *Deciding what's news: a study of CBS evening news, NBC nightly news, Newsweek and Time*, London: Constable.

Golding, P., Middleton, S. (1982), *Images of welfare: press and public attitudes to poverty*, Oxford: Robertson.

Greenberg, D.W. (1985), 'Staging media events to achieve publicity: a case study of Britain's Friends of the Earth', *Political Communication and Persuasion*, 2 (4); pp. 347–62.

Greenberg, M.R., Sachsman, D.B., Sandman, P.M., Salome, K.L. (1989), 'Network evening news coverage of environmental risk', *Risk Analysis*, 9 (1), pp. 119–26.

Hall, S., Critcher, C., Jefferson, T., Clarke, J., Roberts, B. (1978), *Policing the crisis: mugging, the state, and law and order*, London: Macmillan.

Hansen, A. (1991), 'The media and the social construction of the environment', *Media, Culture and Society*, 13 (4), p. 451.

Karpf, A. (1988), *Doctoring the media: the reporting of health and medicine*, London: Routledge.

Lang, G.E., Lang, K. (1981), 'Watergate: an exploration of the agenda-building process', in G.C. Wilhoit, and H. de Bock, (eds) *Mass communication review yearbook*, Vol. 2, pp. 447–68.

Love, A. (1990), 'The production of environmental meanings in the media: a new era', *Media Education Journal*, 10, winter, pp. 18–20.

Lowe, P., Goyder, J. (1983), Environmental groups in politics, London: George Allen & Unwin.

McCarthy, J.D., Zald, M.N. (1982), 'Resource mobilization and social movements: a partial theory', *American Journal of Sociology*, 1, pp. 212–41.

McCarthy, M. (1991), Interviewed by the author, 22 February.

McCormick, J., 1991, *British politics and the environment*, London: Earthscan.

McGinty, L. (1990), Interviewed by the author, 17 January.

McHarry, J. (1989), Interviewed by the author, 17 January.

Moodie, G.C., Studdert-Kennedy, G. (1970), *Opinions, publics and pressure groups: an essay in vox populi*, London: George Allen and Unwin.

MORI (1991), Survey of Britain's environment journalists, London: Market Opinion Research International.

Nohrstedt, S.A. (1991), 'The information crisis in Sweden after Chernobyl', *Media, Culture and Society*, 13 (4), pp. 477–97.

North, R. (1989), Interviewed by the author, 15 March.

Patton, G.Q., (1980), *Qualitative evaluation methods*, London: Sage.

Richardson, S.A., Dowhrenwend, B.S., Klein, D. (1965), *Interviewing: its forms and functions*, London: Basic Books.

Rose, C. (1990), Interviewed by the author, 24 January.

Schatzman, L., Strauss, A.L. (1973), *Field Research: strategies for a natural sociology*, Englewood Cliffs, NJ: Prentice Hall.

Schlesinger, P. (1990), 'Rethinking the sociology of journalism: source strategies and the limits of media-centrism', in M. Ferguson, (ed.), *Public communication: the new imperatives*, London: Sage, pp. 61–83.

Schlesinger, P., Murdock, G., Elliott, P. (1983), *Televising terrorism*, London: Comedia.

Sigal, L.V. (1973), *Reporters and officials: the organisation and practice of news-making*, Massachusetts: D.C. Heath.

Silverman, D. (1985), *Qualitative methodology and sociology*, Hants: Gower.

Solesbury, W. (1976), 'The environmental agenda: an illustration of how situations may become political issues and issues may demand responses from government: or how they may not', *Public Administration*, 54, winter, pp. 379–97.

Strauss, A. (1987), *Qualitative analysis for social scientists*, Cambridge: Cambridge University Press.

Thorp, L. (1991), Interviewed by the author, 22 January.

Tunstall, J. (1971), *Journalists at work*, London: Constable.

Wang, Z. (1988), 'The Chinese mass media: environmental coverage (a case study)', paper presented to the Conference of the International Association for Mass Communications Research.

Warren, S. (1990), 'Aspects of British press coverage of environmental issues in the 1990s', unpublished MSc dissertation, University of Wales.

Wilson, D. (1984), *Pressure: the a-z of campaigning in Britain*, London: Heinemann.

4
Professional practice and organization: environmental broadcasters and their sources

Olga Linné

To say that democracy is only a form of government is like saying that home is a more or less geometrical arrangement of bricks and mortar; that the church is a building with pews, pulpit, and spire. It is true; they certainly are so much. But it is false; they are so infinitely more. (Dewey, 1969, p. 240)

To say that television only is a more or less square box in this geometrical arrangement of bricks and mortar is true, but also false. It is so infinitely more. Television entertains, informs, makes lonely people feel less lonely, is used as an escape from the boredom of everyday life and pulls families together or, conversely prevents families from communicating with each other. People eat, drink, read newspapers, play with children, squabble and make love while the set is on (Linné, 1988, p. 45; Lull, 1990, p. 51).

Concerns over the power and potency of mass media to influence individuals, groups, communities and societies have of course been with us since the turn of this century or rather for every new medium introduced. McQuail (1987, p. 251) goes so far as to say that the entire study of mass communication is based on the effects of the media, yet there seems to be less agreement on this issue than one might expect. Since the early days of radio academics with different assumptions have attributed immense power to the media while others have attributed power to the audience.

The accumulation of knowledge on mass media effects is, of course, greatly influenced by historical and environmental factors. Gitlin summarizes these views:

They [theories] respond, explicitly or not, in the light or darkness of history –

of new, salient forces in the world, social, political and technological . . . thus there are three meta-theoretical conditions shaping any given theoretical perspective: the nature of the theory or theories preceding . . . the normal sociological worldview now current, or contesting the ideological field . . . and actual social, political, technological conditions in the world. (Gitlin, 1979, p. 209)

Carey (quoted in McQuail, 1987, p. 255) has accounted for the cyclical interest in media power in an historical and socio-economic context. During the 1930s powerful effects were sensed because of the Depression and the political events leading up to the Second World War. The perceived normality during the 1950s led to a limited effects model, while the late 1960s were characterized by political disorder and war and the concept of powerful media returned.

Over the last thirty years there has been a gradual rise in public concern for the environment. Hansen and Linné (1986, p. 49) report that public concern about the environment increased dramatically during the latter part of the 1960s up to an initial peak in 1972. Since 1972, although fluctuating up and down, the interest for environmental issues has stayed on the public agenda. They argue, in line with Carey, that this is not surprising when one considers dramatic events which have occurred: Seveso, Love Canal, Three-Mile Island, Bhopal and Chernobyl. They also note how the last five years have witnessed the political climate concerning environmental issues changing in Britain. When, for example, the United Nations document 'Our Common Future' was published in 1987 there was little to show in the British political climate apart from a distinct unwillingness to yield to growing international pressure on such issues as 'acid rain' and 'the pollution of the North Sea'. However, the political climate or rather governmental rhetoric appeared to change dramatically during 1988. A significant political signal was the Prime Minister's 'green speech' in September 1988, but other important events and issues played their part. At the time in Britain there were controversies about the storage of nuclear waste, the reception and treatment of chemical waste, the relationship between pollution and the death of seals in British waters, drinking water standards and the privatization of the water authorities.

This higher profile given to the environment in government rhetoric was most recently demonstrated in governments' attendance at the United Nations Conference on Environment and Development (the 'Earth Summit'), where government representatives from many countries vied with one another to show their 'concern' for the environment.

Jonathan Porritt (then the chairman of Friends of the Earth) had already in 1987 amusingly noticed this change:

Not long ago "greens" were the bits of a golf course where the grass was shortest, or the parts of the main course between the roast-beef and the baked potatoes. Until the early 80s the word rarely passed the lips of British politicians, except among those caring MPs and party leaders who advised their children "go on eat up your greens". These days, however, Greens are a lot less easily digested – but far more politically nourishing. "Green" refers to a rich and extraordinarily diverse movement with new shoots springing up all over the place. Activities as diverse as becoming a vegetarian, signing a petition to stop a motorway or living under a plastic sheet outside a cruise missile base in Berkshire are all held to be green. (Porritt and Winner, 1988, p. 9)

How did this transformation happen? The mass media have been attributed a major role as a forum for public debate in general, where 'various social groups, institutions, and ideologies struggle over the definition and construction of social reality' (Gurevitch and Levy, 1985, p. 19). It is again the mass media, which are often held up as the cause for the higher awareness of environmental issues (Luhmann, 1988, pp. 62–3). Badri (1991, p. 1) notes: 'In Brazil next year, a very heavy responsibility lies on the shoulders of those in the mass communication profession . . . How and what is reported by journalists can mold the public opinion of the world.'

Environmental interest groups are also often offered as being a cause of inreased awareness (Linné, 1991, p. 149; Porritt and Winner, 1988, p. 4). Väliverronen argues:

Environmental groups and organizations play an important role in the formation of this battlefield. They have turned the environmental problems increasingly into social and political problems and formed the core of "new social movements". (Väliverronen, 1992, p. 1)

In this chapter I will examine factors influencing journalists' coverage of environmental issues, the professional codes they use in the selection and presentation of news stories in corporately pro-duced mainstream broadcasting in Denmark (Danmarks Radio) and the UK (the BBC). The discussion is based on findings from a study which examined and compared the extent and nature of environmen-tal issues coverage on the *Nine O'Clock News* and *TV-Avisen*, news broadcast respectively on BBC1 and Danmarks Radio (DR) in October and November 1987, and combined this with a study of broadcast journalists, editors and producers who were involved in the produc-tion of environmental coverage (see Linné and Hansen, 1990, for details).

I will draw on this study addressing journalists' dealings with one type of source: environmental interest groups (more specifically Greenpeace) and how the journalists perceive their relations to these groups have changed over time. I will also look at journalists' perception of how their own reporting on the environment has changed and the constraints they live with. I will briefly report on strategies used by Greenpeace and how they appear to have changed over the years, discussing Stuart Hall's concept of 'primary definers'.

Hall describes news as the end-product of a complex process which starts with selecting events according to a socially constructed set of categories. The social identification, classification and contextualization of news events, 'maps of meaning', help societies to create a consensus. Hall argues:

News journalism, with its addiction to the clean separation of "fact" and "opinion" and its taboo on editorializing; . . . or television, with its pervasive window-on-the-world-effect do not simply transcribe reality to us . . . they all work by using words, text, pictures still or moving combined in different ways through the practices and techniques of selection, editing, montage, design, layout, format, linkage, narrative, openings, closures to represent the world to us. They all work and can only work because they are able to construct the world for us meaningfully in discourse. They are the machinery of representation in modern societies. (Hall, 1986, p. 8–9).

In the study of the Danish and British journalists it turned out that most of them had been professional broadcasters for a considerable period. On average, the Danes had worked in the profession for eighteen years and the Britons for sixteen years. They could thus be expected to have been suitably socialized into their professions by their organization. Had they been asked, they would almost certainly have agreed with Hall's description of them, although they probably would have objected to the language used. However, they emphasized one aspect of their work in particular: that the news coverage of the environment was embedded in an historical context. If one can paraphrase Carey's argument, not only do the 'real events' influence the construction of news, but according to the broadcasters so does one's own experience over time. The fallacy of many descriptions of how news is constructed, is that they overlook the fact that the world is not static, and neither are its citizens, perhaps least of all journalists (Schudson, 1991, p. 155). For example, Hall argued fairly recently:

Some things, people, events, relationships always get represented: always centre stage, always in the position to define, to set the agenda, to establish the terms of the conversation. Some others sometimes get represented – but always at the margin, always responding to a question whose terms and conditions have been defined elsewhere: never "centred". Still others are always "represented" only by their eloquent absence, their silences: or refracted through the glance or the gaze of others. (Hall, 1986, p. 9)

It is the word 'always' I would dispute here because it ignores a historical perspective. The broadcasters in the present study were able to emphasize the importance of this historical dimension drawing from their own experience of covering environmental issues. Hall is referring here to the 'primary definers' or the powerful spokesmen who initiate the primary interpretation of the issue in question. 'This interpretation then "commands the field" in all subsequent treatment and sets the terms of reference within which all further coverage of debates takes place' (Hall et al., 1978, p. 58). Schlesinger (1990, p. 66) points out that the concept of primary definers is more problematic and less powerful than it first appears. The concept doesn't cover what happens if members of the same government have different opinions over a key question, as, for example, in the painful case of the Maastricht treaty. Who are the primary definers, the Prime Minister or those MPs fiercely fighting against it and openly adoring Denmark? Second, what happens with the well-known 'off-the-record' briefings, in which the primary definers do not appear to directly act as such. Third, all representative voices do not always have equal access. Even among privileged citizens, some are more privileged than others! Fourth, there is the longer term aspect, which is particularly important to the above mentioned study. A union can be important in the pre-Thatcher era and less in the late-or-post Thatcher era. This 'atemporal' aspect of Hall's concept (as Schlesinger calls it) is one of the links to the study of the Danish and British broadcasters. Finally, Hall assumes that the media always follow the power centres and never challenge the primary definers, thereby practically neglecting investigative journalism. Add to this the confounding element manifest in the various discourses of the popular and the quality press (Rocheron and Linné, 1989, p. 415) and there is a great deal to be critical of in Hall's formulation.

The broadcasters in the Danish/British study emphasized the significance of interest groups, rather than 'official' sources for stories. Gans stressed as early as 1979 the importance of studying sources, emphasizing that sources should be investigated more closely in order to understand the news fully (Gans, 1979, p. 360).

Having this relevant point in mind I would like to give some information about how the Danish/British journalists perceived their commitment in covering environmental issues. Schudson notes (1991, p. 150) that journalists in news institutions in general are very committed: 'to their ideology of dispassion, their sense of professionalism, their allegiance to fairness or objectivity as it has been professionally defined'. The absolute majority of the interviewed broadcasters in Denmark and the UK expressed the view that they were more committed to and interested in environmental problems than other issues. Two voices from Denmark:

The commitment for environment started very early in my life, before I became a journalist. (journalist from DR, Aarhus)

We have many young journalists who are incredibly committed to environmental issues, and then we have other problem areas which are not at all well covered. (senior editor from DR, Copenhagen)

There were similar statements from the UK:

I'm more personally committed to it than I have been to other issues I've worked on, that's for a number of reasons, I mean one is because I suppose I spent relatively speaking more of my career, I've probably sweated more blood and tears starting the thing, and trying to get people in the BBC interested, because there was a general apathy about these issues. (journalist from the BBC)

However, as one could expect, the journalists in both countries seemed to fight their own commitment either by avoiding issues that might compromise their 'objectivity', as in the example of a committed Danish editor who would not report on local pollution because he was actively involved fighting it, and the British journalist who pointed out that he was not supposed to be a member of a campaigning environmental interest group, and another British broadcaster who hoped he could convey the message with 'detachment' although he had actively been involved in building up the department.

When discussing the question of commitment several broadcasters added the temporal or historical dimension in relation to their own reporting and audiences' awareness of the environment. Two voices again from the Danish Broadcasting Corporation:

I was incredibly biased when I started it in my time, but the situation was different then, because people just had to understand that there was problems with the environment. People just didn't know that at the time. Today it is much more detailed and much more nuanced.

Today all people seem to be specialists on the environment in relation to what they were then – and therefore there are completely different demands on the journalists and legitimate claims at that. Today you can't just stand up and yell: "This is shit, isn't it?", today you have to give a current registration of what happens with the environment.

This awareness of professional values in the media construction of the environment over a period of about twenty years was also explicitly referred to when discussing sources, above all Greenpeace. Hoggart has claimed that news construction should be seen in relation to 'the cultural air we breathe, the whole ideological atmosphere of our society, which tell us that some things can be said and that others had best not to be said' (quoted in Bennett, 1982, p. 303). The usefulness of carrying out comparative research can be illustrated here. Again going back to Carey's notion about the influence of 'real events', one can argue that it is not necessarily true that environmental journalists from two countries develop as identical twins even if the setting is that of 'public service' broadcasting. True, there are many similarities in the construction of news between countries, but there appear also to exist dissimilarities. These might be exceptions from the rule, but as the discussion about Hall's concept of 'primary definers' has shown, exceptions might be useful to analyse and might add to our understanding of the media's role. Part of the objective of carrying out a cross-national comparison, was to attempt to show how, even on a global, cross-border, type issue such as 'the environment', it is not possible to adequately account for differences in environmental coverage without comparing the construction of environmental issues. Hansen and Linné (forthcoming) note that the advantage of comparing journalistic practices and news coverage in countries whose public service broadcast institutions differ relatively little from each other is that one is forced to call upon a wider notion of the general cultural climate framing media coverage, societal factors functioning outside the media but undoubtedly influencing the media.

I will use the case of Greenpeace to illustrate how journalists' own experience can influence their perceptions. We discovered that there was a great deal of uncertainty in Denmark about Greenpeace, which did not seem to exist in the British context. It appeared that the broadcasters in the two countries agreed that 'it is important for interest groups to do their homework', but that they vary more than a little in their evaluation of Greenpeace. Only one of the British broadcasters explicitly said that he would be inclined to check a Greenpeace story more than he would one from another interest group, while half of the Danish broadcasters clearly stated that they would do so. Why this difference between journalists in the two countries?

One explanation lies in the fact that the Danish broadcasters were strongly influenced by their experience in the coverage of a Greenpeace protest over seal culling in Greenland (and later on a story about the pollution of Køge Bay in Denmark) during which they learnt that their source's grasp of the issue in question was not as firm as they might have expected.

A story that came out more than once in the interviews with the Danish broadcasters illustrates this point. The people of Greenland live in a harsh climate where vegetation is sparse and they depend on seal culling for their survival. The seals are not killed for trade or profit. However, the two international representatives for Greenpeace appeared not to be aware of this and on the plane up to Greenland they had conveyed to the editor of the programme covering the Greenpeace protest that the basis of the protest was summed up as: 'Well, one should not kill animals, should one?' To the editor's question: 'But what are they going to live off in Greenland?', the answer was: 'Well, something must be able to grow up there.' The editor described how they managed to take themselves to a little village and the mayor accompanied them to show how important the mission was: 'The two Greenpeace persons stood fifty meters from where it happened. She turned her back on it and he stood there showing how detestable they were. But the people of Greenland can't show how much they detest it, their living depends on seals.' The editor's doubts about Greenpeace were rooted in the knowledge that the international representatives for this organization had not even tried to understand the social context in which seal culling takes place. This sad little story demonstrates that wider historical and cultural differences between the two countries and their broadcasters should be taken into account. The British journalists seemed not to be aware of Greenpeace's role in other societies and, not having similar experiences to their Danish colleagues, appeared to be quite happy to use the interest group as a source. In Denmark one broadcaster referred to the organization as follows:

Greenpeace is an interest organisation, . . . yes, but one has not dealt with it as one, perhaps because the debate about environmental issues is a fairly new one, therefore, one has nothing against the interest groups, it isn't negative to wish for a cleaner environment, it is on the contrary something positive . . . It takes some time before one realizes that these groups have become strong and have a lot of power, power they also could misuse. A small environmental interest group, I wouldn't really scrutinize so harshly, because they only can do something for the better, I almost said. But in the very moment such a tremendously strong million-pound enterprise as Greenpreace is out on the great sea, they can cause damage when they have the power they actually have. Then, when they have this power, they should, God damn it, also endure having their cards checked, of course they yell and protest. You know, the audiences are now much more aware and watch the stuff the news programmes carry, they are much more critical than before and they are much more conscious about what is said.

Only one London-based journalist raised the question about Greenpeace's credibility and that in a quite modest way: 'but generally with Greenpeace, except on a few areas, I find their homework is not as easy to take without confirmation from elsewhere'.

The consequence of the Danish position was for example, according to one editor, that they didn't accept Greenpeace's own coverage of their actions: 'Well, they are smart enough to have it broadcast in different places, but never with me. It is not that I would deny everything they inform us about, but in my view they have become too clever lately, for example, in the unhappy and completely unreliable campaign about seals in Greenland.'

So far it has been stressed that environmental journalists perceive that their reporting on environmental issues has changed over the years as also their relations to interest groups (especially to Greenpeace and especially in Denmark). What about Greenpeace and their strategies over the years?

Officially Greenpeace started in 1971, although as early as in 1969 a group of activists came together to protest over underground nuclear tests on Amichitka Islands in the Pacific Ocean. The organization started as an activist group against nuclear tests, continuing as one for another five years and then incorporating other areas such as whaling and seal culling. Their actions were audacious and the media coverage planned. Greenpeace Communication Ltd was set up in London in 1986. It is meant to be a service division for both international campaigns and national offices. The Annual Report 1990/91 states that Greenpeace Communication Ltd's 'primary objective is to secure maximum media coverage of Greenpeace Campaigns, principally by providing international news agencies with photo, print and video material originated or acquired by Greenpeace'.

Whether Greenpeace has been successful in meeting this objective is one of the many questions for further research. Obviously they have suffered setbacks in Denmark but at the time of the study they seemed not to have done so in the UK. Greenpeace however, appears to be more than willing to change strategies, at least within limits. In 1986 a Greenpeace Science Unit was established at Queen Mary and Westfield College of the University of London and they made a substantial contribution to the laboratory at Lowell University in Boston. It thus appears that Greenpeace is trying to become more 'scientific' while maintaining its reputation for audacious protest which gave it media coverage in the first place.

The television world thus seems far from static or atemporal according to these reports, and contrary to Hall's assertions quoted above. Neither is the pressure on journalists atemporal. A journalist from Denmark remarked: 'And as we are producing more and more stuff about the environment . . . we also have a lot more complaints'. The absolute majority of the Danish broadcasters perceived that they had been subject to pressure as compared to less than half of the British. The pressure, as the Danes perceived it, most often came from the chemical industry, from the farmers' lobby, from interest groups and from management within Danish broadcasting itself. In the UK the nuclear industry, interest groups, the fishing and farming lobbies and BBC management were mentioned.

Self-censorship, sleepless nights, rechecking a story to absurdity, were some of the consequences reported. A journalist from Copenhagen said:

The pressure on me has been anything from that I have been threatened with being beaten up, to that someone actually was causing me trouble because they thought I had given incorrect information.

Another journalist from Copenhagen explained:

We have a chief editor who doesn't do anything else apart from answering lodges of complaints. It's quite incredible, it's headed by the chemical industry. It's nothing really in the criticism and the industry must know, that when we have checked their complaints, we can reject them. But it has something to do with frightening us from touching these stories.

The content analysis showed that in 1987 environmental issues got more than twice as much coverage in the main evening television news bulletin in Denmark as in Britain, and the difference would have been even more marked, had the content analysis not coincided with the event of the 'October hurricane' of 1987 in the UK (which was widely covered, as one might expect).

Again I would like to allude to Hoggart's idea of the 'cultural air we breathe'. Given the smallness of Denmark's population, the centrality of the main and only news on the television, the larger amount of coverage of environmental problems, this notion might be useful in explaning why the Danish broadcasters appeared to feel more harassed and stressed even if the two countries have similar public service broadcasting traditions.

However, let me go back to the discussion about Hall's concept of primary definers. What role does a successful interest group, like Greenpeace, play in the television coverage? Is Greenpeace for ever condemned to being only an interest group, especially in Denmark, and never achieving the role of a primary definer? This is a difficult question to answer. If one asked the Greenpeace movement, they would probably answer that they act as primary definers – at least sometimes. If one asked a British journalist, he, and it is still most often a he, would probably agree. If one asked a Danish environmental journalist the same question they would say that they do not agree.

It seems partly to depend on how one defines the term 'primary definer'. Whatever doubts the Danish broadcasters had about Greenpeace, data from the content analysis indicate that Greenpeace are able to get substantial news coverage in Denmark. They were at the centre of a news story which lasted almost a month and covering nearly a fifth of all environmental news in Denmark during the sample period. This story began by Greenpeace claiming that the incineration of toxic chemicals in the North Sea would take place and that they, together with a fleet of Danish fishing ships, were to halt the operation. As the story moved on to cover the legal, political and ecological implications the actors on television were drawn from the science community, the political parties, and industry (Hansen, 1990, p. 44).

One can argue that this proves that environmental questions are defined largely through established social institutions. On the other hand one can reasonably argue that Greenpeace became a primary definer through drawing attention to the issue in the first place and thereby playing an important role in the story. Other actors took over, not necessarily because they were more legitimate or established, but because the story developed to cover legal, political and ecological implications – but the discussion actually continued to deal with the incineration of toxic chemicals in the North Sea.

This finding complicates Hall's questions of 'which actors are privileged by the media' and 'what voices are left out or go unheard'. The results from this study support Schlesinger's assertions rather than Hall's. Schlesinger (1990, p. 79), drawing on the work of Pierre Bourdieu, notes: 'The main value of Bourdieu's schema, however, lies in conceiving of dominance as a continual struggle for position involving the mobilization of resources in a process of change. Putting it differently, primary definition becomes an achievement rather than a wholly structurally predetermined outcome.' This makes sense to me. In this chapter I have tried to develop an historical perspective in analysing environmental journalists' reporting of the environment and also in relation to their sources. I have also argued for the value of carrying out comparative research because it illuminates phenomena otherwise not understood. The chapter has attempted to demonstrate how complicated the collaboration between environmental journalists and their sources is both currently and historically. The constraints the journalists are exposed to by their own organizations and other agencies indicate what a battleground the media are and probably increasingly will be as the struggle about the environment undoubtedly will continue to escalate as environmental deterioration continues all over the world.

References

Badri, M.A. (1991), 'Mass communication and the challenges on global environmental protection', *The Journal of Development Communication*, 2, pp. 1–16.

Bennett, T. (1982), 'Theories of the media: theories of society', in M. Gurevitch, T. Bennett, J. Curran and J. Woollacott (eds), *Culture, society and the media*, London and New York: Methuen.

Dewey, J. (1969), *The ethics of democracy. The early work of John Dewey, 1882-1898*, Vol. 1, Carbondale, Illinois: Southern Illinois University Press.

Gans, H.J. (1979), *Deciding what's news: a study of CBS evening news, NBC nightly news, Newsweek and Time.* New York: Pantheon Books/London: Constable.

Gitlin, T. (1979), 'Media sociology: the dominant paradigm', *Theory and Society*, 6, pp. 205–53.

Greenpeace annual report, 1990/91.

Gurevitch, M. Levy, M. (1985), Introduction, in *Mass communication review yearbook*, 5, Beverly Hills: Sage.

Hall, S., Critcher, C., Jefferson, T., Clarke, J., Roberts, B. (1978), *Policing the crisis, mugging, the state and law and order*, London: Macmillan.

Hall, S. (1986), 'Media power and class power', in J. Curran, J. Ecclestone, G. Oakley and A. Richardson (eds) *Bending reality: the state of the media*, London: Pluto Press.

Hansen, A. (1990), 'The news construction of the environment' in O. Linné and A. Hansen *News coverage of the environment: a comparative study of journalistic practices and television presentation in Danmarks Radio and the BBC*. Danmarks Radio: Research Report No 1B/90, pp. 4–63.

Hansen, A., Linné, O. (1986), 'Problemas ambientales y medios de communicacion colectiva', *Cuadernos de Communicacion*, 96, pp. 47–55.

Hansen, A., Linné, O. (forthcoming), 'Journalistic practices and television coverage of the environment: an international comparison', in C. Hamelink and O. Linné (eds), *Mass communication research: on problems and policies*, Norwood, New Jersey: Ablex.

Linné, O. (1988), 'Television and the family. A report of the study in Britain', in J.D. Halloran (ed.) *Television and the family in three countries*, Stiftung Prix Jeunesse International, pp. 31–72, Munich.

Linné, O., (1991), 'Journalistic practices and news coverage of environmental issues', *Nordicom Review*, 1, pp. 1–7.

Linné, O., Hansen, A. (1990), *News coverage of the environment. A comparative study of journalistic practices and television presentation in Danmarks Radio and the BBC*, Danmarks Radio, Research Report No 1B/90.

Luhmann, N. (1988), *Okologische Kommunikation*, Opladen: Westdeutscher Verlag.

Lull, J. (1990), *Inside family viewing. Ethnographic research on television's audiences*. London and New York: Routledge.

McQuail, D. (1987), *Mass communication theory: an introduction*, London: Sage.

Porritt, J., Winner, D. (1988), *The coming of the greens*, London: Fontana.

Rocheron, Y., Linné, O. (1989), 'Aids, moral panic and opinion polls', *European Journal of Communication*, 4, (4) pp. 409–34.

Schlesinger, P. (1990), 'Rethinking the sociology of journalism; source strategies and the limits of media-centrism', in M. Ferguson (ed.) *Public communication. The new imperatives*, London: Sage.

Schudson, M. (1991), 'The sociology of news production revisited', in *Mass Media and Society*, London: Edward Arnold.

Väliverronen, E. (1992), 'Environmental controversies. The role of experts and legitimation of science in the debate on forest damages in Finland', Paper presented to IAMCR Conference, 16–21 August, Sao Paulo, Brazil.

5
Communicative action in the risk-society: public relations strategies, the media and nuclear power

Stig A. Nohrstedt

At the same time as we are approaching the end of the millenium the old worldview is being declared outdated and President Bush proclaims that we are experiencing the dawn of a new world order – presumably not the new information and communication world order so heavily resisted by the USA in the heated debate within UNESCO during the 1970s. Will the last decade of this millenium not only mean the global hegemony of the market economy, but also a more solidary capitalism or a more totalitarian one? And how about the ecological dimension of the future: will the military and ideological detente after 1989 lead to increasing concern for the environment?

In this chapter I will focus on the legitimation and communication problems connected with the nuclear power production system as a significant aspect of today's society, the society which also has been called *Risikogesellschaft* (Beck, 1986), the 'risk-society'.

The risk-society

While the traditional modern way to describe the capitalist societies of the twentieth century emphasized the development of material growth as one of the main legitimation factors behind the general popular support for the system, this factor's impact on societal solidarity is far more obscure today. The growth has turned against humankind in a very tragic sense, making humanity's most glorious victory its worst enemy.

What yesterday was distribution of wealth, is today distribution of risks and waste. That is the conclusion of the book written by Ulrich

Beck. And the very dilemma and angst for late modern man, as Beck calls him, is that he is no longer certain that the profit he makes out of nature outweighs the costs he must bear for it. And above that, he is not even confident of being able to make a rational judgement about it (Beck 1986).

Immanent crisis tendencies

The existential difficulties for late modern humanity and its society to come to terms with the extensions of their own capacities and powers amount to an endogenous societal crisis. Some comments about the concept of crisis will clarify the importance of Beck's analysis of the risk-society and the relation between the latter and the former concept.

According to Habermas as well as others the subjective component is central to the concept of crisis (Habermas, 1976). For social science, then, a crisis implies a lack both of trust in the existent authority structure and of a common definition of the situation. From the perspective of the subjective nature of societal crisis, what is at stake is legitimacy. Although some scholars, for example Habermas, mention several types of crisis, I contend that by definition a societal crisis is at the same time a legitimation crisis. It seems appropriate to distinguish between legitimation crisis of a first and a second order.

The first order type of legitimation crisis is a crisis where the very core of the matter is the problems associated with what Durkheim called mechanical solidarity and questions like: who is the authoritative actor to handle the situation, what measures are appropriate, what is the correct definition of the situation and who could be trusted to give the true and relevant information? These problems are all various aspects of legitimacy, and if they are not solved satisfactorily the system's legitimacy is questioned. In essence the crisis is a situation where the relations between different actors in society, and in particular the relations between the citizens and the authorities, are no longer regarded as legitimate. As with any social relations, these are produced and reproduced by communicative acts.

The second order of legitimation crisis is even more fundamental and related to organic solidarity in Durkheim's terms. It goes to the heart of the solidarity dimension of society: the extent to which there is consensus about the values to be realized and by which the outcomes of societal life shall be evaluated. If such a consensus is failing, and that seems to be the implication of Beck's analysis, the communication problems will be immense, as is exemplified below. For in this kind of crisis one can expect the decision-makers to argue for a certain policy from the perspective of economic growth as the primary aim, and to believe that possible doubts concern whether the means suggested are adequate or not, whereas the actual mistrust may very well be related to the goals rather than to the means. In this sense, a diagnosis of the legitimation crises in the risk-society would be that due to normative inertia and a widening value gap between the elite and the more worried part of the general public a latent conflict is increasingly coming into the daylight. The elite tends to rely on the traditional modern strategy of growth, while substantial parts of the public are questioning the rationale and the morality of the goal of that strategy (Inglehart , 1977; see also Etzioni, 1988).

It seems obvious that the systematic legitimation crisis of the risk-society comprises both dimensions above. In general there is lack of confidence that the risks can be managed and that they are distributed fairly. And the other deficiency from a solidarity perspective is the loss of a common value base for what should be considered a just and good society.

The political-administrative response to the crisis is not encouraging, least so from the point of view of the risk-society.

Is information management the answer and, if so, what was the question?

If that which has been said above gives some outline of what are the basic dimensions involved in the more or less permanent legitimation crisis of late modern society, what implications does it have for the political and authoritative leadership? And what are the consequences for democracy?

In most Western countries, and certainly in Sweden, the last decade or so has seen a rapid change of the ruling policy and in fact the whole political culture. Until the 1970s it was still regarded as possible to rule the country by way of laws, instructions and directives – often rather detailed. Social engineering was the slogan. For various reasons, not least ideological, this perspective was opposed, because it had a clear smack of state planning and centralization which ran contrary to liberal-individualistic ideas. The ideological turn-about during the 1980s has at least two important components: (1) decentralization of responsibility within all kinds of organizations, including public authorities, and (2) hegemony for the market model as *the* paradigm for social organizations regardless of aims or substance.

For the public sector this shift has created a completely new responsibility formula with consequences for democracy. The politicians are no longer responsible for the outcomes of the decisions but on the contrary that responsibility is laid on the shoulders of the implementors, i.e. civil servants, social welfare officers, etc. The decision-makers' responsibility is restricted to the intentions or goals of the policy, no more (see Edelman, 1974; see also Thorsvik, 1991). But there is one important exception, namely the financial restrictions and goals. For while this political revolution – and such it is – is claimed to be a decentralization reform, in the economic sense it is centralization; the state's power over for example the expenditures at the municipal level has increased substantially (Elander and Montin, 1990).

The correlate to this changing political management culture and diminishing political responsibility is public relations or information management strategies as ruling techniques. It is no longer regarded as possible to mainly govern by goals, instructions, etc., particularly not in organizations with unclear goals and uncertain techniques, and the alternative strategy is to create a unified culture or spirit which should direct the efforts towards the same end, the policy of management by meaning (Smircich and Morgan, 1982; Bolman and Deal, 1987).

PR and information management comprises several things: diffusion throughout complete organizational structures of the objectives and the 'philosophy' behind them, integration between different parts of the organization mainly by way of a so-called 'corporate or organizational culture' (Deal and Kennedy, 1982; Schein, 1985; Morgan, 1986). It also includes personal leadership with charismatic dimensions and a sort of mental pressure on the staff to devote themselves to the organization's needs and aims. This kind of internal build-up is combined with external public relations efforts to strengthen the image of the organization, which, at the same time as it is designed to influence the general public's and other external target groups' perception, must also consolidate the staff's identification with the organization or the programme (Grunig and Hunt, 1984; James, 1988; Windahl, Signitzer and Olsen, 1992).

To the new management, public relations and information strategies should be added the well-known marketing strategy of life-style advertising. As has often been emphasized this kind of commercial communication aims at improved turnover by the way of linking the commodity to certain life styles and images (Haug, 1987; Meyers, 1984). The common aspect of these processes, in this context, is that they not only intend to influence attitudes towards certain organizations and policies, but basic value structures of society, concerning for example whether material growth or ecological care is the most important value or whether efficiency or democracy should have highest priority. So, in that respect it seems that the question these strategies attempt to deal with is the value base for the growing legitimation crisis in the present society. Will they be successful? Before trying to outline some of the prerequisites for an answer to this question, I will discuss the different explanations of the communication crisis in Sweden after Chernobyl.

How to explain the communication crisis after the Chernobyl accident

Taking the starting point in Jakobson's (1964) famous model it is easy to understand the amplitude of the communication problems in connection with a big nuclear power plant accident, like the one in Chernobyl in April 1986. Besides the usual factors, the sender and the receiver, there are also other factors included in this model which should be considered: the message, the context or the reality out there, the channel and the code. To each of these factors is related, according to Jakobson, a function, i.e. a task which must be fulfilled if the communication is not to fail (Jakobson, 1964). So there is a lot that can go wrong, and if it can it usually does.

For each and every one of these functions, the communication process between the authorities, the media and the citizens was in jeopardy in Sweden after the fallout. The reality out there – the accident itself, the radioactivity, and its consequences for people, animal and crops – was completely unknown for the journalists and the general public. Neither were there, in Sweden or elsewhere, any appropriate channels to inform them since the governments in most countries had denied or neglected the need for emergency plans for such an accident, nor had any familiar code or language been established by which the information could be articulated.

In sum, the situation was almost the worst possible from a communication point of view: a small group of radiological experts, with no experience of supplying information to the general public and the media, were in a crisis situation supposed to communicate with almost the whole Swedish population about things that hardly any of the receivers had any idea about, and do it in a language not understandable to the receivers! It was certainly a formidable task.

Seen against that background it is not remarkable that a crisis evolved also in Sweden after the Chernobyl accident. I have dealt more conclusively elsewhere with the details of the communication problems that emerged (Nohrstedt, 1991), and I will only call attention to some of the more important dimensions of the crisis in order to establish a concrete ground for the discussion, because although pointing to all the communication problems involved clarifies the troublesome situation it does not explain the crisis.

It is important to remember that the general public's confidence both in nuclear power production and in the responsible agencies went down considerably immediately after the accident. In the most affected part of Sweden eight out of ten inhabitants considered the protection to be insufficient, less than half the population had confidence in the SSI's (the national institute for radiation protection) information, a substantial proportion, 42 per cent, thought that the authorities were hiding important facts – even the recommendations from the SSI were met with scepticism from as many as 34 per cent – and 85 per cent found the information from the authorities at least partly contradictory and confusing.

And naturally many citizens were worried. Seven out of ten inhabitants in Sweden were very much or partly worried personally by the Chernobyl accident. And this goes not only for the hardest hit area. The figures are the same for the average Swedish population. As a consequence opinion changed drastically. The anti-nuclear opinion doubled to around 45 per cent for closing down the plants by the year 2010. In the most affected area around the town of Gävle nine out of ten thought that it should be abolished by that year.

Now the question of interest is how the communication crisis should be understood. I have suggested an explanation in the article mentioned above (Nohrstedt, 1991). Let me indicate the main causes of the crisis in the Swedish case. First, and perhaps foremost, it has to be stated that in Sweden, as elsewhere, there were no plans for a situation of the Chernobyl type at that time. Plans were prepared for possible accidents and leakages only at the domestic nuclear power plants. For consequences of accidents abroad there was nothing prepared. The central authority, the SSI, had in fact urged the inclusion of cases of this kind in the disaster plans as early as 1979. Unfortunately, the Government rejected the proposal from the SSI and chose the more restricted scenario of possible threats suggested by the nuclear power industry.

From a formal point of view hardly any authority was responsible for taking the necessary decisions concerning possible evacuation, or other protection measures. If any authority had any responsibility it was the municipalities, which had no resources for it – either with regard to equipment or competence – and were totally unaware of their formal responsibility in this case.

Second, the demands for information heavily extended what was delivered. Not least the local and regional agencies had difficulty in meeting all the questions from the inhabitants for information about radiation levels in their own backyards, about protection recommendations and about the consequences of the fallout. Often these agencies tried to offer the wanted information in spite of their lack of equipment and competence. The situation was not made easier for them by the reluctance on the part of the SSI to support these activities since they could not be effectively coordinated and controlled. The result was not only that the general public received contradictory messages, but that the public also learnt that there were conflicts between different authorities.

Third, the messages from the SSI were confusing for the public in more than one way. This can partly be explained by the lack of knowledge about radiation, its nature and impact on human beings, animals and vegetation, and also the lack of a common code for experts and laymen. But more important in the theoretical perspective of this chapter is the remarkable development of the sequence of information concerning the radiation levels during the first two weeks after the accident. In press releases from the SSI the levels were gradually adjusted upwards. When increased radioactivity was noted on 28 April at Forsmark it was said to be two or three times the natural background level. Two days later the SSI said that the Uppsala-Gävle region around Forsmark had ten times the natural level. And the next day, 1 May, it was reported that the contamination spotwise reached levels of 100 times the normal background level. But in spite of those changes of statement the SSI never changed its first judgement concerning the consequences: 'As has been emphasized earlier, these levels of radiation are below any precaution levels.'

Two problems of understanding were involved here. On the one hand it was difficult for the ordinary citizen to grasp the logic of the changing information and the fixed conclusion. How it could be that the recommendations were the same when the results from the radioactivity measurings were so different, was a question asked by many. On the other hand, no explanation was given as to why the information about the levels changed so much. If the SSI had explained from the beginning that the first estimations were preliminary and based on insufficient data, then the later information would not have been so confusing. But in the press releases from the SSI there was no mention of uncertainty in the information about the radiation levels, probably due to the fear that in the acute phase of the crisis such information would have increased public anxiety. Many people obviously drew the conclusion that the authorities did not have the situation under control and were trying to hide that from the public, which – contrary to the intentions on the part of the sender – increased instead of reduced the worry on the side of the receivers, the citizens.

To a large degree the crisis was a credibility crisis, as has been indicated above. I have pointed to some of the central aspects of the situation in Sweden immediately after Chernobyl. According to my interpretation, the crisis can be explained along the following lines. I make a step-wise analysis, where in the first step I explicate the causality which can be deduced from research about risk communication and credibility problems, and in the second step I return to the theory of communicative acts.

In the debate after the Chernobyl accident several explanations of the communication crisis have been suggested. I will discuss the three most important here for comments. One is that the journalists' reporting was sensationalist and exaggerated the risks as they opened their channels for frightened citizens and anti-nuclear activists who exploited the situation for their political purposes. The problem with this explanation is that it is not supported by the facts. Neither has it been proved that unduly alarmist reporting or biased coverage had taken place. In the Swedish public service system for radio and television these are questions handled retrospectively by a special semi-official bureau, Radionämnden (the Broadcasting Commission). Although there have been several cases of Chernobyl news brought to the commission's attention, none has been criticized or judged to have broken the rules for the media.

The criticism that the journalists contributed to the confusion and anxiety by reporting contradictory estimations of the radiation levels and/or by allowing unauthorized 'experts' or laymen extensive access to the media for diffusion of exaggerated estimations of the risks is not substantiated by the research results. Concerning this it can be concluded that in any case the official authorities did not have any problem in passing the gate-keepers with their messages, and they were certainly not disfavoured considering the space given to other voices (Gröndahl 1986; Findahl and Lindblad 1987; Nohrstedt and Lekare, 1987; Westerståhl and Johansson, 1987).

The second explanation points to the differences between messages from various authorities. It has been a tendency both in Sweden and internationally to take the lack of coordination among authorities as the main explanation of the crisis after Chernobyl (OECD/Nuclear Energy Agency, 1987). It is true that there was not much opportunity for the SSI or any other agency to coordinate all the information activities that took place during the first weeks after the accident, and that consequently contradictory messages and recommendations were spread. Not even the involved central authorities gave unanimous recommendations to the people.

However, there are reasons to doubt that coordination would have improved the situation. My contrafactual argument against the lack-of-coordination explanation is that a policy of strictly coordinated information would have made things even worse, since it would have given the impression of censorship. And if so, the authorities' credibility would have been even lower and people's anxiety would have increased. The theoretical reasons for this will be developed below, but some empirical evidence supports my critique of the lack-of-coordination explanation. First, during the period immediately after the fallout the SSI explicitly dissuaded local agencies from doing their own measuring of the radioactivity levels. The reaction at the local health agencies was great frustration and loss of confidence in the SSI's competence to direct their information efforts. Second, and in this my argument is actually more than contrafactual, the experiences in Norway after Chernobyl reveal the plausible effects of strict coordination of information in crisis situations of this kind. In the Norwegian case one of the central authorities prohibited other agencies from distributing results from radiation measurements to the press and the general public. This decision caused very strong reactions and protests, the so-called muzzle-debate, from several quarters, not only the media, and obviously that wrecked the central authority's credibility (NOU, 1986).

The third explanation directs the light on another aspect of the authorities' management of the communication problems, namely the risk prognosis. And in order to put this in perspective one has to consider the wider background of nuclear power production. Before the Three Mile Island (TMI) accident in Harrisburg in 1979 it had been said that hardly any pollution of the environment could occur due to accidents in nuclear power plants. And the fear of a meltdown of the reactor-hearth was ridiculed as the China syndrome. When, however, the TMI accident revealed the possibility of such a scenario, it was promised that no dangerous leakages could occur and in any case no reactor explosions. Chernobyl falsified this prediction, but now the defence line for the nuclear power production system was that nothing of that kind could ever happen in Western, e.g. Swedish, plants.

This short history of false predictions concerning the risks connected with nuclear power has no doubt had immense impact on public opinion. Due to the shock of the TMI accident, the Swedish government decided to have a referendum in 1980 about nuclear energy production. As many as 40 per cent of the Swedish electorate voted for the abolition of nuclear power by 1990, a strong sign of popular distrust, and the outcome was the decision to dismantle the reactors by the year 2010.

And returning to the Chernobyl case, when the Chernobyl fallout had been discovered it was evident that there were no emergency plans nor adequate preparedness for the situation. Once again a rather flagrant failure of risk evaluation. And the sequence of changing estimations of the radiation levels mentioned above raised doubts about whether the authorities really knew what they were talking about.

Furthermore, during the first two weeks only one isotope with a very short half-life, Iodine 131, was paid attention to by the SSI in its reports about the contamination. Therefore the prognosis said that the problem would be over after a couple of weeks. When the Cesium 137 came into focus in the middle of May it meant that the time perspective had to be changed. Now it became a question of years, not of days or weeks. Since the restrictions on grazing milk cows were prolonged, the difficulties in supplying the cattle with fodder were accentuated. And this fanned the flames of the increasing conflict between the regional board of agriculture and the central authorities, which in its turn contributed to the growing criticism of the latter.

In all, the experience of the risk prognoses for nuclear power both before and after Chernobyl, as well as of the estimations and predictions made after Chernobyl, seems to reflect a sequence of failures, which must have damaged the public's confidence in the authorities responsible for the emergency planning and protection in connection with nuclear accidents. This seems an explanation of the communication crisis after Chernobyl which can be considered both firmly grounded and sufficient. It is hardly necessary to look for any other explanation, unless it be for the sake of avoiding this one.

This is not meant to imply that no other factors, for example lack of knowledge or fear of radioactivity due to its association with Hiroshima and Nagasaki, have contributed to the crisis. On the contrary, the point is that these and other factors are to be understood precisely as contributory causes and not as sufficient causes.

What have the responsible authorities learnt from Chernobyl?

It is revealing to compare the last and most powerful explanation above with the conclusions drawn by the official commission set up in Sweden after Chernobyl and charged with the task of evaluating the experiences (Haverikommissionen, 1987). All the central authorities involved were represented on the commission. Because of the results from several studies about the information crisis after Chernobyl, it could have been expected that the commission would address the questions whether the general public's right to information was satisfied or not, and why opinion polls showed such a loss of credibility for the responsible authorities. But these questions were neither discussed nor answered. This is the more astonishing since studies, as mentioned above, have shown that around 40 per cent or more of the citizens thought that the authorities were hiding important facts about the risks, and around the same proportion did not trust the information from the authorities (Nohrstedt, 1991). It is remarkable that this credibility gap did not motivate the commission to any reflection.

Instead of seeing a communication and credibility crisis after Chernobyl the commission saw administrative and technical problems. The fact that there was no emergency plan prepared for a foreign nuclear power accident with consequences for Sweden before Chernobyl is not denied by the commission. But it is remarkable that while the first report from the commission, published in October 1986 (Haverikommissionen 1986), suggested that the responsibility should be regulated also for foreign accidents, the second and conclusive report, published in September 1987 (Haverikommissionen 1987), completely avoided mentioning both the unregulated situation when the accident occurred and its own recommendation one year before. And regarding technical equipment it proposed automatic instruments for measuring the radiation levels in order to reduce the time-lag. Besides administrative and technical problems the commission also addressed the problem of public fear of the fallout. But this fear is not set in relation to the mismanagement by the authorities as otherwise would have been natural in view of the explanation proposed above.

For example, in connection with the problem of radioactive Cesium in the fallout from Chernobyl, the commission put up smoke screens. Thus, instead of acknowledging the obvious fact that the central responsible authority, the SSI, seriously ignored the Cesium-137 component in the fallout initially and therefore declared that the problems would be over in a couple of days, which later led to great trouble, the commission described it as if the longer duration of the contamination was a surprise for the general public and for the agricultural authorities, i.e. not for the only authority responsible for the judgements and the statements concerning the prolongation of the problems, the SSI.

A serious treatment would probably have included some analysis of the attitudes as well as the 'mental maps' of the staff of the responsible authorities towards the situation and people's fears. However, no such analysis has been presented. But the attitudes of the citizens and the factors influencing people's attitudes and behaviour in dangerous situations are indeed subjected to lengthy discussion in the commission's report. While psychological and mental factors are regarded as so relevant with reference to ordinary people's reactions that six pages are devoted to that subject, not a line or even a word refers to these factors when it comes to the reactions of the responsible authorities!

In conclusion, the commission neither managed to analyse the relations between the events after Chernobyl and the democratic right to information, nor the mental and social factors influencing the activities of the responsible organizations. When some attempts were made to put these questions on the agenda they were rejected. The argument put forward by the dominating interests on the commission as to why they did not find it suitable to deal with these problems was not that they denied the importance of the problems, but that the task was to give recommendations for the future, i.e. practical solutions of administrative problems. While themselves convinced that they were constructively working at solving real problems, they also managed to completely ignore the critical aspects of their own records – as responsible organizations – from the Chernobyl crisis. In terms of the organization's capacity for learning from its mistakes it is not convincing.

In another sense, however, there are signs of conclusions based on the experience from the Chernobyl accident and other problems for continuous operation of the nuclear power system. Public relations strategies have been considered in connection with the future energy production options and waste disposal. The multinational PR firm Burson-Marsteller AB has been consulted by the Swedish power production companies for reconstruction of their image, which now is disengaged from nuclear power.

The decision about a final nuclear waste disposal is coming up on the Swedish political agenda at the end of the 1990s. With this in sight the conflict about nuclear power will flare up again. The industry and the state authorities in this sector are now involved in a public relations process which is based on some of the more sophisticated strategic ideas. Several forms of what in the literature has been labelled the stake-holder analysis and assumption surfacing method (SAAS) (see Pavlak, 1988) have been implemented. For example, in one task group the state of scientific and technological knowledge with relevance for the project of a final waste depository has been scanned. In a presentation of this work, which I personally had the opportunity to listen to, one of the problems dealt with was how to avoid future populations – people living on earth thousands or even tens of thousands of years after us – breaking into the depository and exposing themselves to the radiation. The group 'solved' this tricky problem by way of definition. The conclusion was that if future man is advanced enough to manage to open the waste depository then he will also be so wise that he avoids the radiation risk. This can be compared with the solution suggested by Sebeok, according to whom artificially created legends transmitted from generation to generation by an 'atomic priesthood' could inform our survivors of the dangers connected with the deposits (Sebeok, 1984). Even if this polarized picture of two extreme 'solutions' is too schematic, it gives a relevant image of late modern man desperately seeking ways out of the problems he has created.

In another task group, the so-called dialogue project, technical, economic and social questions of importance for the safety of a final depository are discussed and analysed within a game-approach context where representatives from national and local authorities as well as from the ecological movement participate. In several steps variants of a fictive application for building a final depository will be treated in detail. It should be noted that no representative from the industry participates in the dialogue project.

A third example of the surfacing methods used in the sector is a seminar which took place in Saltsjöbaden outside Stockholm in March 1992. Scholars from various social science disciplines were invited to comment on the political and social problems associated with spent nuclear fuel. A public relations consultant also gave his recommendations on the issue. In English translation the title of his speech was 'The role of horror-scenario exploiters in democratic decision-making'. The title had been suggested by the organizers, i.e. the official authority responsible for unbiased and comprehensive research about treatment and disposal of nuclear waste. The public relations consultant developed an analysis in the direction indicated by the title and consequently described the diffusion of worries among the population in terms of three layers: the 'exploiters', who used people's fear for their strategic aims, for example opposing or stopping nuclear power production, the 'distributors', who spread the fear since they are themselves worried, and the 'victims', who were said to be losers, people who have lost their hope and are manipulated by the exploiters.

Although the intention of the conference was said to be open discussion and surfacing of different aspects of the question of spent nuclear fuel, the effect of the chosen title was – not surprisingly – that two of the three registered representatives from the anti-nuclear movement boycotted the conference and never attended. I have referred to this recent conference in some detail since it illustrates some of the general considerations I will elaborate below in connection with Habermas's theory about communicative acts.

The theory of communicative action and legitimation crisis

In the dialectic thinking of Jürgen Habermas, from the classical work about the public sphere until the recent publications, an essential contradiction in modern and late modern society between instrumental rationality (German *Zweckrationalität*) and value rationality (German *Wertrationalität*) – a distinction taken over from Max Weber – structures the complete theoretical conception, although the distinction and its theoretical context shift from earlier to later works.The culture of modern society is divided into two different and conflicting normative structures. One is the set of humanitarian and democratic values, for example equal value and rights for every human being, the other is evaluation of administrative and managerial appropriateness or efficiency, for example the impact of a certain tax reform on societal cohesion as well as on economic growth and income distribution. The problem Habermas constantly comes back to is the threat of the latter rationality to devaluate the former, that is, that the basic values of our society will be reduced to instrumental values and/or that instrumental values simply will be estimated as more important. In the Frankfurt School tradition of ideology criticism he opposes the ongoing process where late modern society bases its legitimacy first and foremost on its impressive records of increased productivity and material wealth at the same time as the democratic values are expelled to a secondary position. And in the latest works he suggests – contrary to the earlier analysis in for example *Strukturwandel der Öffentlichkeit* – not the ideology criticism approach of contrasting ideas with realities, but in its place the taking of the practice of communication as a starting-point: 'Ich habe . . . vorgeschlagen, die normativen Grundlagen der kritischen Gesellschaftstheorie tiefer zu legen. Die Theorie des kommunikativen Handelns soll ein in der kommunikativen Alltagspraxis selbst angelegtes Vernunftpotential freilegen' (Habermas, 1990a). So, the point is to reconstruct and make visual the rationality realized in the practice of communication.

The format of this chapter does not allow me to explicate extensively the complicated structure of the theory of communicative acts. I will just briefly indicate the bottom-line logic of it and the basic idea. Habermas outlines an ontological-existential worldview with three different worlds: the objective-factual world, the normative-social world and the subjective-expressive world. All communicative acts or meaningful sentences are related to one or more of these worlds. We talk either about the existence of something in external reality in propositional terms (see Jakobson's referential function) or about social and cultural values, for example whether a certain behaviour is right or wrong, whether a decision is fair or unfair or whether a work of art is good or bad, etc., or we express ourselves in terms of our feelings, emotions, experiences, etc. Habermas's concept 'lifeworld' has a complementary position in relation to all these acts of communication. It refers to the tacit preconditions for intersubjective understanding, and they are comprehended as a set of presupposed justification claims in the communication situation which are realizable in principle (Habermas, 1990b).

As I understand this, the basic idea is that any communicative act implies an agreement between the actors that what is said should in principle be open to further justifications: in the case of the statements concerning the objective-factual world expressed in terms of empirical or explanatory evidence; in the case of reference to the normative-social world in terms of explications of the norms and behaviour and their consequences for a good society; and in the case of the subjective-expressive world in terms of veracity, honesty and consistency.

As in earlier works, the paradigm for the communicative rationality in Habermas's later works is the 'ideal speech situation', but in the later works it is clearer that his ambition is to reconstruct the real preconditions for communication practices, though now specified as the practical conditions for a particular kind of communication, i.e. mutual acts oriented towards understanding. The important consequence of his theory in this context is that if the lifeworld prerequisites are not fulfilled or are doubted the presupposed agreement is broken and the communication collapses. For the receiver, the implication would be aberrant decoding and distrust, and for the sender, loss of credibility.

The fruitfulness of Habermas's abstract theoretical reasoning for empirical research may be disputed – is it, for example, in practical life possible and meaningful to establish when something of value is regarded as such from an instrumental or a purely value-rational perspective? However, when one turns to Habermas' contributions to communication theory I think the importance of his works is more distinct. And in the following I will argue for the theoretical – not only meta-theoretical – value of his approach for understanding the communication problems in the risk-society. The experiences from the communication crisis in Sweden after the Chernobyl catastrophe are brought into this discourse as empirical example since they are reasonably well documented in several studies by myself and others.

Developing a theoretical framework for communication in the risk-society

In this section I will try to accomplish two aims: (a) outline the theoretical relations between Habermas's theory of communicative action and communication in risk-society in a conceptual framework, and (b) exemplify spotwise the relevance of this framework for empirical research.

Habermas's theory of communicative action

The concept lifeworld refers to background conditions for communicative acts. These conditions are related to three different 'worlds': the objective, the social and the subjective world respectively. In what Habermas calls acts oriented towards understanding the interlocutors' interaction is based on an implicit agreement, which may be explicated in terms of the world-specific conditions. In Table 5.1 I make an attempt to develop a conceptual framework for the relations between the lifeworld values and their fulfilment.

Table 5.1   *Framework for analysis of communicative action*

	Objective	Social	Subjective
Validity claims	True in terms of correctness and topical relevance	Right in relation to socially relevant norms	Authentic represent-ation of the subject
Condition		Openness	
Criteria for fulfilment	Factual evidence	Morality	Consistency

The framework is probably far from conclusive and the intention is mainly to suggest a structure for further conceptual development. But it seems worthwhile to do this since it holds great promise for communication theory and in particular perhaps for risk communication, as I will soon indicate with some examples.

But first a few comments on the table. What is essential to Habermas's pragmatics is that the implicit validity claims are in principle open to question and that the participants are obliged to fulfil the claims if asked to. Therefore the figure is constructed from a distinction between the claims and the criteria for their fulfilment. And intermediate to claims and criteria is the condition of openness in a sense that seems to be implied by Habermas, namely that no information is consciously hidden or distorted either about the first, the second or the third world. That this is presupposed is evident from the argument that if not, the fulfilment criteria would be meaningless. To fulfil the agreement in terms of presenting factual evidence, argument for the morality or indexes of consistency must at the same time logically imply the preparedness to consider all possibly relevant facts which could be referred to by the interlocutors. Otherwise the postulate of fulfilment vanishes.

The first world, the objective one, is in the implicit agreement linked to validity claims concerning correctness and logical or topical relevance, which could only be fulfilled by factual evidence. Concerning the second world, the social one, the claim is that the proposal, the question or the accusation, in short the communicative act, is right and just according to the norms. The criterion for fulfilment of the obligation is here condensed in the term morality, i.e. the obligation to give moral reasons for the act in question.

Referring to the third world, the subjective one, the implicit agreement states that what you say or indicate about your own feelings, beliefs, intentions, etc., and in particular with respect to the communication interaction, should be truthfully represented in the situation. The commonsense correlates in ordinary life are the mores that you should be honest, open about your motives and truthful about your feelings. The criterion fulfilling this claim is according to Habermas consistent behaviour. One can demand from the other that he or she gives evidence on this point by referring to earlier acts or statements.

The structure of the table relates to communication oriented towards understanding, as mentioned earlier. However, not all communication has this orientation. On the contrary, to mention the trivial, perhaps the dominant part of social communication is not primarily oriented towards understanding but towards influencing and controlling. Habermas calls this success-oriented or strategic action. This is a social type of instrumental orientation in which societal goals are the criteria for rationality. A fundamental conflict between communicative and strategic action is built into the framework extracted from Habermas. He sees a tendency in modern and late modern society for communication to be more and more subordinated to strategy. The consequences of that conflict will now be illustrated.

Implications for empirical research

To exemplify the implications of this framework for understanding communication in the risk-society and also for empirical research in this field, I will return to the experiences from the communication crisis in Sweden after Chernobyl. Within the outlined framework it is possible, at least tentatively, to deepen the explanations of what happened. Starting from the idea of an implicit agreement between the interlocutors in any communication situation as presented above as a prerequisite for the 'listener-effect' (Habermas, 1990b), one can conclude that the crisis developed in all the three worlds.

With respect to the first world, the problem after Chernobyl was first that the authorities could not – at least not during the first, acute phase – supply the information asked for by the public. This probably raised the suspicion that they were hiding information. And when the estimations of the radiation levels started to come they were confusing, as was mentioned above, due to the continuous readjustments. Since other sources presented other estimations and risk-prognoses, the factual truth was far from evident. Added to this was the impression, mainly created by the overload of information and demands, that other authorities and the media had restricted access to the SSI and that the authority was reluctant to take much notice of all the various statements spread during the crisis. Neither the condition of openness nor the criterion of factual evidence seemed to be satisfied.

In terms of the social world, it can be asked whether the SSI actually followed the norms. I am not only thinking of the fact that the responsibility in the actual situation was not regulated by the emergency plans, but rather of whether it, from a normative point of view, was its task to comment on people's fear of the effects of the contamination. My point is not that it was wrong of the SSI to, for example, tell the public how the authority estimated the risk of cancer. The point is that the SSI told the public that there was no reason for fear or extraordinary precautions, and that is highly questionable since the SSI hardly had any foundation for judging on what grounds people were worried or wanted to protect themselves. The hypothesis is that this behaviour was regarded as an offence against the individual and personal right as well as responsibility to take care of one's own physical survival and well-being, acknowledged by our ethical heritage. In sum, the morality criterion was not fulfilled.

The subjective authenticity or truthfulness of the responsible authorities was questioned; people suspected that for example the SSI did not reveal its true strategic motives and interests, i.e. that it was more concerned about calming down people's fear than presenting the truth about the fallout and its consequences. To this contributed obviously also the remarkable sequence of false predictions which created the impressions (a) that whatever the levels of radiation the SSI would never admit its dangers, and (b) that the agency tried to hide its own lack of information and control in the situation. In both cases it looked as if the SSI was more concerned about its own image than the safety of the people. And the way the official authorities have avoided – at least explicitly – learning from their mistakes seems to confirm this suspicion even more. The consistency criterion is not satisfied.

In this case it seems that the crisis started with new information about the objective world, the news about the Chernobyl accident and the fallout, which initiated a process with impacts on all of the three types of justification claims. But in other cases similar processes may very well start in the other worlds. And in any case it seems possible to analyse the processes within the framework suggested here.

Public relations strategies and the lifeworld values

I will finally reflect on the more advanced public relations strategies and their relations to the theoretical approach developed above. What are the implications of the conflict between communicative action and strategic action in this respect? For, obviously, public relations is the business of strategic communication oriented not primarily towards understanding, but towards influence and control.

It is hardly sensational to conclude that the public relations industry is well aware in its practice of some of the implications of Habermas's theory. One would have great difficulty in finding any handbook in this field which did not emphasize the importance of telling the truth, of being open towards the media and of following the rules and norms of the society you are working in (Grunig and Hunt, 1984; Regester, 1989; Dewhurst 1990; Dunne, 1990; Schiller, 1989). That this is the case should not be a surprise, since the theory of communicative action is nothing but a pragmatics developed from the practices of communication. However, the interesting thing about this pragmatics is that it is an instrument for analysis of the limits of the public relations strategies and therefore also a lever for criticism.

Elsewhere I have written about the obstacles to information-crisis management from the perspective of public relations strategies and the problems connected with risk information (Nohrstedt 1990). From the theoretical perspective of communicative acts, these questions should be approached in terms of the threat from strategic intentions which occupy the orientation towards understanding, and therefore jeopardize the validity claims and in the end damage the listener-effect.

The principal theoretical problem here is how to comprehend the meaning of lifeworld values when integrated with strategic acts. Obviously, one implication is that the implicit agreement for communication oriented towards understanding is not valid and as a consequence the communication runs the risk of being damaged. In other words the credibility and reciprocal trust between the participants can be lost, and therefore, even from a purely strategic perspective, the interaction may result in a failure. The argument for this and also for the potential of the approach can be explicated in several ways, but the format of this article only allows me to make some preliminary and short remarks about a field which has to be further cultivated in the future (see Pearson, 1989). The main argument for the sensitive character of public relations strategies that try to exploit lifeworld values is that communication is reflexive and that the suspicion that the other's orientation is not towards understanding but towards power, is alas as vivid for the participants because of practical experiences as it is for Habermas.

One way of indicating the consequences would be to develop and test hypotheses for empirical research or – less satisfactory – to interpret existing research results in terms of this perspective. For example, from the general condition of openness one can deduce the prediction that in a risk communication situation the fear will increase if the responsible agencies are seen as closed or unresponsive towards the public. Or to formulate another but related hypothesis, if the responsible authority is seen as closed its statements and recommendations will be doubted. The first prediction has empirical support in a recent study presented by researchers at the

Environmental Communication Research Programme, Rutgers University. The impact on risk perception of three different factors – seriousness, technical detail and outrage – was tested, and the conclusion was that the outrage factor had more explanatory power than any of the others (Sandman and Miller 1991). The second prediction has not, to my knowledge, been tested, but the experiences from the crisis after Chernobyl confirm it. For instance, the director of one regional agricultural board simply declared in a broadcast interview that the farmers should not bother to follow the recommendations from the national authorities, since he knew that the latter had based their decision on false measuring methods. Several days before the interview attempts were made to bring this information to the SSI, who had no agricultural expertise. But probably because of overload the analysts at the SSI could not be reached and the result was an open conflict between the authorities at different levels. Eventually, the conflict was solved by a decision to decentralize the responsibility for information to the farmers on the regional level (Nohrstedt 1991; see also Amnå and Nohrstedt, 1987).

Another way to point to the fruitfulness of the approach suggested above would be to analyse thoroughly the public relations handbooks from this perspective. Let me give one example. In his well-known book, *Crisis Management*, Regester gives the following advice regarding how to treat the media in an acute catastrophe situation before the facts can be established: 'Never fill the vacuity with speculations or obvious lies.' 'Be prepared to express human regret with regard to what has happened' (translated to English from the Swedish edition; Regester 1989). It seems difficult to find a better illustration of the conflict between communicative and strategic action. One can hardly avoid the interpretation that lies are accepted as long as they are not 'obvious'. And if so, this reveals the fragile nature of the crisis management strategy suggested by Regester, besides its moral deficiencies. The communication acts between human beings are always reflexive, as mentioned before, and because of that one has to count on the possibility that the participants interpret them as potentially strategic. It seems realistic to comprehend the agreement between the interlocutors in terms of a continuous, mainly irreversible process where the interaction could be definitely cancelled at any moment. As public relations strategists usually express it: credibility takes a long time to build, but it can be wrecked in a single moment.

A third argument for the suggested approach is that it is realistic. This has of course to do with its basic perspective, starting from the practice of communicative action as it does. The pragmatics developed by Habermas seems to grasp an important dimension in any kind of communication, i.e. the realitics of built-in expectations of sincerity, truthfulness, accuracy, etc., without which any obligation to take the other seriously will be cancelled.

This dimension is probably central in the present discussions about disposals for nuclear waste. A few comments are in place in connection with the post-Chernobyl debate about this issue and the SAAS-strategy applied. The decisive question is how to accomplish and organize a genuine dialogue in such a way that the impression is not created, on any side, that it is mainly a manipulative strategy for consent. I believe that Habermas's idea about the ideal speech situation can give some guidelines. According to this, all participants should have equal responsibility for fulfilling their validity claims, and have equal rights and possibilities for bringing new questions to the agenda, to give new arguments, to bring forward new evidence, to make conclusions and to formulate standpoints (Habermas, 1976). Perhaps something like the American 'hearings' would satisfy these demands to some extent. In any case it is probably extremely important that not the authorities or the industry in the nuclear power sector are the organizers of the dialogue. Social research has until now presented enough results to make it almost impossible even for authorities with responsibility for supervision to be successful in claiming impartiality and in claiming that they are true proponents of the common good (see for instance the publications from the members of the Norwegian power commission: Hernes, 1978; Olsen, 1983; see also Olsen, 1988). Therefore, it seems inevitable to find organizers that may be regarded as impartial by all the different parties, although this is certainly not easy, if authentic consensus should be reached.

Finally the central question when applying in particular Habermas's abstract, normative theory to concrete realities: is it realistic? Are not the demands far from the practical realities of this world? The answer to this depends on how the meaning of these demands is interpreted. With an absolutist interpretation they are no doubt totally unrealistic. However, with a more relativist interpretation they are both realistic and relevant. And then the challenge is to move in the direction of understanding-oriented communication and not in the opposite direction.

The future will show whether the dominant organizations on the nuclear power sector will be open enough to meet even high demands on a consensus about the energy production system and the methods for dealing with nuclear waste. If they are not the consequence will probably be gradually or even rapidly (in case of new accidents of TMI or Chernobyl magnitude) growing credibility gaps and legitimation problems. The real danger for risk-society is perhaps the possibility of complete loss of organic solidarity together with increased cynicism towards the political processes and democracy. If so, more than the price on energy or where to put the spent nuclear fuel is at stake. Democracy is threatened both from those who think that the practical problems regarding nuclear power and waste disposals are not manageable politically, and from those who believe that the ecological dangers are so great that they can not wait for the general public and the politicians to be aware of them before tackling them.

Conclusion

This chapter analyses the legitimation problems and in particular the ones connected with the consequences of environmental threats on organic solidarity, i.e. the value base for community, in risk-society. focus is on public relations, advertising and information management strategies and their impact on the solidary dimension in this context.

Some Swedish experiences from the consequences of the Chernobyl catastrophe are referred to in order to highlight the credibility and legitimation problems associated with nuclear power production. The main explanation of the information crisis in 1986 is the sequence of false predictions by the responsible agencies, concerning the risks of nuclear energy, the lack of emergency plans for foreign nuclear accidents and the continuously changing statements about the levels of radiation after the fallout. The persistent reluctance by the responsible authorities to consider some of the communicative aspects of the crisis is another noticeable experience mentioned. Also the implementation of some of the most sophisticated public relations strategies to meet the increasing doubts about the system's capacity to manage the nuclear waste problem is discussed in relation to the question of whether consensus will be achieved.

In order to get a perspective on the latent legitimation crisis and the communication problems in risk-society, Habermas's theory of communicative action is taken up and the following points are dealt with. First, when talking about organic solidarity the values connected with communication processes must not be forgotten. In particular, the assumption that there are some validity claims which are constitutive to the communicative acts, and that in principle they should be possible to fulfill on request is essential. Second, and implied by the first point since it seems to be its structural corollary, is the central condition of openness, without which the claims will be doubted and the 'listener-effect' jeopardized. Third, credibility problems can be analysed in relation to the criteria for fulfillment of the validity claims, i.e. accuracy, morality and authenticity. Fourth and finally in association with Habermas, credibility gaps can be explained by the conflict between communicative action and strategic action. Hence public relations strategies will only be successful in dealing with the legitimation crises in so far as they take the communicative demands seriously, i.e. if they are not purely and mainly strategic action. That is the paradox of strategies aiming to influence and control the values of risk-society. And this paradox is clearly visible in the 'stakeholder analysis and assumption surfacing method' applied in Sweden in connection with the issue about nuclear waste disposal.

This book deals with the media and environmental problems. Seen from the perspective of the analysis above the superficial media reporting must be regarded as one of the greater deficiences in risk-society. The often criticized short attention span in media coverage is detrimental to the capacity of systematic learning. For example, the media did not fulfil their role as watchdog when the Swedish authorities evaluated the experiences after the Chernobyl accident. The media did not force the agencies to thorough penetration of those aspects, for example credibility and democratic aspects, which were most delicate for the agencies themselves. Consequently, the learning was unnecessarily reduced to administrative and technical questions, and the authorities were reinforced in their attitude that this was sufficient.

The media are at the same time quick to react on and to enforce any sign of popular distrust towards the authorities. In this alarmist function they certainly contribute to the evolution of legitimation crises, although they do not create them. Perhaps the media are even structurally incapable of realizing the nature and meaning of communicative action, as well as the mechanisms behind credibility and legitimation crises, due to the schizophrenia of journalism, torn as it is between the ideology of freedom and sovereignty, on the one hand, and on the other hand, the realities of suppression under economic restrictions and dependency on access to sources together with the asymmetric and rudimentary relation to the audience.

In short, it looks as if the media are something like the arbitrary searchlight Walter Lippmann wrote about in the beginning of the now ending century. Or, to finish with another metaphor, like a seismograph the press sensitively registers the crisis tendencies but it hardly makes any other constructive contributions when it comes to the destiny of risk-society.

References

Amnå, E., Nohrstedt, S.A. (1987), *Att administrera det oförutsedda*, Stockholm: SPF.
Beck, U. (1986), *Risikogesellschaft. Auf dem Weg in eine Moderne*. Frankfurt a Main: Suhrkamp.
Bolman, L.G., Deal, T.E. (1987), *Modern approaches to understanding and managing organizations*, London: Jossey-Bass.
Deal, T.E., Kennedy, A.A. (1982), *Corporate cultures. The rites and rituals of corporate life*, Reading, Mass.: Addison-Wesley.
Dewhurst, P. (1990), 'Environmental crisis: CFCs and the ozone layer – how ICI handled a major public issue', in D. Moss (ed.), *Public relations in practice. A casebook*, London: Routledge.
Dunne, A. (1990), 'Lilley plc: a crisis in confidence', in D. Moss (ed.), *Public relations in practice. A casebook*, London: Routledge.
Edelman, M. (1974), *The symbolic uses of politics*, Chicago: University of Illinois Press.
Elander, I. Montin, S. (1990), 'Decentralisation and control: central-local government relations in Sweden', *Policy and Politics* 18 (3), pp. 165–80.
Etzioni, A. (1988), *The moral dimension: toward a new ecomonics*, New York: Free Press.

Findahl, O., Lindblad, I.-B. (1987), *40 dagar med tjernobylnyheter i radio och TV*, Stockholm: SR/PUB, No 1.

Gröndahl, A. (1986), 'Myndighetsinformationen om kärnkraftsolyckan i Tjernobyl i svenska tidningar 29.4–21.5 1986, in *Beredskap efter Tjernobyl. Slutrapport*, Stockholm: Haverikommissionen, September 1987.

Grunig, J.E., Hunt, T. (1984), *Managing public relations*, London: Holt, Rinehart & Winston.

Habermas, J. (1976), *Legitimation crisis*, London: Heinemann.

Habermas, J. (1990a), 'Vorvort', in J. Habermas, *Strukturwandel der Öffentlichkeit: Untersuchung zu einer Kategorie der bürgerlichen Gesellschaft*, (18th edn) Frankfurt am Main: Suhrkamp.

Habermas, J. (1990b), *Kommunikativt handlande. Texter om språk, rationalitet och samhälle*, Göteborg: Daidalos.

Haug, W.F. (1987), *Commodity aesthetics, ideology and culture*, New York: International General.

Haverikommissionen (1986), *Beredskap efter Tjernobyl*, Utvärderingsrapport. Statens haverikommission, October.

Haverikommissionen (1987), *Beredskap efter Tjernobyl. Slutrapport*. Stockholm: Statens haverikommission, September.

Hernes, G. (ed.) (1978), *Forhandlingsøkonomi og blandingsadministrasjon*. Bergen: Universitetsforlaget.

Inglehart, R. (1977), *The silent revolution: changing values and political styles among Western publics*, Princeton, N.J.: Princeton University Press.

Jakobson, R. (1964), 'Closing statement: linguistic and poetics', in *Style in language*, T.A. Sebeok (ed.) Cambridge, Mass.: The M.I.T. Press, pp. 350–77.

James, H.J. (1988), 'Introduction: the plight of the pianist', in W. Howard (ed.), *The practice of public relations*, London: Heinemann.

Meyers, W. (1984), *The image-makers: secrets of successful advertising*, London: Orbis.

Morgan, G. (1986), *Images of organization*, Beverly Hills: Sage.

Nohrstedt, S.A. (1990), 'The information system's vulnerability problems in crisis and a general strategy for managing the unforeseen', *The Nordicom Review*, (2), pp. 31–40.

Nohrstedt, S.A. (1991), 'The information crisis in Sweden after Chernobyl', *Media, Culture and Society*, 13 (4), pp. 477–97.

Nohrstedt, S.A., Lekare, K. (1987), *Att rapportera det oförutsedda*, Stockholm: SPF.

NOU (1986), *Informasjonskriser*, 19. Oslo: Universitetsforlaget.

OECD/Nuclear Energy Agency (1987), 'Radiation protection concepts – how should they be communicated', working document (mimeo).

Olsen, J.P. (1983), *Organized democracy*, Bergen: Universitetsforlaget.

Olsen, J.P. (1988), *Statsstyre og institusjonsutforming*, Oslo: Universitetsforlaget.

Pavlak, T.J. (1988), 'Structuring problems for policy action', in L.K. Comfort (ed.), *Managing disaster. Strategies and policy perspectives*, London: Duke University Press.

Pearson, R. (1989), 'Beyond Ethical Relativism in Public Relations: Coorientation, Rules and the Idea of Communication Symmetry', in J.E. Grunig and L.A. Grunig (eds), *Public relations research annual*, Vol. 1, Hillsdale: Lawrence Erlbaum Ass.

Regester, M. (1989), *Crisis management. Krishantering till företagets fördel*,

Stockholm: Svenska Dagbladet. This quote translated to English from the Swedish by S.A. Nohrstedt.

Sandman, P.M., Miller, P. (1991), *Outrage and technical detail: The impact of agency behavior on communication risk perception*, Environmental Communication Research Program, Rutgers University.

Schein, E.H. (1985), *Organizational culture and leadership*, San Francisco: Jossey-Bass.

Schiller, E. (1989), *Managing the media*, Toronto: Bedford House Publishing Corporation.

Sebeok, T.A. (1984), 'Die Büchse der Pandora und ihre Sicherung: Ein Relaissystem in der Obhut einer Atompriesterschaft', *Zeitschrift für Semiotik*, 6 (3), pp. 229–52.

Smircich, L., Morgan, G. (1982), 'Leadership: The management of meaning', *Journal of Applied Behavioural Science*, (18), pp. 257–73.

Thorsvik, J. (1991), 'Målstyrning av offentlig virksomhet', *Norsk Statsvitenskapelig Tidsskrift* 7 (4), pp. 267–82.

Westerståhl, J., Johansson, F. (1987), *Tjernobylnedfallet och myndighetsbyeskeden*, Stockholm: SPF.

Windahl, S., Signitzer, B., with Olsen, J.T. (1992), *Using communication theory*, London: Sage.

Part 2:

Messages, meanings and media coverage

6
Mediating the environment: modalities of TV news

Simon Cottle

Though there is no doubting the recent growth of concern with the environment, the roots of environmentalism are historically long and culturally deep[1]. The environment, from the local to the global, has become a contested terrain. This is self-evident in those innumerable struggles and conflicts of interest, conducted simultaneously across different sites throughout the world, but all in some way involving the relationship between human beings and their use of, and impact upon, the environment. The environment, broadly conceived, thus concerns the physical environment, whether 'natural' or built, and encompasses species of animals and plants and their habitats, as well as climate, landscapes and the world's resources of water, land and air. As a contested terrain the environment is also deeply dependent upon those competing ways of conceptualizing and 'making sense' of 'environmental problems' and 'issues' which in turn inform, and are themselves occasionally mobilized by, the politics of environmentalism. This contested terrain, in other words, is dependent upon the social meanings and frameworks of understanding that circulate within the wider culture, and which are privately and publicly available to a society at a particular point in time. It is through the prism of culture, its language, symbols and 'structures of feeling'[2] that the 'environment' is made to mean.

At least one influential commentator has detected, for example, a long-serving historical underpinning to modern environmentalism which continues to fracture and cohere around positions of ecocentrism and technocentrism (O'Riordan, 1981). However, if the complexities, subdivisions and ideologies of modern day environmentalism can usefully be explored through such a schema, it is less certain to what extent wider public perceptions and understanding of the environment line up behind one or other of these organizing ideological positions. What is clear, though remaining in need of systematic and detailed investigation, is that the mass media are likely to be of major importance in the selection, transformation and circulation of environmental meanings in modern society. It is all the more surprising therefore that, with a few notable exceptions, the study of mass mediated images and representations of the environment has remained relatively unexplored, though commentators have been keen to establish a causal relationship between environmental media coverage and shifts in public opinion. (For an excellent critical review of this and other related media-environment research see Hansen 1991, as well as Burgess 1990.)

More particularly, in relation to one of the most central of preoccupations of mass communications research, the production, dissemination and reception of news, the relative paucity of environmental related research has, until recently, been noticeable and in any case largely confined to press reporting. Two major exceptions deserve reference here, first a study by Lowe and Morrison in which the observation is made that 'popular sentiment towards the environment ensures that many issues have a strong emotive and moralistic appeal', which is thought likely to influence their media portrayal (Lowe and Morrison, 1984, p. 79), and second, a recent comparative study in which differences of national culture are thought to have influenced differences of environmental coverage across the BBC *Nine O'Clock News* and Denmark's *TV-Avisen* (Hansen 1990).

Towards a framework for the analysis of TV news environmental coverage

To what extent and in what way the environment is mediated across the spectrum of TV news programming remains unexplored, and undertheorized. By way of a preliminary examination this study sets out to examine the extent and character of environmental portrayal on British television news, across the spectrum of available TV news programmes, to see to what extent differences of news programme form and character impact upon the news mediation of the environment. Though it is commonly accepted that the press, both 'serious' and 'popular', is characterized by distinctive market orientations, readership appeals and political allegiances, TV news has tended to be ignored as a differentiated news medium with findings from studies of selected main channel national news programmes (BBC1 and ITN) serving as exemplars of 'TV news', as if all forms of TV news were essentially similar. British TV news now includes major breakfast news programmes on three channels; the midday BBC1 and ITN programmes; long-established and popular regional news programmes; the longer (and some would suggest more analytic) *Channel 4 News* and BBC2 *Newsnight* programmes, in addition to the main evening BBC1 and ITN programmes; and not forgetting the potential, for some at least, of satellite and cable TV news services.

The study of news has traditionally preoccupied scholars of mass communication and continues to do so. This is perhaps unsurprising given those central claims and responsibilities placed upon the mass media by liberal-democratic theory, as well as those more critical claims advanced from within variants of radical social theory in which issues of media ownership and control, processes of legitimation and ideological hegemony have come to the fore. Whether news is approached in liberal-democratic terms as a medium safeguarding the interests of representative democracy by providing a citizenry, in the best traditions of the fourth estate, with the requisite information and knowledge on which political opinion formation depends and the democratic will can be implemented; or whether approached in more critical terms as a central purveyor of images, representations and ideologies thought to offer legitimacy to the status quo, simultaneously undermining the basis for participatory democratic involvement and advancement, both approaches make implicit reference to the idea of a public sphere.

In more recent years, however – and perhaps reflecting the unease with monolithic conceptions of the mass media and its correlate of an imposed 'dominant ideology' as much as an increased recognition of the constant struggle over meanings waged upon the media stage – mass communication researchers have begun to turn, in more explicit terms, to Jürgen Habermas's concept of the public sphere. By the term 'public sphere' Habermas has referred to a realm of social life in which citizens can come together as a rational body, in which general interests can be discussed, debated and decided upon. This provides, following some critical elaboration and revision, a useful theoretical framework for the analysis of TV news environmental coverage. In an oft-quoted statement Habermas outlines his understanding of the public sphere as follows:

> By "the public sphere" we mean first of all a realm of our social life in which something approaching public opinion can be formed. Access is guaranteed to all citizens . . . Citizens behave as a public body when they confer in an unrestricted fashion – that is, with the guarantee of freedom of assembly and association and the freedom to express and publish their opinions – about matters of general interest. In a large public body this kind of communication requires specific means for transmitting information and influencing those who receive it. Today newspapers and magazines, radio and television are the media of the public sphere. (Habermas, 1974, p. 49)

Four characteristics can thus immediately be identified which together constitute Habermas's public sphere, these comprise: the public expression, debate and formulation of public opinion; the openness of access to such public discussion; the availability of public fora on which to stage such public discussion; and lastly, in recognition of the increasing importance and centrality of the mass media, a means by which such public debate and deliberation can publicly be sustained. While each provides a useful starting point for the analysis of TV news forms and, in this instance, their mediation of the environment, a few critical observations are first called for.

As numerous commentators have pointed out, Habermas's concept is not without its difficulties (Elliott, 1986; Garnham, 1986; Jensen, 1986; Thompson, 1990; Curran, 1991; Dahlgren and Sparks, 1991; Tolson, 1991). Though Habermas was concerned both to recover the idea of the public sphere via its historical emergence, development and subsequent demise, as well as elucidate its 'ideal' or normative form, rarely approximated in practice and thus serving as an ideology of liberal/bourgeois society and interests, it has been suggested that even here Habermas over-estimated the degree of original democratic involvement. If historically the public sphere is thought to have been inflated, attention to the dynamics and commercial contexts of media industries has frequently been observed to distort and undermine the pursuit of the 'public good', with institutions compelled to pursue their corporate and commercial interests within the market place. While such findings have informed political economy approaches to the media industries for some time, so too have sociologists and political scientists recognized the increasingly stratified and organized nature of society where powerful social groups and vested interests, including the state, pursue particular interests, though often advanced via the mass media, as of more universal benefit. Furthermore, the historical emergence of 'professional' politicians as well as professional journalists – two privileged groups of 'rhetors' and opinion formers often deemed essential to the idea of the public sphere – may themselves be seen as inhibiting its wider potential for democratic participation.

Moreover, contrary to the ideal of the free exchange and rational deliberation of ideas, knowledge and information have increasingly become commodified and therefore less than freely available to all, while the differences of social and political competence stratifying the 'public' also qualifies notions of equal participation and universal access. Underlying such empirical considerations, which appear to undermine the practice if not the ideal of the public sphere, is its overly rationalist epistemology. The emphasis upon rational public debate and deliberation leading to public opinion and consensus formation lends itself to what James Carey has recently coined a 'transmission', as opposed to 'ritual' understanding of media impact and influence: 'If a transmission view of communication centres on the extension of messages across geography for purposes of control, a ritual view centres on the sacred ceremony that draws persons together in fellowship and commonality' (Carey, 1989, p. 43). In such terms, it can be suggested that the mass media may well sustain and help constitute 'publics' and public understanding, but this need not be confined to processes of rational opinion formation based upon information exchange and engaged debate. Working more at the levels of sentiment, myth and ritual, shared realities can be publicly appealed to, affirmed and even celebrated at a less than rational level.

Taken together these criticisms indicate that the public sphere cannot simply be assumed to be operative with the existence of a mass media universally available to all. While the public sphere is thought to be constituted by the mass media, it cannot be deemed to be coincident with the disparate roles and functions of the mass media in entirety. Herein lies both its dependency and potential corruption. Habermas himself, of course, was more than aware of such contemporary failings which arguably prompted his historical recovery of the concept in the first place. In particular his concern with the transformation from what he discerned as 'a culture debating to a culture consuming public' (Habermas, 1989, p. 159) is a concern which has animated the writings of others. None the less, while the historical and contemporary practice of the mass media may be found to fall far short of the normative understanding of the public sphere, the concept does provide a useful critical benchmark with which to approach the mass media generally, and its news function in particular.

To return to the four constituents identified as central to the public sphere, it is now possible to outline four central lines of analysis informing this discussion of TV environmental news. First, it is necessary to chart the extent and array of environmental concerns finding public expression across the news media. This represents a more focused concern than Habermas's public opinion, but for the reasons already noted is thought to be a more adequate way of addressing public communication and provides the means of gaining an initial overview of environmental news coverage without assuming that such coverage in fact succeeds as communicated 'opinion'. In addition to the non-rational appeals of news programming already referred to, it can also be suggested that news provides a prioritized view of the world, the environment being no exception, with a public agenda of issues and frameworks of understanding informing environmental news treatments. These do not necessarily, of course, function in terms of deliberate and articulated opinion but may well provide the potential resources for wider environmental interpretations and understandings.

Second, conditions of access are deemed integral to the formation of the public sphere. This implies, at the very least, that the means of communication must be universally available, and not prohibited by price, scarcity or perhaps geography. Conditions of universal access also demand that programming should not demand specialist or esoteric knowledge nor a level of exclusive cultural competence. The medium of British TV has for some time approached conditions of universal availability in such terms, though satellite broadcasting has yet to establish itself (the problem being one of price rather than level of expected cultural competence). If the underpinning premise of the public sphere is social difference and disagreement, such differences frequently find expression through representative voices. While such differences need not necessarily be assumed to be neatly sealed within identifiable social groups, classes or status positions as if, to borrow an image from Nicos Poulantzas, they could be easily recognized from the ideological number plates displayed on people's backs, it remains evident that 'who gets on', often determines 'what gets said'. In addition to the array of substantive environmental concerns finding expression across the news medium, then, attention is also paid to the environmental actors finding a public stage from which to advance their concerns and points of view.

Third, the idea of the public sphere implies a public arena in which issues and concerns find wider public expression. This immediately raises questions concerning the nature or form of the forum itself and how this may impact upon public communications. The news fora or arenas of the TV news public sphere are here thought to be of considerable relevance to the discussion of environmental news portrayal, since it is here that the public sphere is essentially enacted and brought to life. Surprisingly little attention has so far been addressed to these differing types of news presentational formats and their impact upon the communication of public concerns.

Fourth, Habermas's discussion of the public sphere raises the issue of the 'means of communication' by which the public sphere is constituted. Confining the analysis to the 'moment' of environmental news treatment, and placing in abeyance both questions of informing contexts of production[3], as well as consideration of audience reception, the analysis seeks to address the modalities of TV news and their impact upon the extent and character of TV news environmental portrayal, perhaps in line with characteristic programme appeals, and involving differing journalistic strategies of story telling. With these four lines of inquiry set in place the analysis begins by outlining its basic method, sample of TV news programmes reviewed and overall findings concerning the extent and priorities of environmental news coverage found across the TV news spectrum.

The research frame, TV news and environmental presence

For the purposes of this analysis a sample of news programmes was sought that would encompass all main news programmes which, on the basis of general availability, are currently broadcast across the four main British channels. This excluded satellite and cable TV news, but included all variants of breakfast news, midday BBC1 and ITN news programmes, instances of BBC1 and ITV early evening regional news, BBC1 and ITN early evening programmes, and *Channel 4 News* and BBC2 *Newsnight* programmes, as well as early evening weekend news broadcasts, both national and regional, across the four main channels. The sample details are included in Table 6.1.

Table 6.1 *TV news programme sample (a)*

	Times	Weekly Sample hours(b)hours		Programme 'stories'
Weekdays				
BBC1 Breakfast	6.30–9.05 am	12.55	25.50	269 (c)
Channel Four Daily	6.00–9.25 am	17.05	34.10	280 (c)
TVAM	6.00–9.25 am	17.05	34.10	239 (c)
ITN Midday	12.30–1.10 pm	3.20	6.40	108
BBC 1 Midday	1.00–1.30 pm	2.30	5.00	119
ITN	5.40–6.00 pm	1.40	3.20	89
BBC1	6.00–6.30 pm	2.30	5.00	125
ITV Regional	6.00–6.30 pm	2.30	5.00	133
BBC1 Regional	6.30–7.00 pm	2.30	5.00	98
C4	7.00–7.50 pm	4.10	8.20	128
BBC2 *Newsnight*	10.30–11.15 pm	3.45	7.30	85
		Hours	140.00	N 1673
Weekend				
BBC1 (Sat)	5.00–5.10 pm	0.10	0.20	12
BBC1 (Sun)	6.25–6.40 pm	0.15	0.30	22
ITN (Sat)	5.00–5.05 pm	0.05	0.10	10
ITN (Sun)	6.30–6.35 pm	0.05	0.10	10
BBC1 Regional (Sat)	5.10–5.15 pm	0.05	0.10	11
HTV (Sat)	5.05–5.15 pm	0.10	0.20	20
HTV (Sun)	6.35–6.40 pm	0.05	0.10	13
BBC2 (Sat)	7.50–8.05 pm	0.15	0.30	16
C4 (Sat)	7.00–7.05 pm	0.05	0.10	12
		Hours	2.30	N 126
		Total Hours	142.30	Total Stories 1799

(a) The selected sample weeks were 25 November–1 December 1991 and 13 January–19 January 1992. These were deliberately separated to avoid the possible distortions of overlapping major running stories, and were thought not to be unduly influenced by seasonal news values. They were selected, in so far as such can be gauged, as 'typical' environment news weeks.

(b) These duration times are total broadcast durations which include, of course, the intermissions of advertisements on all ITV and Channel 4 news programmes, excluding weekend programmes.

(c) As all insomniacs no doubt will realize, all breakfast news programmes contain considerable repetition of news items. For the purposes of this analysis all identifiable news stories, and not their repetition within a single programme, were coded.

With 142 hours of news programming selected for review from two weeks of news broadcasting, and representing all main news programmes transmitted across each of the four existing channels, it is apparent that even a relatively small sample captures an impressive outpouring of news. In terms of both overall programme news stories and programme durations, it is immediately evident that certain programmes, and breakfast news programming in particular, dominate the news schedules. This raises the question, to what extent does environmental news feature both within the sample as a whole and, in relative terms, across different news programmes? It is also interesting to inquire to what extent similar programmes, whether breakfast, midday or evening main channel or regional or subsidiary channel night programmes, convey similar amounts of environmental news? Is it the case, for instance, that certain news programmes and types of news programme convey differing amounts of environmental coverage, perhaps in absolute as well as relative terms?

Table 6.2 *TV news programmes and environmental presence*

Programme	Total programme items		Environmental items	Per cent
HTV Regional	166		23	13.9
BBC Regional	109		11	10.1
			Regional 34	Sample % 43.6
Channel Four Daily	280		11	3.9
TV AM	239		9	3.8
BBC1 Breakfast	269		9	3.3
			Breakfast 29	Sample % 37.2
ITN Midday	108		3	2.7
BBC1 Midday	119		2	1.7
			Midday 5	Sample % 6.4
C4 Evening	140		3	2.1
BBC2/Newsnight	101		2	2.0
			Night 5	Sample % 6.4
ITN Evening	109		0	0.0
BBC Evening	159		5	3.1
			Evening 5	Sample % 6.4
	Total 1799		Total 78	(4.3 %) 100.0%

As Table 6.2 indicates, with seventy-eight environmental news stories found within a total sample of 1,799 news stories, the environmental presence at 4.3 per cent is not great. However, differences between programme types are also revealing, suggesting that programmes can indeed be grouped as 'types' and that this results in remarkably similar patterns of relative environmental coverage within them. In absolute terms it is clear that regional news and breakfast television programming together carry 81 per cent of all environmental items broadcast. Clearly, this is a finding of some interest, particularly perhaps to those researchers who have confined their analyses to ITN and BBC1 evening news programmes, which together comprise only 6.4 per cent of all environmental news items broadcast.

Such findings cannot simply be accounted for in terms of the total number of broadcast news items carried by these different programmes, since the relative presence of environmental coverage is not related to overall news items. It is apparent, then, that particular news programmes tend to share similar relative degrees of environmental coverage when approached as programme types, notwithstanding the differences between particular programmes in terms of overall news items carried. Such findings, even at this basic level of absolute and relative environmental item frequencies, indicate that the spectrum of TV news programming exhibits remarkable diversity, and within types noticeable consistency, concerning the amount of environmental news coverage broadcast.

TV news and the hierarchy of environmental concerns

If such differing patterns of environmental coverage indicate that TV news is far from being a homogeneous form of broadcast journalism, it is also instructive to examine the array of environmental concerns finding news expression. Clearly, there are many ways in which environmental themes and issues could be categorized, often with considerable degrees of overlap. For the purpose of this analysis all news items were identified which involved environmental themes as defined by the news treatment itself. While differences of interpretation can challenge the validity of such news frames when approached from one or other of available environmental ideologies, it is possible to discern, though not necessarily to accept, the basic environmental issue which informs the news definition of the environment. The classification of items was developed from the environmental stories themselves, therefore, rather than from extrinsic categories. Table 6.3 shows the emphases revealed.

Table 6.3 *TV news environmental concerns*

		N	Per cent
Pollution: air	6		
water	9	18	23.1
land	3		
Animal habitat/	5		
Animal exploitation	11	16	20.5
Land conservation/	12		
Cultural heritage	2	14	17.9
Urban squalor/congestion/			
Development		14	17.9
Natural disaster		6	7.7
Environmental party politics		4	5.1
Radiation/nuclear		3	3.8
Nutrition/food		2	2.6
Mineral exploitation		1	1.3
	Total 78		100.0 %

A hierarchy of environmental news concerns emerges from the

sample. With nearly a quarter of all news items concerned with pollution, typically reporting the latest major polluting spillage or contamination of land, air or sea, the event orientation of news observed across many studies of news – with its associated displace-ment of background issues, informing context and wider social processes – finds further confirmation in relation to environmental news coverage. Interestingly, however, when such findings are examined across programme types it is noticeable that half of all pollution items are carried by midday, early evening and night programmes, notwithstanding that together they convey less than one-fifth of total environmental items. In addition to finding that such programmes, when compared to other TV news forms, portray environmental concerns relatively infrequently it is also the case therefore that their reporting appears to be dominated by the major and dramatic events of pollution coverage. When examining those relatively few items of environmental news covered by BBC1 midday and early evening news programmes, for example, all but one concern pollution 'events' with the remaining item referring to a 'natural disaster' (yet another form of event reporting which typically displaces consideration of those contributing social processes and inadequacies of response which may inform such natural events).

Turning to the second largest category of TV news environmental concerns, animal habitats and exploitation, which comprise over a fifth of all sample environment stories, it was found that the bulk of these were confined to breakfast news programmes (9), and regional news programmes (5), with a further two items in BBC1 and ITN midday programmes (though these were dropped from the later BBC1 and ITN evening broadcasts). Concern with animal exploitation and the loss of habitats, frequently involving popular species and/or wild scenery provide an opportunity for good pictures. They also provide an opportunity to indulge engrained cultural sentiments and nostalgic feelings for the loss of a natural order and way of life in which man and nature are thought to have enjoined in a less complicated, if often vitalistic, relationship. Interestingly, while such stories routinely figure within breakfast and regional variants of TV news, and often bring up the 'soft news' rear of national midday news broadcasts, they appear less likely to be selected for national early news programme transmission. The inference that this particular news construction of the environment is often included as a means of building a particular form of popular appeal cannot be discounted.

Similarly, the news interest in land conservation and/or themes of cultural heritage are also noteworthy to the extent that nearly all such items are found within regional news programmes (9), while a further two items were found within the breakfast programme *TVAM*, and midday ITN programme. Once again, it seems, the opportunity to reproduce idyllic countryside scenes is rarely lost upon regional and breakfast news producers.

Also constituting a fifth of all environmental coverage is the concern with the urban environment and its development. Though some may object to its inclusion as an environmental concern given its urban focus, the fact that such stories refer to the human and environmental costs of urban planning and modern way of life lends support to their inclusion. Moreover, to the extent that such items frequently resonate with those known and deep-seated cultural oppositions known to sociologists since Tönnies as *gesellschaft* and *gemeinschaft*, and in which the modern, individuated, industrialized and alienated way of life associated with the urban is implicitly contrasted to the traditional, collective, natural and communal way of life associated with the rural, enhances their popular news value. This is particularly so concerning the regional news variant of TV news in which such mythic values are regularly indulged.

With 'natural disasters' breaking through the relatively disinterested environmental news thresholds of early evening national news programmes, and finding some inclusion within breakfast news, this category of environmental news, as suggested above, tends to be confined to immediate aftermath damage counts, often including graphic eye-witness accounts.

Environmental party politics was found to play a small role within the overall picture of environmental news, with three items confined to the major announcement by the Green Party of its new form of leadership reported in regional, breakfast and Channel 4 night variants of TV news. During the two week sample period, only three items directly addressed issues of nuclear power and its environmental impact or consequences, though one of these, reported by *Newsnight*, provided an in-depth analysis of over ten minutes duration concerning the emerging revelations about nuclear accidents and continuing hazards associated with nuclear installations within the former Soviet Union and Eastern Europe. With the remaining items concerned with nutrition and health, focused in relation to wider environmental concerns and consumption habits on *TVAM*, and one other breakfast item taking the opportunity of a geological find of gold in Devon, to indulge popular images of Devon's 'green and pleasant land' incongruously alongside references to the 'Wild West', the priorities of environmental coverage, though based upon a relatively small sample appear pronounced and, importantly, differentiated by type of TV news programme.

Clearly, established programme forms appear to determine in considerable measure both the extent and nature of environmental coverage. Notwithstanding such opening programme cliches as: 'This is the midday news from ITN bringing you the latest news from Britain and around the world'; or 'Here is the BBC with the latest national and international news', it is clear that the environment is mediated according to existing programme interests which do not simply reflect, in empiricist fashion, what is 'out there'.

Out of seventy-eight environmental news reports, nine stories were found to have also been reported by other news programmes, though most by only one other news programme, and with twenty-one news items in total belonging to those which had also been reported elsewhere. In other words fifty-nine news reports, or 76 per cent were not found reported elsewhere across the sample of news programmes at all. As far as TV news reporting of the environment is concerned, therefore, and with the exception of major pollution and disaster stories, the coverage of the environment is largely dependent upon the selection decisions of the particular news programme in which such stories are found.

If concern with the environment, as suggested earlier, extends from the local to the global, it is also the case that such spatial considerations inform the programme types of environmental news coverage. Here it is apparent that different TV news programmes have differing reaches of environmental interest. For example, if a news item reports a pollution leak from a local factory, and is treated as a localized problem, then such an item can be said to have a local environmental reach, though possibly of more widespread audience interest. If an item reports a major incident of river pollution, as with the recent pollution of a Cornish estuary, then such an item can be said to have a regional reach, unless explicitly concerned with the wider scene of national river pollution and/or central government responsibility, in which case its story reach extends to the national terrain. Environmental stories which pertain to a foreign country, such as the political success of a foreign national Green Party, or the reintroduction of wolves into the American wilderness, have a foreign national reach, while stories which report, say, a new international agreement on the use of drift nets in an attempt to halt the unnecessary killing of dolphins, or fears concerning the increasing international trade in wild horses, have an international environmental reach. Lastly, news stories reflecting the growing concerns over world impacts of global warming and other concerns which effect the planet can be said to have a global environmental reach. Such dimensions of environmental news reporting are important to the extent that the 'environmental problem' is mediated as one of say, local, national, foreign or global impact and concern.

Table 6.4 *TV news and environmental reach*

	N	Per cent
Local	26	33.3
Regional	14	17.9
National	11	14.1
Foreign National	15	19.2
International	9	11.5
Global*	2	2.6
Other	1	1.3
	Total 78	100.0

TVAM item on 'body ecology' not allocated

Interestingly, as Table 6.4 shows, it is clear that the problems of the environment find unequal prominence in relation to such spatial considerations. As might be expected, the regional news programmes tend to monopolize the reporting of local environmental matters, bringing back home, as it were, the more socially immediate and geographically proximate impacts of environmental issues and concerns. While both regional and national environmental stories are found across the spectrum of TV news forms (notwithstanding the mistakenly named 'regional' news programmes, which could, on present findings, more accurately be termed 'local-parochial' news programmes), it is interesting to note that the presence of national environmental stories is relatively infrequent, no doubt reflecting the priorities of national government and news reporting practices. When it comes to foreign national environmental stories however, reporting is increased, particularly within breakfast news programmes where such stories are commonly found, in addition to the foreign environmental disaster stories found on other main channel news programmes. With both BBC1 breakfast and the Channel 4 Daily programmes scheduling a routine foreign news element within their overall programme design, increased numbers of foreign environmental stories are likely to be, and are, generated. The fact that they are included, however, may say more about their perceived contribution to the programme composition and disposition than their status as 'major' foreign news stories.[4]

Environmental stories with an international reach are also relatively infrequent, though stories with a global reach find the least of all TV news exposure, with the two sample global items found, in this instance, on *TVAM* breakfast news. Such findings, no doubt, reflect the daily exigencies of news production, established programme contours and the external realities of existing source organizations and political and institutional arrangements.[5] For the purposes of this analysis, however, the major finding is that the environment, from the local to the global, finds unequal expression across the TV news spectrum.

TV news access and environmental voices

It has long been a central claim of much news research that news operates a 'structured over-accessing to the media of those in powerful and privileged institutional positions' who are thereby able to advance 'definitions of social reality' in accordance with dominant social interests (Hall et al., 1978, p. 58). While this basic finding has frequently been rehearsed, it has less frequently been put to empirical test across both different forms of news media and different social issues. It is instructive, therefore, to consider the array of 'primary definers' finding their way on to the environment news stage. To what extent is it the case, for instance, that political and social elites dominate the environmental news agenda? Looking at Table 6.5, the notion that a hierarchy of social and political elites 'define' environmental issues in accordance with dominant interests becomes problematic, not least because the catch-all category of 'elite' proves too elastic to provide much analytic, much less explanatory, power in this area while tending to impose a spurious semblance of unity upon a differentiated number of institutional and organizational domains and social interests – many of which will be characterized by internal as well as cross-organizational divisions of interest and opinions. In other words, while an environmental 'hierarchy' can be discerned, the constituent elements do not appear likely to produce a closure around a dominant viewpoint, but rather reflect the organized expressions of vying social, political, economic and cultural interests. Indeed, within such a contested context it is difficult to imagine what a dominant viewpoint, much less 'definition of reality' would be.

Table 6.5 *Access: environmental 'primary definers'*

	N	Per cent
Environmental pressure/interest group	25	14.6
Individual non-affiliated citizen	23	13.5
Local authority representative/official	20	11.7
Foreign government representative	18	10.5
Scientists/expert	18	10.5
Public authority	15	8.8
Industry/business representative	15	8.8
Central government representative	12	7.0
Agriculture/fisheries industry representative	6	3.5
Farmers/fishermen as individuals	5	2.9
Trade unions	4	2.3
Police	4	2.3
Other*	4	2.3
EEC/UN representative	2	1.2
	171	100.0 %

*Others: 2 military, 1 royalty, 1 Opposition MP

What does appear to be the case from Table 6.5, is that environmental news depends in large measure upon a number of organized bases and sites of environmental opinion and activity, whether environmental pressure groups or different levels of formalized politics and administration, whether scientific and expert viewpoints or simply 'representatives' of non-affiliated individual citizens/consumers. Clearly, such general findings do not indicate a situation of open and equal access, but then neither is it the case that a dominant elite monopolizes the environmental media stage.

It was also found that regional news tends to routinely access more non-affiliated voices in relation to environmental concerns than other types of news programming, while scientific and expert opinions find increased prominence in other types of news programmes. Business and industry voices find most representation in national evening news programmes, and environmental pressure groups within breakfast news programmes. These findings, given the sample size of environmental actors, are admittedly only provisional at present but they suggest that the notion of an invariant and relatively closed hierarchy of access, defining the social agenda of environmental concerns and issues across the TV news medium, is less than adequate when approaching the differentiated nature of TV news and its mediation of the environment. Moreover, as discussed below, such generalized claims concerning the role of accessed voices in 'social definition' fail to address the way in which such voices are put to work within differing journalistic strategies of story organization and telling[6].

TV news and the forums of environmental coverage

In delivering news stories, TV news programmes employ a number of different standardized formats or 'forums' which variously enhance or inhibit the free expression of contending environmental points of view. A news item is a combination of visual and verbal elements produced under the authorship of professional newsworkers. For the purposes of this discussion, the manner in which 'outside' voices are given an opportunity to develop their point of view, or not, is thought crucial, and in large measure dependent upon the array of presentational formats deployed. The first format can be termed 'restricted' because it permits little or no accessing of outside voices, with the telling of the story entirely dependent upon the news presenter's account. Examples of such restricted newsdesk formats are included below.

An inquiry is to be held into a chemical leak at a government explosives factory in Somerset early today. Emergency services spent nearly five hours at the plant at Puraton in Somerset after the escape of sulphuric acid. Officials say no one was injured. In recent weeks there has been a number of chemical leaks from the factory. Now there is to be talks with local residents to improve the warning system. (HTV regional)

In this instance the form of the news delivery permits no questioning of either the activities or the location of the government's explosive factory. Moreover, given the history of previous leaks, the response may appear, to some at least, to be an exercise in mediated symbolic reassurance which fails to grapple with the major issue at stake: the leaking of dangerous gases into a local residential area. What local residents or others have to say about this situation, however, remains unknown within this format of news delivery.

The Belgian prime minister, Wilfred Martins, has offered his resignation after his coalition government lost seats to an anti-immigration party and environmentalists at yesterday's election. Mr Martins, who is Europe's longest serving prime minister, has agreed to head a caretaker government until a new one can be assembled. (Channel 4 evening news)

Similarly, this item also remains entrapped within the narrow confines of its news format. With its focus upon the Belgian prime minister's political downfall as an event, rather than the outcome of informing political processes involving, in this instance, what might appear to be the odd alliance between anti-immigrationists and environmentalists, the audience is offered no understanding of the background needed to help explain this account.

A fire at a Lucozade bottling plant is believed to have been started deliberately. A senior fire officer said that the blaze at Little Holton in Greater Manchester yesterday was certainly not an accident. No one's admitted starting it. Two weeks ago Lucozade withdrew five million bottles from sale after a poison scare. Police said they had uncovered a plot by animal rights activists. (BBC1 breakfast news)

Reading the last example above, it again becomes apparent that the voices in play are offered restricted possibilities within this presentational format. Why would animal rights activists start this fire? How would such an action fit into the wider politics of environmental direct action? Why has no animal rights spokesperson admitted, even anonymously, to this action? Are there grounds for doubting police claims? From within the confines of this restricted format such basic questions remain imponderables.

TV news increasingly works with another form of standardized format, however, which provides more 'limited' scope for voices to contribute to and, on occasion, contest the viewpoints of others. Consider the following, not untypical, regional environmental news involving a form of environmental protest.

News presenter Rush hour traffic came to a standstill in Bristol this
(studio)   morning when over a hundred and fifty cyclists blocked
                the M32. They were protesting at traffic congestion and
                high pollution levels. The demonstration closed one of the
                main routes into the city. But it was over almost as soon as
                it began. Clive Mairy reports.

Reporter   Bristol city centre at eight thirty this morning and a latter
(video film)   day King Canute is directing the rush hour traffic.

King Canute   Go back, go home. Bristol doesn't need you. We're
(to halted traffic) coughing with your fumes every morning.

Reporter   An obvious gimmick but for the Bristol Cycle Campaign
                behind the fake royal patronage lies an important issue:
                traffic pollution and congestion. The demonstrators claim
                traffic flows into Bristol have increased by 80 per cent over
                the last 20 years, and that pollution is so bad in the Old

	Market area of the city that carbon monoxide emissions are 77 times higher than World Health Organisation limits.
Protester	We're having more roads, more roads generate more traffic, that's well known. You only have to look at the M25. What we actually need is more facilities to take people off the roads, because Bristol cannot continue to accommodate more cars ad infinitum.
Reporter	But while the tide was kept at bay, others just wanted to get to work.
Motorist	Well it's a good idea but I don't know what my boss is going to think when I'm late for work. Yeah, it is a good idea; obviously something has got to be done about the travelling in Bristol, it's stupid, it takes you three quarters of an hour to get in to work in the morning. But like I said, I don't know what my boss is going to think when I'm late for work.
Reporter	The campaigners want Avon County Council to freeze all new building and ban cars with only one occupant entering central Bristol in the rush hour. To end the proceedings King Canute then rallied his troops.
King Canute	I beseech you, to go home and rest to prepare for the struggles to come.
Assembled protestors	(Cheering). (BBC regional news)

As the transcript of this item indicates, the format of electronic news gathering (ENG) video and clipped interview 'bites' provide enhanced opportunities for advancing contesting points of view. Though still reliant upon the overall frame of reference which remains within the editorial control of the news team, such 'limited' formats none the less provide increased discursive opportunities. This particular news report appears to have been self-consciously drawn to the 'staging' props of the demonstration and in part actively becomes complicit to the development of the analogy of King Canute, but it also appears undecided as to the item's essential news value. Is it principally about the effects of a morning protest upon motorists, the effects of traffic congestion and pollution, or even the dramatic device informing the demonstration? Though the protesters in this instance have won considerable news access, they remain dependent upon the overall narrative framed by the news producers.

Occasionally a third form of presentational format is employed across TV news programmes which offers more 'expansive' opportunities for discursive engagement and contest and which, furthermore, if it is broadcast in its entirety or 'goes out' live is not subject to the imposed editing and packaging process of the above. This expansive format involves more lengthy, often studio-based, interviews in which the interviewee can deliver and build his point of view in engaged discussion, often contesting the interviewer's agenda and informing viewpoints. Consider the following studio discussion extract in which the announcement of a new government scheme to subsidize Somerset farmers in order to conserve animal habitats and wetlands is discussed.

News presenter So can farmers survive this latest attack on their methods and livelihood? Can man and nature live together on the Levels? Earlier I asked the National Farmers Union policy adviser Anthony Gibson.

NFU adviser I believe they can perfectly well. After all it's only in the last thirty or forty years there's been this conflict. I think the challenge for the future is to devise systems of farming there which produce food, job satisfaction for farmers and keep and enhance the wildlife of the area.

News presenter But farmers haven't been too ready to take up these government schemes, how are they going to react to this one do you think?

NFU adviser It depends on how much money there is on the table. I think the problem with the scheme in the past is that there hasn't been enough money on offer. There was half as much again offered in the Norfolk Broads and the take-up was one hundred per cent. It won't be a hundred per cent on the Somerset Levels because there will always be farmers who want to farm up to maximum efficiency. But there is room for them as well in this sort of mosaic approach with some areas left for the birds, other areas are farmed at low intensity, and areas around the fringe are farmed to their full potential.

News presenter But there remains a conflict doesn't there? A lot of conservationists would say stop farming completely and manage this as a proper nature reserve.

NFU adviser They'd be wrong to say that for two reasons. First of all it's actually essential to wildlife interests that the area is farmed, albeit in a certain way. Secondly, while breeding waders is very, very important to the character of the Somerset Levels, I believe breeding farmers is equally important. If we lose them, we lose the whole character of the Levels.

News presenter Anthony Gibson, thanks very much.

The interviewee develops his point of view by countering the informing perspective of the news presenter which appears to entertain a fundamental conflict model of man versus nature, always a useful journalistic ploy when seeking to maximize news values of conflict and controversy. Though still having to respond to the presenter's agenda, the interviewee builds his point of view at some length and, though not visible in this instance, has some opportunity to shift the interview agenda. Clearly, each of these standardized news formats present very different degrees of opportunity for the portrayal and public contests that surround the environment. They also appear from Table 6.6 to be differently deployed across the spectrum of TV news programmes in their environmental coverage.

Table 6.6: *TV news and presentational formats**

	Restricted	Limited	Expansive
Regional news	15 (44.1)	17 (50.0)	2 (5.9)
Breakfast news	5 (17.2)	17 (58.6)	7 (24.1)
Others combined	4 (26.6)	10 (66.6)	1 (6.6)
Total	24 (30.8)	44 (56.4)	10 (12.8)

*Given the infrequency of environmental items found within the sample for certain news programmes other than breakfast and regional TV news forms, the remaining national news programmes have been combined. In fact there are also interesting differences to be found between *Channel 4 News* and *Newsnight* which employ more expansive and restricted formats when compared to the predominance of limited formats found on BBC1 and ITN evening news programmes.

Important differences can be discerned concerning the array of presentational formats, and their enhancing or constraining role in the mediation of the environment across programme forms. Interestingly, though variations are evident, opportunities for expansive environmental coverage, with the exception of breakfast news, are limited, while most environmental portrayal across the TV news spectrum tends towards the limited opportunities of tightly edited and packaged news formats.

Towards the modalities of TV environmental news

Enough has been indicated above concerning the differentiated portrayal of environmental concerns across the TV news spectrum to suggest that news mediation of the environment is internally differentiated, structured and open to further detailed exploration. The above has done little more than indicate, in aggregate and broad terms, that the environment has found differential news treatment according to the established priorities and forms of existing TV news programmes. Whether concerning the salience of the environment as a news issue, the array of substantive environmental concerns, the spatial 'reach' of environmental portrayal, the hierarchy of environmental voices finding news access, or, lastly, the enhancing or constraining impacts of standardized presentational formats, each has been found to be differently distributed across the spectrum of TV news. Finally, this last discussion raises some further points of variance concerning environmental news treatment, simultaneously rendering problematic a few orthodox views of news as essentially about information dissemination, confined to the prominent issues and concerns of the public sphere and delivered by journalists invoking an objectivist epistemology. On all three counts, the TV news portrayal of the environment points to a more differentiated and nuanced state of affairs.

At the beginning of this study it was suggested that popular understanding and responses to the environment are culturally informed, that is to say, the 'structures of feeling' through which the environment is apprehended are often deeply embedded within the wider culture and available for news mobilization. In other words, and contrary to professional journalist, liberal and occasional radical claims to the contrary, news is not confined to its information (or ideological) function. In popular variants of TV news, most notably breakfast and regional news forms though not exclusively confined to these, environmental portrayal is frequently found to resonate with affective appeals. Consider the following for example.

News presenter Farmers and environmentalists in the south western United States are gearing up for a battle of survival – the survival of an endangered species. It follows the government's plans to reintroduce wolves into their natural habitat which now borders prime farming country.

(film sequence: sound of howling wolves)

News presenter It's a sound which becomes rarer each year, wolves
(film/voice over) howling across the great American west. At one time there were thousands, the great predator of the Rocky Mountains. But they began to decline when a greater predator, man, came along. None suffered as badly as the Mexican wolf whose population fell to just seven captive animals. Now there are forty-four and scientists are preparing to send them out to fend for themselves.

Scientist We are hoping their numbers are strong enough so that they can return to what I feel is their rightful place. Our children have some right to see these things. To see them stuffed in a museum is not the way I want my children to grow up seeing them.

News presenter But farmers resent the new competition, especially when the wolves' new home is next door to their prime breeding herd.

Farmer With a major predator introduced and thrust into that situation, I don't think anybody knows what is going to happen.

News presenter The US government says it's bound by law to reintroduce the wolves to the wild. The result will be the renewal of the battle between the two great predators of the west (sounds of howling wolves). (Channel 4 Daily)

Clearly this news story does provide, at an informational level, detail of a new scheme to introduce American wolves back into their original habitat. However, it is also apparent that the story works at a deeper level than this, and that this is a product of its journalistic story treatment. Affirming good intentions and deeds, the item celebrates rather than reports. Activating popular apprehensions and myths of wolves, no doubt sustained within the wider mythologies of the 'taming of the wild west', not to mention the symbolism of the wolf and wolf howls found in Gothic horror tales, the story also dramatizes the popular conception of man against nature in the renewed 'battle between the two great predators'. By invoking the popular myth of this 'eternal' struggle for survival, apparently for the most part beyond history, economics, culture or reason the outcome of such a contest is left unclear. What is suggested is that man and nature are pitted in deadly opposition more at the level of blind instinct than from the competitive pressures for land use. Needless to say, if the social realities informing the abstract idea of man are rendered invisible by such a metaphor, the positioning of wolves as engaged in battle is to once again invest the forces of nature with supernatural cunning. This may be a journalistic device to convey information in a succinct and entertaining way. It simultaneously trades however in cultural mythology and it is this which gives it its popular resonance.

In another story carried by both regional news programmes, popular sentiments towards deer and their natural habitat are indulged while simultaneously juxtaposing the age-old custom of poaching against the modern technology of surveillance equipment deployed with the calling in of the Royal Marines. The evening programme was introduced with the final 'tease': 'And the Royal Marines go hunting a new enemy in Somerset':

News presenter   Royal Marine commandoes have been called in to help track down poachers of the Quantock Hills in Somerset. It's hoped the Marines will be able to bring to an end an illegal trade in venison which is threatening the future of the Quantocks Red Deer population. This report from Clinton Rogers.

Reporter   This is the security force which will be facing poachers on the Quantock Hills in Somerset. From now on the hunters will become the hunted, in an exercise designed to stamp out a crime which threatens the future of the Quantock's Red Deer population. No one is sure how many deer fall victim to the poachers rifle (sound of rifle shot), but it's bound to run into hundreds every year . . . (Regional BBC1, *Points West*)

In fact, the Royal Marines were permitted to only report the whereabouts of any spotted poachers, but this did not hinder the use of the dramatic device: 'the hunters become the hunted'. Once again, it is apparent that the story works at a deeper level than simply reporting the latest strategy to combat the illegal trade in venison.

Attending to the different forms of TV news portrayal of the environment also raises questions concerning the assumed political function of the news media and its role in imparting important information. If Habermas forewarned of the tendency of the modern news media to debase the public sphere, transforming a 'culture debating' society of citizens into a 'culture consuming' society of consumers oriented within a 'pseudo-public sphere', evidence from *TVAM* suggests that such is already at hand. Whether concerned with Green tourism, the growth in sales of natural mineral waters, the impact of global warming upon British holiday weather or 'body ecology', the environment becomes refracted through a journalistic prism frequently seeking to appeal to the immediate domestic and leisure concerns of ordinary consumers. Consider, for example, how in this *TVAM* introduction even global warming can be reduced to those more mundane concerns of the British weather and holiday prospects.

News presenter A little later on we will be discussing the latest warnings about the aah, the warnings about the global warming and the greenhouse effect. All of which sounds pretty dramatic but judging from the weather we are going to get at the end of this November it doesn't sound like global warming is here to stay or affecting us very very greatly, at least at this time . . . Now as you've heard from Ulrika [weather woman] the British weather is very unpredictable at the moment. We've certainly had our share of cold weather and you might be surprised to learn that this year is set to be the second warmest on record. Remember those long hot summer days by the seaside, they're little more than a distant memory now. I don't remember too many long hot days, but anyhow, some scientists say many more are on the way because of global warming and the greenhouse effect. Changes to the world's climate may also bring more intense storms such as those which have caused such havoc in the Philippines last week. And some experts believe unless action is taken to stem the greenhouse effect right now, areas of the Mediterranean and American Midwest will become deserts, if you can believe that, in the twenty-first century. Well, joining us now is freelancer environmental journalist and author Fred Pearce . . . We've heard these scare stories before – deserts and parts of England are going to look like a jungle. How can you take any of these reports seriously, people can't believe when we're facing one of the coldest Novembers on record possibly, that the greenhouse effect can be having much effect at all. (*TVAM*)

Delivered with accompanying background mellow music and lush tropical scenes the following *TVAM* holiday item, makes no pretence to be oriented to the news public sphere, deliberately appealing to private leisure ambitions as a means of escaping the pressures of urban living.

Reporter   When you think of holidays in Australia you probably think of beaches and sunshine. But only a short hop from the coast there's this: the Australian rain forest. According to my guidebook it's only for the really intrepid traveller, but if you want to be intrepid in comfort you can come and stay here, Silky Oakes. There are a number of hotels like this here which have been built to fit into the scenery, like the huts we stayed in. It's really only a form of Green tourism, a way of getting closer to nature without having to rough it or destroy the environment. And because of strict planning regulations these hotels have to be small, which unfortunately means they are expensive. But as we found out small can be beautiful. If you want to treat yourself, you can come here for a luxurious break and really get away from it all ... (*TVAM*)

Though perhaps assuming their most pronounced form in the breakfast programme of *TVAM*, such consumerist appeals are not confined to this news programme alone. Moreover, as the extracts above illustrate, not only is the substance of their concern oriented to the private sphere of individual and family consumption and leisure, but so too is their style of delivery and mode of appeal differentiated from other news programmes. Delivered in the familiar, at times chatty, idiom of common sense reasoning and feelings, environmental items can often eschew those professional claims to objectivity and impartiality, deliberately appealing to emotive responses and adopting a position of moral partisanship. This populist strategy of news delivery and 'way of knowing', or underpinning news epistemology, can be contrasted to the objectivist epistemology usually thought to inform news accounts with their accessing of authoritative expert opinion and the marshalling of reason and statistical facts, all delivered in the detached tones of a neutral observer. Whether addressing concerns of environmental pollution with a representative of the World Wide Fund for Nature, or the leading campaigner and author against the mass killing of baby seals, *TVAM* is disposed to adopt a championing position. Consider the following interview extracts:

Programme   Children must wonder when they look at, what I think are
presenter   amongst the most obscene films that you can see, and that is the toxic poisons flowing into waters not just in Britain, but right across the industrialised nations of the world, I wonder why we can't embarrass the government? ...

            And let's hope the government's given a huge ear trumpet so they can hear you loud, loud and clear. You sometimes think that's what they need.

In an interview with a leading campaigner against the killing of baby seals the presenter adopts a position of moral outrage, and feels able to give full vent to his feelings. Such a declaration would surely sound strange if introduced into the more authoritative and detached tones of evening BBC1 or ITN news programmes. Included below are just a few of the programme presenter's typical style of questions and prompts found within a lengthy studio interview.

Programme presenter	Now let's be clear about this. The killing's not for any sound ecological purpose is it? It's for adornment, yes? . . .
	Earlier you had seen mile upon mile of bloodstained ice hadn't you? . . .
	I bet you would like to carry all those who do have any seal fur out to the ice floes and make them watch what you have seen . . .

And in concluding the interview, the refrain continues thus:

Programme presenter	Brian Davies, you emigrated to Canada, you're still a Welshman thanks for joining us.
Co-presenter	Well said, they look better on seals, of course they do. And what a wonderful holiday to go to Canada and just take photographs of seals and watch them. I think that would be great.

The purpose of including such extracts is not, of course, to criticize their obvious populist appeal and informing strategy of affective engagement, but to draw attention to the fact that TV news forms can and do work according to differing informing news epistemologies, and it is here that environmental news portrayal finds characteristic journalistic inflection. The discussion above has highlighted such popular-based journalist strategies given the usual privileging of the objectivist/authoritative news epistemology subjected to detailed discussion within the news literature (Tuchman, 1972; Hackett, 1985). Both, of course, inform the spectrum of TV news programmes, often in permutation and to varying degrees as news programmes modulate stories from so-called 'hard' news issues to 'soft' news concerns. Given that there are good grounds for suspecting that many environmental stories are used in exactly this way, bringing up the rear of different news programmes, such subjectivist/experiential ways of dealing with environmental concerns are not thought to be confined to *TVAM*, though perhaps this programme, more than any other, has deliberately courted populist appeal.

With these final observations, it is clear that TV news programming provides a differentiated array of programme forms, each with its own modality of telling stories, and that such have been found to impact upon the mediation of environmental concerns. The above has offered no more than a preliminary investigation of existing news forms and their contribution to environmental portrayal within the TV news public sphere; more detailed studies have yet to be completed in which the specificities of particular programmes as well as illustrative examples of environmental news stories can be discussed in greater depth than was possible here. What is clear is that the news portrayal of the environment does not simply function at an informational level, imparting rational discussion and resources for environment opinion formation important though this may be, but can also frequently be found to work at a deeper cultural level in which widespread, if rarely articulated, structures of feeling towards nature and the environment are mobilized. If this study has sought to make a claim for recognizing the differentiated nature of TV news programming, it also calls for increased sensitivity to the cultural expressiveness of news which, in relation to environmental portrayal, appears to regularly inform its popular news mediation.

Notes

I would like to acknowledge the assistance of Bath College of Higher Education and its contribution towards the costs of this research, and thank my good friend Sargs and my Dad who generously volunteered to help record the news sample.

1 See D. Pepper (1984) *The Roots of Modern Environmentalism* for an account of the historical development and ideological formations of environmentalism.
2 The phrase 'structures of feeling' is, of course, from Raymond Williams's *Marxism and Literature* in which he sought to pay increased recognition to the affective dimension of consciousness as continual flux and process, informing thought but not confined within fixed ideological boundaries. 'The term is difficult, but "feeling" is chosen to emphasize a distinction from more formal concepts of "world-view" or "ideology". It is not only that we must go beyond formally held and systematic beliefs, though of course we have always to include them. It is that we are concerned with meanings and values as they are actively lived and felt' (Williams, 1985, p. 132). In the context of this study with its particular concern with popular forms of TV journalism and their activation of affective responses and environmental resonances found deep within the wider culture, this phrase is thought to be particularly apt.
3 Though it is not part of the purpose of this study to engage with debates within media theory which seek to account for news forms and output, the fact that differently styled news programmes can be produced by the same, or similar, news producers suggests that such differences cannot be entirely explained by variants of the main explanatory approaches. In short, the generalized claims of political economy approaches, culturalist frameworks and the notion of imported dominant codes, as well as production studies of news organization and bureaucracy and studies of journalist backgrounds, beliefs and professional socialization all fail to address the professional adaptation to, and purposeful pursuit of, different news forms as established forms of news genre. This argument is developed in my study of regional news production and its coverage of the inner city (Cottle, 1993).
4 A recent study of global newsrooms and the use made of such TV news

agencies whether Visnews and WTN, and others also reveals how foreign news stories can now readily be accessed. An American news executive has aptly commented 'The sky is full of stuff . . . We just take it down from the satellites' (Gurevitch, Levy and Roeh, 1991, p. 197). Questions of established programme ambitions as much as increased sources of TV news need to be considered here however.

5 Here reference can also be made to the known journalist attractions to such different 'news scenarios' as demonstration or government announcement recently documented in Hansen 1990.

6 For a detailed illustration of the manner in which accessed voices are sought, interviewed and subsequently edited and repackaged according to the informing professional journalist conception of 'the story' and its requirements, see my discussion 'The Rushdie Affair: A case study in the orchestration of public opinion' (Cottle, 1991).

References

Burgess, J. (1990), 'The production and consumption of environmental meanings in the mass media: a research agenda for the 1990s', *Transactions of the Institute of British Geographers*, New Series 15 (2), pp. 139–61.

Carey, J. (1989), *Communication as culture*, London: Unwin Hyman.

Cottle, S. (1991), 'The Rushdie Affair: A case study in the orchestration of public opinion', *Race and Class* 32 (4), pp. 45–64.

Cottle, S. (1993), *TV news, urban conflict and the inner city*, Leicester: Leicester University Press.

Curran, J. (1991), 'Rethinking the media as public sphere', in P. Dahlgren and C. Sparks, (eds) *Communication and citizenship*, London: Routledge.

Dahlgren, P., Sparks, C. (eds) (1991), *Communication and citizenship*, London: Routledge.

Elliott, P. (1986), 'Intellectuals, the "information society" and the disappearance of the Public Sphere', in R. Collins et al. (eds), *Media, culture and society: a critical reader*, London: Sage.

Garnham, N. (1986), 'The media and the public sphere', in P. Golding, G. Murdock and P. Schlesinger (eds), *Communicating politics*, Leicester: Leicester University Press.

Gurevitch, M., Levy, M.R., Roeh, I. (1991), 'The global newsroom: convergences and diversities in the globalization of television news', in P. Dahlgren, and C. Sparks (eds), *Communication and citizenship*, London: Routledge.

Hackett, R.A. (1985), 'Decline of a paradigm? Bias and objectivity in news media studies', in *Mass communication review yearbook*, London: Sage.

Habermas, J. (1974), 'The Public Sphere', *New German Critique* 3, Autumn.

Habermas, J. (1989), *The structural transformation of the public sphere*, T. Burger (trans), Oxford: Polity Press.

Hansen, A. (1990), *The news construction of the environment*, Leicester: Centre for Mass Communication Research, University of Leicester.

Hansen, A. (1991), 'The media and the social construction of the environment', *Media, Culture and Society*, 13 (1), pp. 443–58.

Jensen, J. (1986), *Making sense of the news*, Aarhus: Aarhus University Press.

Lowe, P., Morrison, D. (1984), 'Bad news or good news: environmental politics and the mass media', *Sociological Review*, 32 (1), pp. 75–90.

O'Riordan, T. (1981), 'Environmentalism and education', *Journal of Geography in Higher Education*, 5 (1), pp. 3–18.

Pepper, D. (1984), *The roots of modern environmentalism*, London: Routledge.

Thompson, J. (1990), *Ideology and modern culture*, Oxford: Polity Press.

Tolson, A. (1991), 'Televised chat and the synthetic personality', in P. Scannell (ed.) *Broadcast talk*, London: Sage.

Tuchman, G. (1972), 'Objectivity as a strategic ritual: An examination of newsmen's notions of objectivity', *American Journal of Sociology* 77, pp. 660–79.

Williams, R. (1985), *Marxism and literature*, Oxford: Oxford University Press.

7
The Canadian press and the environment: reconstructing a social reality

Edna Einsiedel and Eileen Coughlan

Despite the relatively recent emergence of 'the environment' as a social problem, the subject has provided enough grist for the analytical mill. Like other kinds of problems, 'the environment', particularly as portrayed in the mass media, is a social construction, and the documentation and understanding of such a process has been a central task of researchers.

In this chapter, we will describe a research effort on the Canadian press and the environment that has looked at environmental coverage and environmental news writers. In examining environmental coverage, we were particularly interested in answering two questions: first, how does media coverage of a social movement evolve; and second, what factors help explain the media's social construction of the environment?

Such analytical frames as organizational analysis (for example Tuchman, 1978), professional assumptions (Weaver and Wilhoit, 1991), psychological approaches, structural approaches (Tichenor, Donohue and Olien, 1980), and ideological-hegemonic paradigms (Hall, 1977) have, at one time or another, been applied to understanding media coverage. All of these approaches have made some contribution, albeit in a limited way, to assisting our understanding of why coverage is as it is. We approach our discussion on press coverage of environmental issues from the point of view that a fuller picture of this process might emerge by drawing from these multiple explanatory frameworks. This approach proposes that news-making is a process that might be better understood by examining the interaction of a variety of factors.

First, news can be viewed as an individual product, an outcome of what a particular journalist – with her beliefs, experiences and training – brings to the news production process. Second, it may be seen as an organizational-professional product. It is shaped by the norms of a profession, its cultural practices, the professional values it espouses. These professional values are further shaped or redefined by the reporter's news organization which can provide opportunities, resources, rewards and punishments. Third, it can reflect the network of activities designed to catch public and policy-maker's attention, to educate these publics, to lobby for their support in favor of particular public decisions. Some of these activities require gaining and influencing the direction of media coverage to a greater or lesser extent. Finally, it may be viewed as a cultural and ideological product, often reflecting the values of the dominant culture.

These various perspectives have been found individually to shape the news and in examining environmental news in particular, we tried to keep in mind these different analytical frames. We also used a multi-method approach to answer the questions we posed. In order to gain some historical perspective of 'environment' coverage in the Canadian press, we undertook a headline analysis of environmental subjects in the Canadian Newspaper Index from 1977 to 1990. We combined this with a previously conducted content analysis of environmental news in seven major newspapers in Canada. Finally, we conducted in-depth interviews with six reporters who covered the environment either as a beat or as part of their reporting assignments.

The structure of an environmental story

We examined a sample of science stories in seven metropolitan newspapers between 1986 and 1987.[1] This sample included a variety of science story categories that included 'Medicine and health' and 'Environment', among others (see Einsiedel, 1992). From this larger study, we did a more focused examination of environmental stories in particular, looking at their overall tone, their pattern of source use, the diversity of sub-topics covered, and the problems and benefits portrayed. We also conducted a qualitative analysis of environmental stories to describe narrative styles employed.

On the agenda of science issues, it was clear that the environment occupied a prominent position, coming second behind medicine and health stories. Unlike other science stories, however, environmental stories tended to exhibit a negative tone: only one in five environmental stories were positive stories while about half were predominantly negative. These negative stories tended to be about environmental problems such as the occurrence of accidents (oil or chemical spills), pollution problems, or some warning about a potential disaster or ecological problem.

Where do the stories originate? About four in ten environmental stories were generated by the local paper; the rest tended to be from

Canadian and international wire services. In terms of pattern of source use, environmental stories showed a heavy reliance on institutional sources. Government officials were the predominant first and second source cited, followed by scientists, or so-called 'experts'. About 45 per cent of the first source cited in environmental stories were government officials; about a quarter of the first source mentioned were scientists. Much less prominent at this time were interest group sources and those from private industry.

We decided to do a follow-up on attention paid to environmental groups in the headlines by comparing their mentions in the headlines as listed in the Canadian Newspaper Index. Comparisons were made between 1979 and 1991.[2] In 1979, Greenpeace was the only environmental interest group mentioned in the headlines and it received two mentions, both in the context of the seal hunt debate. In 1991, seven interest groups were specifically mentioned in the headlines; six were mentioned only once while Greenpeace was named in twenty-four separate headlines. Five of these instances had to do with the organization's twentieth birthday, a recognition of its unique status among environmental organizations in the press.

A qualitative look at the environmental stories in the seven newspapers was undertaken. In examining these stories, we found a strong event orientation typified by an action–response sequence. That is, news stories tended to be about an occurrence (for example, an oil spill, a report released, a policy adopted), or some response to an occurrence. Typical is a story about a provincial minister publicly condemning the inconclusiveness of a toxic waste dump report, portraying the action–reaction pattern.

We also found that these environmental stories for the most part did not deviate from the news format typically employed in other kinds of stories. This format was of the who-said-what-when-and-where variety and the ritual of 'balance' engaged in by reporters, particularly on more controversial issues. The latter involves the practice of balancing a controversial position with a response from an opponent. For example, a story reporting a provincial government decision to consider using chemical insecticides on small test areas of the province's forests includes a response from a major environmental interest group, Pollution Probe, decrying the proposal (*Globe and Mail*, 4 January 1987, p. A3).

Over and above these conventions, however, we also observed the practice of 'framing' an issue, which perhaps illustrates more clearly how the media can impose its own meaning frames and symbols to a given event. By calling a policy 'controversial', by highlighting a dispute, by suggesting a benefit and excluding risk information, the media can legitimate positions and project images with considerable power. A full page devoted to the Brundtland Report including four stories, two diagrams and a background analysis, plus an editorial on the editorial page (*Globe and Mail*, 27 April 1987) conferred an importance to this Report not often seen in the dissemination of other international reports.

A more extended analysis of a controversial activity, the seal hunt, vividly illustrates the media's ability to cast a story in compelling ways. Lee (1989) analysed coverage in the *Globe and Mail* and the *Toronto Star* and demonstrated the significant role played by opposing sides in framing the debate in strong moral terms. More interesting, however, was the additional role played by the media in injecting its own voice in the debate. The opponents to the seal hunt led by Greenpeace claimed the hunt was a 'slaughter' of 'endangered baby seals'; the hunters, on the other hand, succeeded in gaining support for their cause by presenting the attempts to stop the hunt as 'cultural genocide'. Lee further demonstrated that the largest amount of moral keywords presented were not from the competing claims-makers but in the reporters' own voices. He concluded thus:

The moral reality of the seal hunt is communicated in the apparently objective voice of the news reporter rather than . . . in the voices of the moral contestants, a profoundly significant comment on the power of the newspaper to construct moral social reality. (p. 43)

The environmental news producers

We interviewed six reporters from the newspapers we analysed in order to understand their backgrounds, how they received their assignments, their views on their jobs, their audiences and their news sources. Three of the reporters had environmental beats whereas three did not; the three reporters we interviewed in the papers that did not have assigned beats had the environment as one of their assignments. The seventh paper was not represented as there was no one on the staff who was identified as covering the environment on an occasional-to-regular basis.

Interestingly, everyone had been assigned to the environment beat. One of the three environmental reporters we interviewed was leaving his newspaper because the beat assignment was being rotated and he was not allowed to remain on the beat as he had requested. This reporter was told the reassignment was necessary as he had become 'too close' to the issue and was no longer considered by his editors to be sufficiently objective.

All six came from a social science, humanities or journalism background. The three environmental reporters specifically mentioned the lack of a science background as a handicap because of the increasing number of technical reports a reporter had to go through to understand certain environmental issues.

In various ways, all except one of these reporters considered themselves reporters first, environmental reporters second. The majority seemed to think the routines of newswork served them well.

That is, for most hard news stories, accuracy and balance were considered key to doing a good job. One of the three environmental reporters said it was developing expertise on the job that was most important. Two specifically agreed they could be seen as advocates for the environment, putting them outside the norm more typically espoused by members of their trade. However, one justified this by saying, 'but who would be against the environment?' The second environmental reporter observed:

There is something about the beat that would reinforce the characteristic of "advocacy" because of the knowledge one gains from covering the beat. But I certainly don't see myself as an advocate for environmental groups. In fact, I'm constantly under considerable pressure from the more radical groups in this province to be more sympathetic. (Bohm, 1989)

Comparisons of environmental content in the papers with full-time environmental writers and those without revealed some interesting differences. In general, there were more stories on the environment in the former than in the latter. The mean number of items in our constructed week sample was 41 versus 32. While this disparity may not be surprising, there were interesting differences in the stories generated by both groups of reporters. We examined between eight and sixteen stories written under the byline of each of the reporters interviewed. The environmental beat writers were more likely to write longer pieces, more analytical pieces, more likely to generate a story on their own rather than depend on an external source to initiate the story, and more likely to 'challenge' conventional institutional wisdom. They were also more likely to include background or contextual explanatory material and to recognize uncertainty in scientific findings.

The following illustrates a major story initiated by a west coast reporter:

The US and Canada have signed an agreement on trans-boundary shipments of hazardous wastes, the Sun has learned. The international accord compels each nation to give written notice before sending toxic chemicals across the border . . . Environment Canada officials in Vancouver and Ottawa on Tuesday refused to disclose details of the five-year agreement . . . but officials with the US Environmental Protection Agency in Washington DC confirmed that the accord was signed Friday [by Canada and the US's federal environment administrators]. (*Vancouver Sun*, 5 November 1986, p. A3).

A story initiated by a reporter in the east which illustrates a challenge to institutional 'wisdom' is the following:

Excessive amounts of radioactive radon gas are believed to be seeping into as many as 80,000 Canadian homes and causing 500 to 600 lung cancer deaths each year. Living in one of these contaminated homes could be as dangerous as smoking more than a package of cigarettes a day, yet federal officials have no plans to notify Canadians about a problem many health specialists say is the most serious radiation threat facing the public. (*Vancouver Sun,* 10 January 1987, p. A13).

A story by an environmental reporter about the shutdown of a city's water supply following the discovery of a cancer-causing chemical in water beneath part of the city was a good illustration of contextualizing. The reporter proceeded to explain that the chemical called benzo(a)pyrene belonged to the family of polycyclic aromatic hydrocarbons and was found at levels of nine parts per trillion. He included the fact that the World Health Organization guideline for the maximum amount of this chemical in drinking water was 10 parts per trillion. He further explained that this chemical was described by WHO as a human carcinogen (*Globe and Mail,* 26 July 1986, p. A5).

One environmental reporter incorporated uncertainty in his lead as follows:

A widely used chemical in western Canada could have severe effects on wildlife but studies proving suspicions of scientists are not complete. (*Edmonton Journal,* 7 September 1986, p. B1).

These interviews demonstrate some of the ways in which organizational and professional factors interact with individual differences, resulting in similarities and differences in environmental coverage. The similarities occur in the more formulaic approaches to the timely, event-oriented kinds of news stories (or hard news stories). The differences seem to manifest themselves in opportunities to explore issues in greater depth, in the development of expertise such that the reporter is able to contextualize more, to challenge expert positions, or to develop and follow up on a wider array of sources and story ideas.

A longitudinal perspective on the environment

Our examination of the Newspaper Index focused on every second volume. This Index provides annual listings of all article headlines that appear in seven metropolitan newspapers.[3] There are obvious limitations in simply examining the headlines of newspaper stories. On the other hand, these headlines were used quite broadly to signal the general nature of the topic and to describe the first level of 'framing' an issue for the readers. The way an issue is 'framed' refers to format elements (headline size, location in paper, etc.) as well as content features (language features, narrative qualities, etc.) that tend to portray a given story in a particular light.

The analysis was designed to provide indicators of the nature of environmental coverage over this time span and to describe the general evolutionary pattern of environmental topics. By looking at the various subject headings on environmental topics, it was possible to trace this pattern via the development of second- and third-order sub-topics.

There were three distinct patterns that were discernible in our analysis of headlines. The first was that environmental coverage could be described in terms of problem categories and in terms of specific issues, each of which had its own characteristic life cycle. In the earlier years of our analysis, the problem categories included such things as 'air pollution', 'water pollution', 'waste management', and 'wildlife conservation'. The disparate and seemingly unconnected nature of these topics changed with the emergence of more holistic or integrated categories of 'ecology' and 'environmental protection'. This more systemic approach is supported by a second observation relating to the increased tendency after 1985 to present environmental problems in global context. This was signalled by greater use of such keywords as 'global', 'earth' and 'planet'.

We found that messages inherent in the headlines in the 1970s and early 1980s tended to focus on local environmental issues rather than global ones. One indication was that the keywords 'world', 'earth', 'planet' and 'global' hardly appeared in any of the headlines in 1977, 1979 or 1981. For example, there were only two references in all of 1977. 'Global' appeared once and for the first time in the 1983 sample. The keyword 'ecology' also appeared once in 1979.

Toward the end of 1983, however, new descriptor terms began to appear in headlines such as 'global catastrophe', 'environmental order', and 'environmental ethics'. Increasing use of the terms 'global', 'planet' and 'earth' after 1983 may have signified a rising consciousness that environmental problems transcended geographic boundaries. In 1989, at least one of these keywords appeared in each of 98 headlines.

Environmental issues were also characterized by varying life cycles of specialized issues: acid rain, global warming, the ozone problem and the issue of tropical deforestation are examples of such issues which rise and wane in the various media fora but which fall within the general rubric of 'the environment', keeping this broader topic in the public eye (see Figure 7.1).

Taking acid rain as an example, there were two articles on the subject across the seven newspapers in 1977; in 1981, there were 53, and in 1985, 299 pieces. While acid rain was peaking in 1987 (with 354 stories), then declining, problems of the ozone layer and the greenhouse effect were beginning to rise in media attention, with each issue generating its own public and institutional sets of actions and reactions.

The second pattern discernible in the headlines relates to the apparent meaning vested in the concept 'environment' during the time period of our study compared to earlier depictions. Earlier studies on environmental coverage have demonstrated what might be interpreted as a cyclical pattern to media attention to the environment

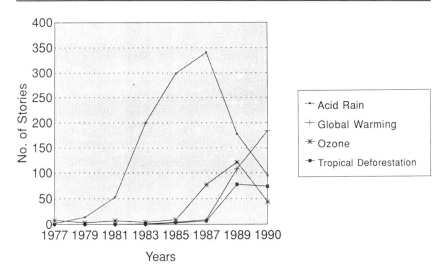

Figure 7.1 Number of stories in Canadian newspapers on
four environmental topics

as well a narrower interpretation of 'environment' as an issue. In an
analysis of media coverage of environmental issues in Canada from
1960 to 1972, Parlour and Schatzow (1978) documented that prior to
1965, coverage was low and sporadic. In the latter half of the 1960s
through 1970, coverage steadily increased, with an explosive rise
between 1968 to 1970, followed by a dramatic decline. Schoenfeld,
Meier and Griffin (1979) similarly demonstrated a somewhat cyclical
pattern of attention in two major American newspapers from 1962
through 1977, with coverage rising and waning according to a variety
of major occurrences such as the energy crisis.

A number of earlier studies have also documented the 'conservation' focus of the environmental issue (see Bowman and
Hanaford, 1977; Parlour and Schatzow, 1978; Schoenfeld, 1983). What
seems to differentiate the more recent period of the late 1970s
through the early 1990s is that 'the environment' has been vested with
a more global character, encompassing attributes that include holism
and interdependence, and the finiteness of resources.

The increase in second-order and third-order sub-topics during the
1980s further illustrates the variety of ways that 'the environment'
was being codified. In 1989, for example, there were twenty
second-order topic headings such as 'Environmental   protection',
'Environmentally friendly products', 'Environmental crimes', 'Environmental law', and 'Environmental studies'. Under the sub-heading
of 'Environmental protection', there were twenty-six third-order
sub-topic headings such as 'government relations', 'international
aspects', and 'public opinion'.

We examined the sub-head 'Environmental protection' more closely and found that the number of stories under this sub-head expanded quite a bit between 1987 and 1990. This sub-topic heading had 62 per cent of the stories under 'Environment' in 1987, 81 per cent of the total in 1989, and 78 per cent in 1990.

This proliferation of sub-topics was an indication of how much 'the environment' had permeated a wide range of fora – from the legal arena to tourism, from construction to consumerism, from feminism to terrorism. Witness, for example, the appearance of such terms as 'environmental law', 'eco-tourism', 'environmentally sick buildings', products that were 'environmentally friendly', 'eco-feminist' and 'eco-terrorist' in the headline lexicon.

Our final observation has to do with the process of constructing a social problem. There was a discernible pattern of increasing urgency to the portrayal of 'the environment' as a social problem. We looked at headline content patterns in terms of particular keywords and their descriptors to gain some understanding of how 'the environment' as social problem was being framed. Headlines are useful for 'framing' a story or putting the story within a certain context. In this respect, we examined the following keywords: 'earth', 'ecology', 'environment', 'globe' (or 'global'), 'planet', and 'world'. Descriptors were defined as words or phrases preceding or following these key words. For example, the headline, 'Civilized people killing the earth' would have the verb 'killing' as the key descriptor for the keyword 'earth'.

The seriousness of environmental problems was highlighted by the increasing appearance by 1985 of descriptor phrases such as the following:

- threatens world
- state of world
- save earth
- heed environment
- tiny world
- study environment
- environmental risks

By 1987, there were increasing reports of actions being taken to help protect the environment. The following list is illustrative:

- environment campaign
- environmental law
- environmental strategy
- environmental review
- environmental report
- environmental task force
- environmental bill
- environmental research
- global pact
- global study

1987 also marked the appearance of war and dominance metaphors. For example, the phrase 'environmental crusader' appears for the first time. Environmental efforts were more frequently being described as a 'war', a 'fight', involving 'victories', 'battles', 'survival' and 'defeat'. 'Environmental terrorists' became part of the landscape and certain problems were categorized as 'public enemy no. 1'. 'Rescues' had to be mounted and problems had to be 'tackled'.

The seriousness with which the problem was being portrayed may have brought to the fore a flurry of activity or responses from the private sector. At this time, economic and financial metaphors also began to appear: there were 'environmental debts' to be faced, 'environmental funds' established, 'exemptions' made, and 'environmental spending' conducted. Furthermore, the responses of the corporate sector were marked with such heads as 'environmentally safe' products, the 'environmentally friendly label', and even 'planet marketing', suggesting that the efforts of the corporate world at claims-making were meeting with some success.

It was clear that by the late 1980s, the social construction of environmental degradation was no longer a matter of speculation but a harsh reality. Such phrases as 'environmental mess', 'global clean-up', 'environmental ruin', 'decaying world' were typical.

By 1990, the patterns described earlier had become solidified. Even more economic and business metaphors were in use ('environmental economic challenge', 'environmental dividends', 'environmental industry', and 'environmental backers') and so were the war and dominance images. For instance, the terms 'eco-spy' and 'eco-fighters' had become part of the headline lexicon.

As well, the new ailing or sick-planet metaphors that began to emerge in the headlines during this period communicated the message that the environment was indeed in serious trouble and that it was no longer a matter of cleaning up but 'nursing the planet back to health'. The phrases 'wounded earth', 'scars on earth', 'battered planet' and 'nursing mother earth' were more prominent at this time.

As a potential indicator of a general consensus on environment-as-social-problem, we decided to look at the signalling of mobilizing information in the headlines. 'Mobilizing information', according to Lemert et al. (1975) is information which allows people to act. It might be suggestions about where to go, what to do or whom to contact. In Lemert et al.'s analysis of news and editorial items, mobilizing information was missing in negative and controversial contexts. An earlier study by Hungerford and Lemert (1973) showed that one in five items in their environmental news sample contained mobilizing information.

We compared mobilizing-information signals in 1977 and 1989 headlines. 'Ten ways to recycle and reuse' is an example of a headline with a clear indication that the story contains mobilizing information. In 1977, there was no headline that contained mobilizing information. In 1989, however, under the sub-head of 'Environmental protection' alone, we found 24 per cent of the headlines alerted readers to things they could do. It is likely this is a conservative estimate of what actually appears in news stories because mobilizing information could be present in the story without the reader being alerted in the headline.

The following headlines exemplify the kind of signalling information available to readers:

- Action on household products and packaging is crucial
- 50 ways you can help save our earth
- Environmental action should start at home
- More and more people turning green
- What you can do to help
- Make sacrifices for planet's sake
- Dreaming of a green Christmas: This season give gifts that aid environment

It is difficult to imagine the use of mobilizing information in political stories or other kinds of stories involving controversy or lack of consensus. It is, in fact, part of the ritual of objectivity not to be seen to promote causes or organizations. This observed pattern could indicate the newspapers' perceived general consensus among its audiences that doing something to save the environment was critical.

In sum, our analysis of the evolution of environmental topics suggests that the environment incorporated an increasing range of issues and was incorporated in a variety of fora, each of which generated its own set of activities and accompanying claims to media attention. Over time, 'the environment' as a social problem was increasingly framed in tones of urgency and the perceived widespread acceptance of this urgency was signalled by the greater frequency of mobilizing information.

Multiple perspectives on the environment

In looking at coverage of the environment, we raised two questions earlier: how does a social issue evolve in the mass media? And what factors might help explain the media's social construction of the environment?

With regard to the development of a social issue, Strodthoff and his colleagues (1985) suggested that three adaptive phases are characteristic of media processes: disambiguation, legitimation and routinization. Disambiguation is a process whereby the basic tenets of the social movement become defined. This might involve conceptual development of the issues or concerns via specializied media channels. Legitimation is a process whereby communication gatekeepers, particularly in general audience channels, recognize the various concerns characterizing the movement to be topics valid for coverage. Routinization describes the phase where content about the movement becomes institutionalized into the channel's regular space, time, personnel allocation. This might be evident in changes in formats (for example, an 'Environment' section) or the creation of a regular newsbeat.

We found some evidence of this structural evolutionary pattern from our interviews with environmental journalists and examination of news coverage. In addition, our examination of content demonstrates that content routinization is more than regular attention to an issue. It accommodates such processes as amplification and specialization as well. Amplification involves continuing attention to an issue (for example, provision of background analysis, follow-up articles, and so forth). Specialization involves sub-topics that fall under the rubric of 'environment' but are separable yet interrelated. For example, tropical deforestation achieved some prominence as did the greenhouse effect and biodiversity. These issue labels were categories of environmental problems but also had interconnections among each other.

The three phases as presented by Strodthoff, Hawkins and Schoenfeld (1985) also appear to be more linear and sequential than what seems to be the case. For example, environmentalism in its early years (1960s and 1970s) focused on the theme of conservation. In Canada, concern for the environment during this period was in the context of the issue of leisure and was a middle-class concern (Parlour and Schatzow, 1978). The 1970s saw a diminution of attention to the environment which continued until the mid-80s. The renewed interest in the environment resulted in different foci which related to such principles as the fragility of the ecosystem, the interconnections between its parts, and the acceptance of limits to growth.

What factors help us understand the nature of environmental coverage? There are both macro-level and micro-level factors that help explain coverage patterns.

News as organizational-professional product

McQuail (1992) has argued that news analysis cannot be fruitfully accomplished without some understanding of the professional-organizational context of newswork. We agree with this view and our own examination of environmental news supports the notion that newswork is indeed conducted within professional routines.

The environmental stories we examined were for the most part routinized chronicles, providing a record of noteworthy happenings. Whether one is a sports, political or economic reporter, the formulaic routines which provide a record and present an image of 'balance' (defined as the presentation of opposing views) serve as professional devices that are as much for the benefit of the reporter as they are for the reader.

Professional factors similarly impinge on environmental news reporting. Environmental beats afford an opportunity for the reporter to develop expertise that can translate into different approaches to news coverage. Although not documented in our study, there is evidence that even within the reporting specialty, there are hierarchical differences in levels of expertise and influence. Dunwoody (1979) demonstrated, for instance, that an inner club of influential journalists operated within the science writing profession.

Organizational factors have some impact as well. A news organization that decides to have an environmental beat and/or decides to allocate a regular column, section or page to environmental news, or allocates resources to cover special topics provides ways of signalling attention and importance. Similarly, organizational control is exercised when editors impose constraints, such as rotation of assignments, imposition of what they perceive to be important organizational-professional norms or audience considerations. Such control has in fact, also been interpreted as ideological control.

Environmental news production as claims-making

Hansen (1991) has rightly argued that news production reflects a complex pattern of claims-making activities. Indeed, the reliance on a variety of sources, particularly those who speak in an official voice (government officials) and those dealing in the currency of expertise and authority (scientists), reflects this element.

The influence of claims-makers on the news product has been documented elsewhere in environmental news production. Sachsman (1976) demonstrated that over half (53 per cent) of some 200 environmental stories in mass media channels in the San Francisco Bay area were results of public relations efforts.

On the other hand, some claims-making activities are clearly more effective than others. Greenpeace, for example, has been extremely successful in garnering media attention precisely because it understood the media's rules and requirements and played to these factors (Cassidy, 1992).

The claims-making activities of various individuals and groups and the media's representations and further elaborations of various claims is a complex transactional process. It is clear from the studies described earlier (Lee, 1989; Cassidy, 1992) that the interplay between competing voices and media activities of framing and elaboration needs further examination. As Hansen (1991) has argued, the linear media-to-public representations do little justice to the more complex process of claims-making. On the other hand, the media also play an active and important role beyond simply serving as a forum for claims-makers.

Environmental news as symbolic system

It is easy to view various environmental stories as disparate chronicles. Much of the work on environmental news, however, neglects to address the important role of symbolism to the news production process. In this process, journalists' narrative activities have to be imbued with concepts, definitions and descriptions that are often culturally determined. How else to elicit resonance with the audience? At the same time, journalists are able to provide categories of meaning for events and to assign actors into hero or villain roles. The urgency with which 'the environment' has been portrayed in recent years via metaphors of the battlefield reflects this ability to symbolize. While much media coverage has been portrayed as promoting the ideology of the status quo and the affirmation of power structures (Hall, 1977; Barkin, 1984) one might also argue that the paradigm shift said to have occurred within the environmental movement regarding limits to growth (see Caldwell, 1990) has also been helped along by media coverage.

The use of metaphors can also frame an issue in ways that project greater importance, urgency or heightened emotion. Portraying the environment in terms of war and dominance metaphors tends to imbue the issue with an urgency that might be absent had the issue been portrayed in gentler terms. For example, a 'battle for global survival' is clearly more compelling and dire than 'a clean-up of the environmental mess'. This is not to say that the issue was no less urgent ten or twenty years ago. Some have, in fact, argued that these ways of framing environmental stories are part of the inherent alarmist or sensationalizing tendencies among media players.

Environmental news as ideology

An ideological framework also has some utility to explaining news production. Two arenas where this framework has demonstrated utility occur in journalists' patterns of source reliance and in their presentation of alternative courses of action. In the case of source reliance, the sources that obviously have *routine* access to the media forum are those with power. This could be the power of scientific expertise, shoring up the dominant view of epistemic hierarchy which ranks scientists above other actors in the public arena (see Hilgartner, 1990). Government and industry have similarly been quite influential in gaining access to the media platform (see Molotch and Lester, 1975).

A second arena is reflected in the range of alternatives offered to audiences. Luke (1987) has argued that the representations of the Chernobyl accident were 'packaged' in such a way as not to call the future of nuclear energy into question.

To say that the media simply reproduce the dominant field of ruling ideologies (see Hall, 1977) is too simplistic, however. The evolution of the environment as a topic of coverage and as a social issue demonstrates, as some would argue, an important paradigm shift that sees limits to growth imposed where these might have been unthinkable in the past.

Notes

1 The seven newspapers analysed included one national newspaper (the Toronto *Globe and Mail*) and six metropolitan papers, including one French-Canadian newspaper. These newspapers were the *Vancouver Sun*, the *Edmonton Journal*, the *Winnipeg Free Press*, the *Ottawa Citizen*, Quebec's *La Presse*, and the *Halifax Chronicle-Herald*, representing six provinces. (For a more detailed description of the methodology employed in this phase of the research, see Einsiedel, 1988). The larger study from which these data were taken was supported by a grant from the Social Sciences and Humanities Research Council of Canada (No. 410-87-0493).

2 The later section on headline analysis covers the period 1977 through 1990 as the 1991 index was halfway completed then. This examination of interest group coverage in the headlines was done after completion of the 1991 index so we were able to look at 1991 as the comparison point.

3 The analysis started in 1977 because this was the first year that the Canadian Newspaper Index (CNI) was published.

References

Barkin, S. (1984), 'The journalist as storyteller: an interdisciplinary perspective', *American Journalism*, 1 (2), pp. 27–33.

Bohm, G. (1989), personal interview, 24 November

Bowman, J., Hanaford, K. (1977), 'Mass media and the environment since Earth Day', *Journalism Quarterly*, 54 (1), pp. 160–65.

Caldwell, L.K. (1990), *Between two worlds: science, the environmental movement and policy choice*, Cambridge: Cambridge University Press.

Cassidy, S. (1992), 'The environment and the media: two strategies for challenging hegemony', in J. Wasko and V. Mosco (eds), *Democratic communications in the information age*, Toronto: Garamond Press.

Dunwoody, S. (1979), 'Newsgathering behaviors of specialty reports: a two-level comparison of mass media decision-making'. *Newspaper Research Journal*, 1, pp. 29–41.

Einsiedel, E.F. (1988), 'The Canadian press and the environment', paper presented to the International Association for Mass Communication Research, Barcelona, Spain, 25–9 July.

Einsiedel, E.F. (1992), 'Framing science and technology in the Canadian press', *Public Understanding of Science*, 1 (1), January.

Hall, S. (1977), 'Culture, the media and the "ideological" effect', in J. Curran, M. Gurevitch and J. Woolacott (eds), *Mass communication and society*, London: Arnold, pp. 315–48.

Hansen, A. (1991), 'The media and the social construction of the environment', *Media, Culture and Society*, 13, pp. 443–58.

Hilgartner, S. (1990), 'The dominant view of popularization: conceptual problems, political uses', *Social Studies of Science 20* (3), pp. 519–39.

Howenstine, E. (1987), 'Environmental reporting: shift from 1970 to 1982', *Journalism Quarterly*, 64 (4), pp. 842–6.

Hungerford, S., Lemert, J. (1973), 'Covering the environment: a new Afghanistanism?' *Journalism Quarterly*, 50; pp. 475–81, autumn.

Lee, J.A. (1989), 'Waging the seal war in the media: toward a content analysis of moral communication', *Canadian Journal of Communication*, 14 (1), p. 37055.

Lemert, J., Mitzman, B., Seither, M., Cook, R., Hackett, R. (1975), 'Journalists and mobilizing information', *Journalism Quarterly*, 52, pp. 721–6.

Luke, T.W. (1987), 'Chernobyl: the packaging of transnational ecological disaster', *Critical Studies in Mass Communication*, 4, pp. 351–75.

Lundburg, L.J. (1984), 'Comprehensiveness of coverage of tropical rain deforestation', *Journalism Quarterly*, 61 (2), pp. 378–82.

McQuail, D. (1992), *Media performance: mass communication and the public interest.* Newbury Park, CA: Sage.

Molotch, H, Lester, M. (1975), 'Accidental news: the great oil spill as local occurrence and national event', *American Journal of Sociology*, 81 (2), pp. 235–60.

Parlour, J.W., Schatzow, S. (1978), 'The mass media and public concern for environmental problems in Canada, 1960–1972', *International Journal of Environmental Studies*. 13, pp. 9–17.

Sachsman, D.B. (1976), Public relations influence on coverage of environment in San Francisco Area, *Journalism Quarterly, 53*, pp. 54–60.

Schoenfeld, C., Meier, R., Griffin, R. (1979), 'Constructing a social problem: the press and the environment', *Social Problems*, 27 (1), October.

Schoenfeld, A.C. (1983), 'The environmental movement as reflected in the American magazine', *Journalism Quarterly, 60* (3), pp. 470–75.

Strodthoff, G.C., Hawkins, R.P., Schoenfeld, A.C. (1985), 'Media roles in a social movement: a model of ideology diffusion', *Journal of Communications*, 35 (2), spring, pp. 134–53.

Tichenor, P., Donohue, G., Olien, C. (1980), *Community conflict and the press.* Beverly Hills, CA: Sage.

Tuchman, G. (1978), *Making news: a study in the construction of reality.* New York: Free Press.

Weaver, D., Wilhoit, G.C. (1991), *The American journalist.* Bloomington: Indiana University Press.

8
Greenpeace and press coverage of environmental issues

Anders Hansen

The rise, in the 1960s, of modern environmental concern owed much of its initial impetus to scientists and claims-making activities in scientific and specialist fora. Likewise, the emergence on the environmental agenda of new emphases and foci has often started initially in the form of claims and warnings put forward by scientists (examples of the latter include original fears voiced in the early 1970s about ozone-depletion, and the renewed emphasis on this following the discovery by British scientist Joe Farman and his colleagues of a hole in the ozone layer over the Antarctic in the early 1980s). Scientists are not, however, primarily (or at all) in the business of translating science-based findings, discoveries and warnings into political action. The continued, although fluctuating, emphasis on environmental issues in public and political debate and concern over the last twenty to thirty years would thus have been unthinkable without the persistent claims-making activity of environmental pressure groups.

One of the key characteristics of the new environmental groups (see Lowe and Goyder, 1983), established in the late 1960s and early 1970s – and a characteristic which amongst other things distinguishes them crucially from the older established 'conservation' groups – is their focus on and use of the mass media as a primary forum for their claims-making. Deprived of the political lobby connections of established groups, the new environmental groups, as Lowe and Goyder (1983) point out, from the outset saw media publicity as a key to 'their own continued buoyancy and legitimacy' (p. 78), as a means of influencing 'an impending decision or course of action', and as a means of improving 'the climate of opinion for environmental issues through long-term educational and propaganda campaigns' (p. 79).

The success of environmental groups in securing media coverage has been noted and celebrated not just by the groups themselves but also by academic studies of the relationship between the media and environmental pressure groups (Lowe and Goyder, 1983; Lowe and Morrison, 1984; Greenberg, 1985; Grant, 1989). Lowe and Goyder note: 'What was striking in our survey was the extensive media coverage enjoyed by the majority of groups, and yet their appetite for more' (p. 74). Greenberg (1985), in his analysis of coverage of Friends of the Earth (FOE) in *The Times* between 1971 and 1982, argues:

The strongest indicator of FOE's success has been its media coverage. The coverage FOE has received in the press has been overwhelmingly favourable. Since the first article appeared in *The Times* on May 11, 1971, there have been a total of one hundred and five items in *The Times* concerning FOE. (Greenberg, 1985, p. 348)

To know how much coverage a pressure group receives in the various media, however, tells us little about how successful or otherwise it may be in terms of influencing the media agenda. Taken on its own, the amount of coverage tells us even less about how successful a pressure group is in its campaigning. The amount of media coverage thus clearly has to be seen in the context of questions about the overall degree of media attention to specific issues, questions about the coverage-seeking activities of the pressure groups, and questions about the degree of definitional power enjoyed by pressure groups within such coverage.

It is one thing for environmental groups to achieve massive media coverage for a short period of time and in relation to specific issues. It is quite a different task to achieve and maintain a position as an 'established', authoritative and legitimate actor in the continuous process of claims-making and policy-making on environmental matters. This requires skills of a rather different magnitude of sophistication (as well, of course, as resources) to those needed for capturing short-term media interest. The ascendance of such groups as Greenpeace and Friends of the Earth to the status of authoritative and legitimate actors in the field of environmental definition is clearly confirmation of such skills.

In their useful review of 'The Role of the Press in the Dynamics of Social Movements' Kielbowicz and Scherer (1986) point to some of the key skills and factors which are in play in the relationship between pressure groups and the media. Drawing on classic studies of news-making practices they note:

Among the more important findings are the media's preference for dramatic, visible events; journalists' reliance on authoritative sources, often those connected with government; how the deployment of newsgathering resources and news cycles or rhythms affect the probability that an event will be covered; the influence of reporters' professional values or orientations on their work; and how the media environment, mainly the degree of competition, influences news decisions. (Kielbowicz and Scherer, 1986, pp. 75–6)

Aims and methods

It is the aim of this chapter to begin to assess the success of one particular environmental pressure group, Greenpeace, in terms of its coverage in the press over an extended period of time (the five-year period of 1987 to 1991). I wish to examine, and account for, the extent and nature of Greenpeace coverage and to consider this in relation to questions about media and news-making practices and questions about the agenda-building power of Greenpeace. I take as my reference points theories of the production of news, and of social movements and their relationship with the mass media. At a more general level, I take my point of departure in social constructivist theory, and in the fundamental assumption that action on environmental problems depends principally on a complex process of social construction and negotiation, the construction of such problems as problems for public and political concern.

The empirical basis for this chapter is a content analysis of the entire coverage of Greenpeace, in the period 1 January 1987 to 31 December 1991, in two British national daily newspapers, *The Guardian* and *Today*.[1] Using the electronic database FT-Profile, which stores the full text of a range of national and regional newspapers (although *Today* is the only national daily tabloid paper covered in full), all articles containing the word 'Greenpeace' were identified and the full text of these articles was retrieved for analysis. The FT-Profile database was further used for searches to establish the overall extent of coverage of key issues. The retrieved articles were content analysis coded on a number of key dimensions, including: analysis of the extent to which Greenpeace was a focus of the article, or simply referred to in passing; the main subject or issue focus of articles; the news scenario or forum giving rise to the coverage; the 'actor' status of Greenpeace in the article (direct quotation, indirect quotation, reference only); and the type of reporter.

The rise of Greenpeace in the 1980s

Greenpeace was one of the most successful environmental pressure groups of the 1980s. From being one of the smallest environmental groups in terms of membership in 1980, Greenpeace's membership figure grew gradually during the first half of the 1980s and experienced a massive increase during the latter half of the 1980s. McCormick (1991) has recently noted that while the membership of most environmental pressure groups grew during the 1980s and experienced a boom in the period 1987 to 1989, Greenpeace had the largest percentage increase in the period 1980–89 and grew from being one of the smallest – with a membership of less than Friends of the Earth, and a mere fifth of the World Wildlife Fund (WWF) in 1980 – to being one of the biggest in 1989 with a membership figure more than twice that of FOE and more than one and one half times that of WWF.

Since the early days of Greenpeace in the beginning of the 1970s, much of its success has been ascribed to its astute publicity and communications strategies, including a particular emphasis on using visually stunning and daring actions as a device for drawing media attention to its campaigning issues. But it is also clear that while the visually stunning strategies of protest action may have largely characterized Greenpeace in the early years of its existence, the Greenpeace of today enters into media discourse in much more varied ways, ways which are themselves closely linked to the organizational transformation of Greenpeace during the 1980s. As Eyerman and Jamison (1989) have pointed out, successful environmental groups have been characterized by significant changes in the last twenty years:

After a period of declining membership and a relative lack of media attention in the early 1980s, environmental organisations have recently been riding on a new wave of public concern over nuclear energy, air and water pollution, and natural resource exploitation.

It is striking, however, that the expansive organisations of the late 1980s are, in most countries, not the same organisations that achieved the status of "new environmental movements" in the second half of the 1970s. Instead of the usually leftward-leaning anti-nuclear alliances and action groups that brought environmental issues into the centre of political discourse, the current environmentalist wave is characterised, on the one hand, by a revitalisation of the older, more traditional conservation societies and, on the other hand, by the meteoric rise of a multinational environmentalist corporation, namely Greenpeace International. (Eyerman and Jamison, 1989, p. 99)

The extent of press coverage of Greenpeace

While Greenpeace has generally been successful in getting media coverage, it interestingly trails slightly behind Friends of the Earth in the amount of exposure achieved. Thus, in the period 1987–91, Friends of the Earth was mentioned in 1031 articles in the two newspapers (*The Guardian* and *Today*) compared with Greenpeace in 896 articles. By comparison, two of the more traditional conservation groups received considerably less coverage: The World Wide Fund for Nature appeared in 304 articles, and the Royal Society for the Protection of Birds (RSPB) in 328 articles.

Of the articles mentioning Greenpeace or Friends of the Earth, only 120 articles mentioned both. It is thus clear that, although there is some overlap between the two environmental pressure groups, they gain coverage independently of each other in the large majority of articles. This indicates that these two key environmental pressure groups may play rather different, and perhaps complementary, roles in terms of the issues which they help to put on the media agenda and bring to public attention. It also provides an indirect indication that intergroup rivalry and competition – a highly newsworthy aspect of the development of social movements, and one that has proved fatal to many groups in their relationship with the media (see Kielbowicz and Scherer, 1986) – have not been allowed to play a significant role in the coverage of these two prominent environmental pressure groups.

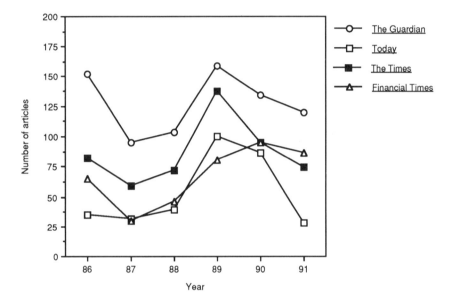

Figure 8.1   Greenpeace coverage 1986-91

Looking at the amount of coverage of Greenpeace in four national newspapers during the six-year period of 1986–91 (Figure 8.1), it is clear that while Greenpeace does not get the same amount of exposure in different papers, the longitudinal trends of coverage follow patterns of considerable similarity. Falling to a temporary low in 1987, the coverage crept up again in 1988 to reach a peak in 1989 (or in the case of the *Financial Times*, in 1990), since when it has been on its way down again.

The broad similarity in the trends of coverage for different newspapers indicates most of all the success with which Greenpeace has been able to insert itself on the media agenda. While Greenpeace may achieve more coverage in some papers than in others, the ups and downs of coverage follow similar paths. Clearly, it would be a mistake to assume that Greenpeace is the sole agent or engineer of such ups and downs, but the patterns do provide a first indication of the central role played by Greenpeace itself as an originator of topics for media coverage. I shall examine this aspect more closely later in the chapter.

The parallel trends in amount of coverage, identified above in the annual coverage in four national newspapers, is also found at the more detailed level of a mapping of the amount of coverage per quarter in the period in which the two papers *The Guardian* and *Today* were analysed. Although the coverage of Greenpeace in *Today* does not really get off the ground until the third quarter of 1988 – coinciding with the popular press panic over the mass deaths among the seals around Britain's coasts, and with the environment achieving prime political status through the then Prime Minister, Mrs Thatcher's, appropriation of environmental rhetoric[2] – the pattern thereafter follows a trend broadly similar to that of *The Guardian*.

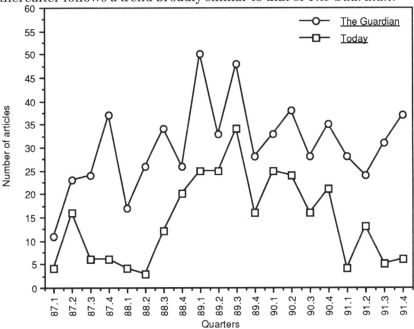

Figure 8.2 Greenpeace in *The Guardian* and *Today* 1987-91

The peaks of coverage seen on Figure 8.2 are generally, although not exclusively, closely related to major campaigns, actions and claims-making by Greenpeace (see the annotations below to the various peaks) which, when considered together with the broadly similar trends of coverage in the two papers, confirms the ability of Greenpeace to influence the media agenda.

87.2   Nuclear demonstrations/protests, including Greenpeace attempts at blocking Sellafield waste pipe.

87.4   The North Sea: Greenpeace leads a major campaign against chemical incineration and sewage-dumping in the North Sea;

the London North Sea Conference in November 1987; court case against Greenpeace for blocking Sellafield waste pipe.

88.3   Seal deaths around Britain's shores: Greenpeace 'rescue' campaign in the form of the creation of a seal sanctuary; Greenpeace blocking of chemical waste pipes; Margaret Thatcher's green speech.

89.1   Greenpeace campaign in the Antarctic: bases, pollution, disturbance of wildlife, mineral exploitation, Japanese whaling.

89.3   Greenpeace campaign against toxic waste shipments/imports.

90.2   Greenpeace campaigns: against ICI; against nuclear waste imports; on company cars. Whales, dolphins, seals. Oil spill in Devon.

90.4   Greenpeace protest to halt nuclear test explosion; *Rainbow Warrior* campaign at French testing site in the Pacific; government policy on Antarctica and government's record on green issues.

91.3–4 A major contributor to the increase in *The Guardian* articles during the latter half of 1991 is the reporting on Gulf war-related pollution and environmental damage – *The Guardian*'s environment correspondent Paul Brown travels (as in the 1989 campaign in the Antarctic) with a Greenpeace team in the Gulf. *Today*, by contrast, has no Greenpeace-related coverage of the Gulf.

Media issues/'Greenpeace issues'

Greenpeace becomes part of media coverage in relation to a very broad range of issues, but while the types of issues range widely, it is also possible to identify a number of dominant issue areas in which Greenpeace serves a prominent role. These issue areas are outlined in Figure 8.3. The issue areas identified are not necessarily logically mutually exclusive; they are principally a classification based on the main focus or main thematic emphasis of individual articles. Thus, for example the 'Conservation/endangered species' category includes a large number of articles about the rapidly declining dolphin/porpoise population in British waters; a considerable number of these articles are also about 'Sea/beach pollution', but they have been categorized under 'Conservation/endangered species' because the main emphasis or focus is on the decline of the dolphin population, and sea/beach pollution is a subsidiary explanatory focus. While it needs then to be recognized that the various issue areas are not defined by clear and sharp borders, they are an indication of the primary foci/emphases of coverage. The single most prominent issue area associated with Greenpeace coverage is anything nuclear or radiation related, whether nuclear arms, nuclear weapons-testing

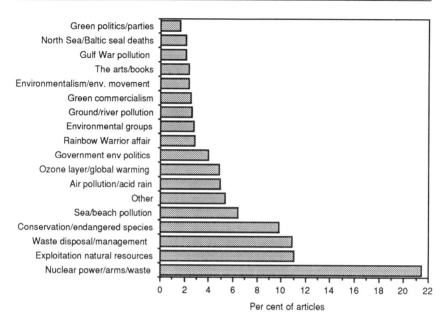

Figure 8.3 Greenpeace-environment issues 1987-91

and development, nuclear power, nuclear waste or nuclear and radiation-related pollution, illness, and danger to health and safety.

Nuclear and radiation-related issues, accounting for just over a fifth of all articles, are nearly twice as prominent as the second, third and fourth most prominent issue areas: 'harmful exploitation of natural resources' (including such key campaign issues as mineral and other exploitation of Antarctica, industrial whaling, overfishing and harmful industrial fishing practices (for example, the use of driftnets)); non-nuclear 'waste disposal and waste management' (including the dumping of dangerous chemical waste at sea, release of untreated sewage into the sea, land/sea incineration and processing of toxic waste); 'conservation and protection of endangered species' (including, most prominently, campaigns to protect dolphins/porpoises and seals). 'Sea and beach pollution' more generally is the key focus in just under seven per cent of the articles, followed by 'air pollution/acid rain' (including articles which focus on automobile-related air pollution, carbon and sulphur emissions generally, and attendant health/asthmatic consequences) and 'ozone layer/global warming/greenhouse effect' articles more specifically, each at just over five per cent of the articles. Finally, articles focusing on the Government's environmental policies, rhetoric and action (including the then Prime Minister, Margaret Thatcher's sudden adoption of an 'environmental perspective' in the autumn of 1988, and the Conservative Government's White Paper on the environment) constitute just over four per cent of the articles.

Figure 8.3 then gives an indication of the major issue areas with which Greenpeace is associated in press coverage, and in this respect, it also gives a tentative indication of the issues on which Greenpeace has been successful in its campaigning and in influencing media coverage. It is, however, necessary to examine this more closely: the relative prominence of issue areas shown in Figure 8.3 may thus simply be a reflection of the wider prominence, whether Greenpeace related or not, of particular issues in media coverage. In the following, two specific ways of analysing this aspect more closely will be adopted. One approach is to examine whose activities in which fora drive the coverage, and more specifically to examine what proportion of each of the most important topics appear principally as a result of Greenpeace/pressure-group claims-making or action. A second approach is to consider in broad terms what proportion of all coverage of selected specific topics Greenpeace appears in.

Articulating the environment: news scenarios and news fora

The environment and 'environmental issues' do not ordinarily – other than in the form of major disasters and accidents – draw attention to themselves (Hansen, 1990; Yearley, 1991). Instead, environmental issues become issues for public and political concern when claims are successfully made about them in public arenas, including arenas which routinely serve as foci for media coverage, and including, of course, the media themselves.

The coverage in *The Guardian* and *Today* in the period 1987–91 was analysed with a view to determining, for each individual article, what kind of activity in what kind of forum had caused this coverage to appear. In other words, whose activity in which (news) forum had given rise to the article? In 7 per cent of the articles, it was not possible to determine what the forum was or whose activity had caused the article to be written. In another 8 per cent of the articles, the coverage was a product principally of the newspaper's own 'diary routines' or an editorial decision to focus on a particular issue which was not otherwise 'in the news'. But in the remaining articles, coverage was governed by activity in relatively well-defined news scenarios.

Given that these articles were selected on the basis of whether they referred to Greenpeace, it is perhaps not surprising that 'Environmental pressure group action' and 'Environmental pressure group claims-making' were the two most prominent fora, accounting jointly (see Figure 8.4) for just over a third of all articles. 'Parliament and government politics' was the main cause of coverage in 10 per cent, and the following fora each accounted for between 8 and 10 per cent of the coverage: 'Science', 'Non-UK-government action or rhetoric', and 'Agriculture/industry/business action or rhetoric'.

Less prominent fora included 'Major environmental accidents/ disasters' at 4 per cent (for example, the *Exxon Valdez* oil spill), and

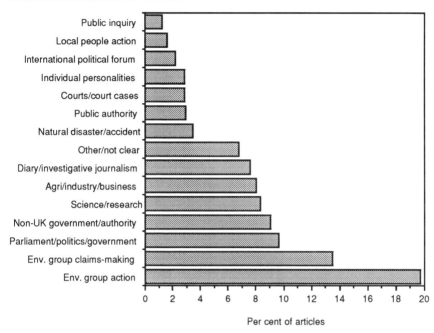

Figure 8.4 Forum analysis

'The courts/legal proceedings' and 'Public authorities' (each accounting for 3 per cent). 'Local people taking action' (for example, in the form of a protest march, blockade or petition), and 'International political discussions/conferences/negotiations' were less prominent fora, accounting for about 2 per cent each.

For most of the less prominent fora, there is relatively little variation over time between 1987 and 1991. Their relative prominence is in fact remarkably stable overall, even if some fluctuations do occur from year to year. Thus, 'Science' for instance fluctuates in the narrow band of 6–10 per cent between 1987 and 1991, while 'Agriculture/industry/business' fluctuates in the even narrower band of 6–9 per cent.

Five specific fora, however, deserve some comment in terms of their development over the period of analysis. Table 8.1 shows these five fora and their corresponding percentage of articles for each year. While the relative prominence of environmental group action and claims-making coincides, not surprisingly (although it does confirm the importance of these), with major Greenpeace campaigns, notably in 1987 the blocking of waste pipes and incineration ships, and in 1989 the major Greenpeace campaign in the Antarctic, it is also clear from this that in the absence of such major campaigns the claims-making and news-making role of Greenpeace decreases.

Table 8.1 *Selected fora as a percentage of all articles by year*

	1987 (%)	1988 (%)	1989 (%)	1990 (%)	1991 (%)
Environment group action	25.5	15.1	26.3	17.1	11.5
Environment group claims-making	10.0	15.9	16.3	11.6	12.2
Parliament/politics/government	8.2	6.3	7.5	12.6	13.7
Diary/feature/investigative article (no obvious external forum)	7.3	7.1	5.4	7.5	12.2
International politics/negotiations/ conferences	.9	.8	.4	3.0	6.9

The decrease in prominence of these two types of fora is particularly noticeable against the steady increase in the extent to which environmental coverage is brought on by activities and developments in the forum of formal politics (Parliament/politics/government), from a low in 1988 toward an overall peak in 1991. These trends give some indication that the news-making initiative has increasingly been seized by the government and the forum of formal politics. Likewise – although the number of articles in this category is small (see Figure 8.4) – the importance of international negotiations, conferences and bodies in defining 'news-worthy' environmental issues is evident in the increase from less than 1 per cent to nearly 7 per cent for this category between 1987 and 1991. Finally, the increase in the general category of news-organization initiated articles – no obvious external cause for covering a particular issue at the particular time – points to the need to fill the news hole created by the establishment of environmental beats (and in the case of *The Guardian*, a weekly 'Environment Section').

While the prominence of environmental group claims-making, as a primary news forum, changes over time, there are also considerable differences from issue area to issue area in the extent to which Greenpeace is a primary articulator of these issues (or, conversely, acts on, reacts to, or is drawn into commenting on developments in other primary fora).

Thus, environmental group claims-making or action is the main forum in close to half of the articles on 'Waste disposal and waste management' (see Figure 8.5), but in less than a third of articles about 'Conservation/endangered species' and 'Air pollution/acid rain'. Not surprisingly – given Greenpeace's major campaigns/expeditions to stop development in Antarctica and Japanese whaling near Antarctica – a relatively high proportion of the articles on 'Harmful exploitation of natural resources' are generated by Greenpeace. Environmental group claims-making is also a prominent catalyst for articles about the government's environmental policy and record. This prominence is in large part a result of the major environmental pressure groups' close monitoring and publicizing of how well the Government is meeting its own targets, as set out in the Government's White Paper on the environment.

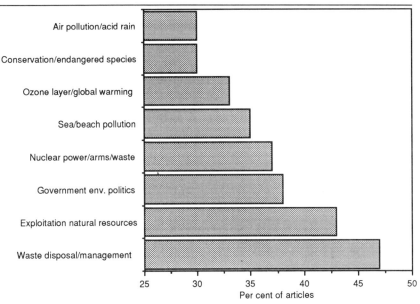

Figure 8.5 News forum: environmental group claims-making or action

Greenpeace and the press agenda on selected key topics

The relative prominence of Greenpeace in press coverage of certain environmental issue areas may not necessarily tell us much about the extent to which Greenpeace is a significant factor in placing such issues on the media and public agenda. It may simply be a reflection of the overall prominence of such issues, whether Greenpeace originated or not. A clearer indication of the agenda-building power or potential of Greenpeace comes from examining Greenpeace coverage in relation to overall coverage of selected key issues.

A number of more specific topics, which figured prominently in the Greenpeace coverage, were selected for a more detailed analysis with a view to determining how prominently or otherwise Greenpeace figured in the overall coverage of such topics. The topics selected for this analysis were topics which could be examined by using relatively unique keywords or search terms on the FT-Profile electronic database. The four specific topics selected were: nuclear issues (identifying articles which included either one of the words 'nuclear' or 'radioactive' (or derivates thereof), but excluding articles with the term 'nuclear family/families'); whaling (identifying articles which included any variant of the words 'whale' or 'whaling'); global warming (identifying any articles including either of the terms 'global warming' or 'greenhouse effect'; and Antarctica (identifying any article including either 'Antarctic' or 'Antarctica').

Table 8.2 shows the number of articles in *The Guardian* and *Today* about each of the selected four topics in each of the five years, 1987–91, and it shows the percentage of articles which mentioned Greenpeace. Table 8.2 shows that relative to overall coverage on each of the selected issues Greenpeace is most prominent in relation to coverage of issues relating to Antarctica (18 per cent of articles on Antarctica make reference to Greenpeace), and least prominent in coverage of nuclear/radiation-related issues (only 3 per cent of such articles refer to Greenpeace). Greenpeace appears in 12 per cent of articles about whales or whaling, and in 6 per cent of articles referring to global warming/greenhouse effects.

Table 8.2   *Amount of coverage of selected topics, 1987–91*

	1987	1988	1989	1990	1991	Total 1987–91	% articles mentioning Greenpeace
Nuclear issues	2605	1802	1884	1581	1727	9599	3
Global warming	17	118	443	473	189	1240	6
Whaling	117	184	256	280	206	1043	12
Antarctica	57	62	140	111	75	445	18

The coverage of nuclear issues, while at a much higher level than other issues in terms of the sheer number of articles, declined dramatically during the period studied from over 2600 articles in the two papers in 1987 to just over 1700 articles in 1991. For each of the three other issues, coverage rose – most significantly so in the case of 'Global warming/Greenhouse effect' – to a peak in 1989–90, and then declined again in 1990–91. It is clear from these figures that the singular prominence of nuclear issues in the Greenpeace coverage (as seen in Figure 8.3) is predominantly a function of the overall prominence of nuclear issues in press coverage.

From these figures, a broader underlying indication seems to be that environmental issues coverage in general peaked during the 1988–9 period (coinciding with, and in large part as a result of, the Government's adoption of environmental rhetoric as a central feature of its policy programme), and has since gone into a decline (it may be too early to pronounce the 'environmental boom' of the late 1980s over, as undoubtedly, although not possible to show on the basis of this data, another surge would have taken place in the period leading up to the 'Earth Summit' in Brazil in June 1992).

Figure 8.6 shows the breakdown for each year of the percentage of articles which mention Greenpeace in the coverage of the four topics. On 'nuclear issues', Greenpeace has maintained a relatively stable profile despite the dramatic overall decline in nuclear issues coverage. On 'Global warming', Greenpeace seems to have played no significant agenda-setting role: the coverage of global-warming issues rose dramatically to a peak in 1990, but the percentage of such coverage mentioning Greenpeace increased from nil in 1987 to only between 4 and 7 per cent in 1988–91.

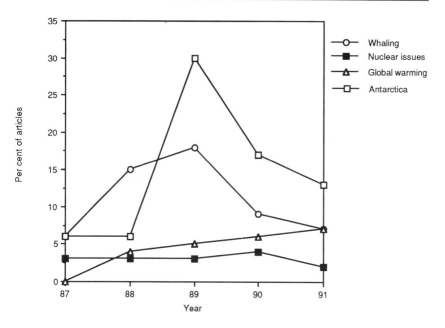

Figure 8.6   Greenpeace articles as a percentage of total coverage

The pattern in relation to 'whaling' and 'Antarctica' is not surprisingly – given the major campaigns conducted by Greenpeace on these issues, particularly during 1988–9 – rather different, although still far from simple. Coverage of 'Antarctica' peaked in 1989, coinciding with a massive increase (from 6 per cent in 1987 and 1988 to 30 per cent in 1989) in the percentage of such articles mentioning Greenpeace. The pattern for Antarctica coverage points to an absolutely key role played by Greenpeace as an agenda-setter on this issue: as Greenpeace's major campaign on Antarctica (in the form of actions built around a trip to Antarctica in the Greenpeace ship the *Gondwana*) came to an end, so too did the issues relating to Antarctica begin to recede from public view. On 'whaling' and whale-related issues the percentage of Greenpeace articles increased to a peak in 1989 in parallel with an overall increase in coverage. Overall coverage continued, however, to increase to a peak in 1990, while the percentage of Greenpeace articles began to fall back sharply after the peak in 1989 and the end of the Greenpeace campaign to obstruct the work of the Japanese whaling fleet operating in Antarctic waters.

These analyses, then, demonstrate quite clearly that a simple account of the amount of media exposure which a pressure group receives is, on its own, a relatively poor indicator of its successfulness. Not only is the news-generating/news-framing role of pressure groups (in the form of the news for a 'pressure group claims-making' and 'pressure group action') highly differentially associated with different types of issues, but it is also clear that the proportion of coverage, on any one issue, which refers to Greenpeace at all varies considerably from a very small proportion in relation to the prominent coverage of nuclear issues, to a large proportion of less visible issues such as 'Antarctica' or 'whaling'. Major campaigns by Greenpeace clearly have a visible influence on the amount of media coverage, and in this respect Greenpeace can be said to be a successful claims-maker. More remarkably, it seems that through its campaigning Greenpeace has the power to influence or boost its coverage across different newspapers. It is also, however, clear that Greenpeace is very dependent for its media coverage on major and often resource-demanding campaign initiatives: when major campaigning initiatives on specific issues come to a close, the Greenpeace-related coverage of such issues would appear to drop off rather more quickly than the overall coverage of the issues themselves. It remains however, and despite these qualifications, that compared with other environmental groups – with the exception of Friends of the Earth (see the beginning of this chapter) – Greenpeace has been remarkably successful in gaining media coverage. While the dependency on active campaigning and resource-demanding actions, noted above, could be interpreted as a symptom of 'low' legitimacy status (as a news source) and as a symptom that Greenpeace is not yet a routine news forum, a closer analysis of the nature of Greenpeace coverage points in the opposite direction, toward a pressure group of increasing legitimacy and authority status.

Legitimating coverage: Greenpeace as a legitimate and authoritative source of media coverage

The consolidation of Greenpeace as a legitimate and authoritative source of information, and as a credible commentator, surfaces in a broad number of ways. Most notable are perhaps the extent to which Greenpeace is quoted directly in coverage, and the fact that Greenpeace representatives are occasionally the authors of articles (this was the case in 6 out of the 611 *Guardian* articles – it did not happen in *Today*, although *Today* did publish a total of two letters written by Greenpeace representatives).

Greenpeace is quoted directly in just under half of all articles, and quoted indirectly in another 20 per cent of articles. In just over a third of the coverage, Greenpeace is not quoted, but simply mentioned or referred to. These figures confirm that, when Greenpeace does receive coverage, it does so primarily as a primary definer, an actor who gets to actively define what issues or situations are about. The overall trend for Greenpeace's role as a central defining actor seems to be on the increase, although not in a simple linear way. The percentage of articles quoting Greenpeace directly rose from around 40 per cent in the first two years of the analysis period to between 45 and 49 per cent in the last three years. The percentage of articles in which Greenpeace was simply referred to but not quoted either directly or indirectly declined from 41 per cent in 1987 to 31 per cent in 1991.

Two particular aspects stand out as remarkable in the coverage of Greenpeace in the two papers: one is the generally favourable light in which Greenpeace is portrayed; the other is the extent to which Greenpeace has been successful in deflecting media attention away from itself as an organization to keep such attention focused instead on the issues on which Greenpeace is campaigning.

The 'favourable' portrayal of Greenpeace is evident in a number of ways, not least of which is the frequency with which it is quoted directly as shown above. At a more semantic level, the favourable portrayal surfaces through the relative absence of explicit criticism of Greenpeace. Rarely, if ever, is Greenpeace itself the subject of press criticism (see also below). Criticism of Greenpeace in the coverage tends to come from other key players on the 'environmental issues scene' (notably industry and government) rather than from journalistic or editorial comment. Where criticism is reported, it adds to – rather than detracts from – the consolidation of Greenpeace as a legitimate player because it shows that Greenpeace needs to be reckoned with by key players such as Government and industry.

> **Greenpeace 'bias' puts Patten in rage: Environment Secretary scorns Britain's 'dirty man' tag**
> A Greenpeace report reinforcing Britain's image as the dirty man of Europe so enraged the Environment Secretary, Christopher Patten, that he accused the group of being politically partisan and distorting the facts.
> Mr Patten took the unusual step of rubbishing the document before it was officially published yesterday on the eve of the Government's Environment White Paper.
> He said: "Whatever their (Greenpeace's) past record, they have become increasingly shrill and partisan, and their latest publications are the worst sort of political pollution replete with distortions, exaggerations and worse". "They (Greenpeace) go on asserting that we are the dirtiest country in Europe, a libel for which there is not a shred of evidence." . . .
> But Lord Melchett, executive director of Greenpeace, said the dirty man tag was wholly justified: "There is nothing in Britain's future plans that will rid us of that tag." He said Britain was opposing serious action on cutting carbon dioxide emissions to control global warming.
> *(The Guardian, 25 September 1990)*

> **Clash ahead on toxic sea waste: Danes and Greenpeace seek ban on incineration**
> . . . The Association of Maritime Incinerators will clash with the Danish Government and Greenpeace in a private confrontation at the scientific committee of the London

Dumping Convention, the international body which
regulates waste disposal at sea.

. . . the AMI accuses the Danes and Greenpeace of
"prejudice, propaganda and an abject lack of scientific
objectivity." It says Greenpeace "do not hesitate to lie"
and claims that Danish fishing practice is "one of the most
pernicious threats to the environment of the North Sea."

. . . Other Greenpeace-commissioned research deals
with the accumulation of poisonous residues in the
microscopically thin layer which forms the ocean surface.

. . . The AMI says the report is "tendentious and
misleading," ignores any evidence which does not support its conclusions, and is based on work which has been
discredited by all serious researchers.

(*The Guardian*, 25 April 1988)

Japan hits at high seas 'terrorists'
Greenpeace was yesterday accused of acts of "terrorism
on the high seas" by Japan's Agriculture, Forestry and
Fisheries Agency for its attempts to prevent the Japanese
whaling fleet killing minke whales . . .

Mr Junichiro Okamoto, assistant director of the
agency's deep sea division, called for such direct action to
be outlawed. "We need international pressure to prohibit
such terrorist activity," he said . . .

Mr Peter Wilkinson, Greenpeace campaign director, dis-
missed the Japanese authorities' attacks and said: "We have
achieved a victory for peaceful direct action, for the environment and for the whale conservation movement". . . .

(*The Guardian*, 3 February 1989)

It is significant that the two strongest criticisms above, Mr Patten's
and Mr Okamoto's, are both 'denied' through direct counter-quotes
from Greenpeace representatives. In the middle excerpt, Greenpeace
is drawing on scientific research commissioned from a University
scientist. The AMI's disagreement with the findings of this research
forces them rhetorically to create a new category of scientists, namely
'serious researchers'. The AMI's strong critique of Greenpeace is
'undermined' partly by the 'authority' conferred on Greenpeace by its
siding with a whole nation, 'the Danes', and partly by the alliance with
science – that is, the fact that they are making claims on the basis of
scientific evidence. In terms of the overall 'legitimacy' of Greenpeace
in the coverage the main point of the above excerpts is, however, that
such criticisms are rare and exceptional occurrences in the coverage.

Even where Greenpeace is clearly in breach of the law, the
coverage – while making this clear – also gives prominence to the
possible justifications for such breaches (for example on the grounds
of legitimate beliefs, conscience or moral stands: 'Gaoled Greenpeace
activist faces £125,000 pounds claim: The unbowed campaigner who

regards himself as a prisoner of conscience', *The Guardian*, 2 January 1988).

A second aspect of Greenpeace's favourable image in the press is the success with which Greenpeace has managed to deflect attention away from itself as an organization, and to keep, instead, media attention focused on the issues and causes on which it campaigns. Only a relatively small number of articles (notwithstanding the lingering coverage about or associated with the French Secret Service sinking of the Greenpeace *Rainbow Warrior* ship in Auckland Harbour in 1985) are *about* Greenpeace per se. And the articles that are specifically about Greenpeace or Greenpeace personalities are more likely to highlight, in tones of thinly veiled admiration, the uniqueness and commitment of the people involved:

> **Tuesday Women: Maggie – the real McCaw/Green for one environmental worker means only one thing – action**
> *(The Guardian*, 21 March 1989)

> **Tuesday People: Greenpeace skipper looking forward to blue seas after weathering grey skies – Peter Wilcox**
> *(The Guardian*, 15 August 1989)

> **Saturday People: On the crest of a green wave – Peter Wilkinson**
> *(The Guardian*, 6 January 1990)

> **Green Today: Green Power – Lord Peter Melchett means business**
> *(Today*, 4 July 1989)

Or the success of the environmental movement and the ingenuity of the Greenpeace organization and its communication skills:

> **The Media: Go with the floe but get the copy out – The problems of communicating from the bottom of the world**
> *(The Guardian*, 20 February 1989)

> **Volunteers for the Green Army: 20,000 people are joining Britain's environmental groups each month**
> *(Today*, 7 April 1989)

Unlike other social movement groups, whose coverage over time has deteriorated into a media focus on personality clashes, internal schisms and breakaway groups (see Gitlin, 1980, on the students' movement; see also Kielbowicz and Scherer, 1986), Greenpeace has successfully avoided such publicity and retained the focus of media attention on its campaign causes and issues.

Kielbowicz and Scherer (1986) have noted the importance to media coverage of 'having identifiable leaders authorised to speak for a large following; they seem authoritative, like the head of a large business or government agency' (p. 87). It may be thought then, that Greenpeace, which has always made a point of *not* having a single charismatic leader, could be disadvantaged in this respect. This, however, would not seem to be the case. The strategy adopted by Greenpeace has been one of having clearly identified spokespersons for each of their major campaign issues, including local and regional spokespeople for international issues. Invariably, these are the people who are accessed by the press for comments, readily providing knowledgeable and authoritative quotes which, as was shown at the beginning of this section, often end up as direct quotes in the coverage itself.

This organization of spokespeople clearly secures that Greenpeace speaks with a uniform voice, or at least, and more to the point, it secures that potential differences within Greenpeace are not publicly on display in media coverage. It also, however, adds additional weight and legitimacy, particularly on issues in other countries where the official government or industry defence of whaling or seal-culling will be tied rhetorically to questions of the preservation of traditional cultural customs and communities, whose livelihood would be undermined by or disappear altogether if the kinds of bans that Greenpeace is campaigning for were implemented. In this context, the Greenpeace arguments inevitably carry more weight if they're seen as coming from spokespeople who are intimately familiar with – and/or themselves part of – the local/national culture, rather than aficionados sent out from an international organization to pronounce on the rights and wrongs of local/regional communities and their practices.

The media legitimation of Greenpeace takes place in a number of other ways: *The Guardian*'s environment correspondent, Paul Brown, travelled with Greenpeace on the Greenpeace ship the *Gondwana* on the long campaign, starting out from New Zealand in 1988 and culminating in actions at a French Antarctic base in January 1989 and interruptions of Japanese whaling ships in Antarctic waters during the first months of 1989. The fact that the paper devoted a specialist correspondent to travel with Greenpeace for an extended period of time – with a visible increase in Greenpeace articles during this period (see the peak in Figure 8.2 in the first quarter of 1989) – in itself confers legitimacy on the operation and on Greenpeace. Similarly, although on a more modest scale, *Today* reporters joined Greenpeace on a Greenpeace ship at various stages during the group's campaign to draw attention to the pollution of Britain's coastal waters and to the decline of the dolphin and porpoise populations around Britain's coast. In other places *Today* describes *joint operations* with Greenpeace:

> **Secret nuclear ship in 90 mph storm**
> A SHIP carrying a deadly secret cargo of nuclear waste was marooned outside Dover by gales and mountainous seas yesterday. . . . At Dover, coastguards admitted they had no idea that 4.5 tonnes of atomic waste was on board the nuclear ferry, exposed in a joint operation by TODAY and Greenpeace. . . .

> Greenpeace claimed the incident highlighted the menace of the multi-million pound reprocessing business that has made Britain the world's nuclear dustbin.
>
> (*Today,* 8 February 1990)

One of the most significant signs of the established and legitimate role which Greenpeace has achieved is the way in which Greenpeace has become perhaps *the* sign and signifier of everything environmental. In other words, Greenpeace has become the popular shorthand for environmental caring, for green lifestyles, and for environmentally conscious attitudes. The excerpts below show this use of Greenpeace as a signifier in articles which in other respects say nothing about Greenpeace claims-making.

> **Society Tomorrow: The whole truth – Wholistic living**
> . . . Breaking through into our daily lives, green ideas are making steady progress. . . . Greenpeace is edging into the cultural mainstream.
>
> (*The Guardian,* 15 July 1987)

> **Saturday People: Memoirs from a dutiful daughter – Rhonda Paisley**
> Greenpeace supporter and vegetarian Rhonda Paisley is eager to be more than just her father's dutiful daughter . . .
>
> (*The Guardian,* 17 September 1988)

> **Guardian Tomorrows: A blast from the brass section – We know they've done better than anyone else from the Thatcher years but what are the wealthy like?**
> . . . Mr Hudson, latterly famous as, briefly, Ian Botham's manager, could afford several Porsche 959s but he prefers a Jeep and a deep blue Rolls-Royce with a Greenpeace sticker on the bumper . . .
>
> (*The Guardian,* 15 February 1989)

> **Style Eternal assets – Silicone implants are here to stay. . . in more ways than one**
> Brigitte Nielsen is a walking environmental hazard and I fear for my babies, or at least I would if I had any. . . . [S]he has set an example to millions of people who now believe the prosthesis to be the ultimate route to happiness. Forget Sellafield; it's Beverly Hills that Greenpeace should be concentrating on . . .
>
> (*The Guardian,* 22 January 1990)

> **Lingua Franca reaching futon man**
> In the thrusting, acquisitive Eighties, advertisers created yuppies and dinkies for the way you lived today. Now, they assure us, we're into the caring, sharing Nineties – with kinder, gentler consumers replacing the old 'lifestyle' categories.
> . . . 'Creatives' lately favour futon man, whose needs are largely organic, but not fully-fledged Greenpeace warriors – of little use to advertisers, as their dogged

environmental commitment makes them rather sceptical
consumers . . .

(*The Guardian*, 24 March 1990)

**Green Living: Fashion Wearing What Comes Natu-
rally**
A SOCIAL conscience is back in fashion. The new breed
of environmentally aware trendsetters are led by Katha-
rine Hamnett and French designer Agnes B.
. . . The top British designer and Greenpeace member
says: "I like to work with natural fabrics and use
non-toxic processes like stone-washing instead of
bleaching."

(*Today*, 10 September 1988)

Amanda Donohoe's sexy gospel of true love
Amanda Donohoe's eyes burn with missionary zeal. The
subject is sex and her position couldn't be more clear. "I
don't embarrass easily over sex. Let's face it, it is so
important to all of us," she says. . . . A part-time CND and
Greenpeace activist, she goes as far as to say: "Really, I'm
quite boring. Who needs to go around jumping into
BMWs, raving it up and that kind of thing.". . .

(*Today*, 2 June 1990)

I have already, above, hinted at the use of 'science' as a legitimating
and authority-reinforcing factor for Greenpeace in claims-making. In
the final section I discuss this more closely, together with the
argument that Greenpeace gains coverage by engaging established
news fora.

The alliance with science and the engagement with established news fora

Theatrical stunts and visually daring protest action may have a degree
of inherent news-worthiness, but such actions cannot in themselves
explain the long-lasting and sustained accessing of Greenpeace in
media coverage. Nor can such access be explained by additional
arguments concerning Greenpeace's catering to the needs of media
organizations in terms of news cycles, provision of sources, provision
of visual material, exploitation of deadlines, etc. These aspects are not
unimportant, but in order to explain Greenpeace's sustained success
as a claims-maker and in terms of getting media coverage, we need
to look further. More particularly, we need to look to what we may call
'the alliance with science' and we need to look to the way in which
Greenpeace continuously links into or latches onto developments in
existing established and legitimate news fora.

Most of the issues on which Greenpeace campaigns and successfully gains media coverage are issues which already have an
institutional forum rather than completely new issues which have not

been problematized in some form or other before. The success of Greenpeace as a claims-maker is partly explained then by its careful timing of press releases and publication of reports to coincide with (or often, slightly precede) political events (for example, in debates in Parliament; publication of the Government's White Paper on the Environment), international meetings (for example, the London North Sea Conference in November of 1987), treaty renewals (for example, the Antarctic Treaty Nations and the protection of the Antarctic wilderness; the International Whaling Commission's consideration of applications from Norway, Iceland and Japan for 'scientific' whaling; GATT trade negotiations with implications for bans on tuna fish caught with driftnets); industry or public authority announcements (for example, announcements of nuclear industry decisions concerning suitable sites for storage of low-level radioactive waste).

In this respect Greenpeace's effectiveness as a claims-maker arises from its exposure of agenda items which are part of the routine and legitimate fora of politics, public authorities, international politics, etc., but while they are routine fora for media attention, it is the claims-making activity of Greenpeace which helps direct the attention of the mass media to aspects and interpretations which might otherwise have gone unnoticed or might have been deliberately glossed over. In short, Greenpeace's claims-making activity is often at its most effective not so much in terms of constructing entirely new problems for social and political attention, but in terms of framing and elaborating environmental dimensions which are already in the public domain as issues or problems.

At one level this is a simple process of gaining coverage by attacking or making claims about people, institutions and fora which are already by themselves newsworthy and the focus of routine interest (see also Molotch and Lester, 1975, and Kielbowicz and Scherer, 1986, on this dimension of pressure-group news-making). At a more complex level, it points to the way in which Greenpeace's successful claims-making is built on intelligence-gathering and surveillance of developments in environmental policy-making and decision-making – in the broadest sense of the term:

Greenpeace can be defined primarily by its transformation of knowledge into an organisational weapon. . . . Knowledge, for Greenpeace, is at one and the same time very limited and very crucial. Without strategic information, its campaigns would be merely media shows and they would long ago have stopped making news. It is the selective gathering of campaign-related facts, the selective dissemination of arguments to the media and other public fora, the selective testimony at hearings and conferences and international meetings that gives Greenpeace its enormous influence. . . . [Professionals are hired to work for Greenpeace] because of their ability to get the information that Greenpeace needs: in a word, they are intelligencers, environmental agents. As such, they can either be scientific experts by training or activists; in either case, those who continue to work with Greenpeace become a kind of new-fangled hybrid between a professional scientist and a movement activist, not so much producing "science for the people" as producing intelligence: strategic information for the people. (Eyerman and Jamison, 1989, p.p 113–14)

Journalists, even specialist journalists (science, environment, health, medical, consumer affairs, agriculture journalists), could not hope to even begin to monitor systematically the wide range of institutions, industries, bodies, political fora, etc. involved in decision-making about environmental issues. This requires an organization or organizations with expertise and resources for precisely such a task. Seen from this perspective, it is perhaps not surprising that an organization such as Greenpeace enjoys a great deal of positive resonance with journalists. Greenpeace in many respects helps make the journalists' task less impossible by drawing attention to significant developments which might otherwise have remained buried in the mountain of propaganda, information, and press releases landing on the desk of a journalist every day.

It may be sufficient for Greenpeace to simply shine its selective spotlight on developments in, for example, international negotiations about whaling, carbon-dioxide emissions and the greenhouse effect, acid rain or pollution in the North Sea. The excerpt below is an example of Greenpeace exploiting information in another forum (a report commissioned by the Department of the Environment) for claims-making against the nuclear industry:

> **BNFL urged to clear 'cancer risk' sediment**
> Greenpeace today urged British Nuclear Fuels to recover radioactive contaminated sediment from the Irish Sea to reduce the cancer risk to people in Cumbria from the plutonium being brought ashore by wind and tide.
> A report commissioned by the Department of the Environment says that plutonium from the Sellafield plant in Cumbria is seriously polluting the Solway coast in southern Scotland.
> *(The Guardian,* 14 August 1989)

A variant of this type of claims-making is the form where Greenpeace is actively used by other fora or institutions (or individuals within such institutions) for leaking information and bringing it to the attention of the media. Greenpeace acts as a conduit or as a vehicle for information, a role which in itself confers legitimacy and prestige on Greenpeace:

> **Voting shift backs non-nuclear power: Private industry survey reveals Chernobyl switch**
> Almost half the population is prepared to pay more for electricity in order to phase out nuclear power, according to an internal opinion survey commissioned by the nuclear industry and leaked to the environmental group, Greenpeace.
> *(The Guardian,* 29 February 1988)

Penguins that face death on the rocks: French plans to
start blasting for a new airstrip later this month
threaten many of the birds breeding on the site
The French Government is resuming blowing up six
islands in the Antarctic this January, the breeding ground
of penguins and other birds, in order to build an airport
to take giant Hercules transport aircraft. . . . Greenpeace,
the environmental group, now see Dumont d'Urville,
founded as a scientific research station, as a first bridge-
head for the new Klondike which the mineral-rich
Antarctic is set to become. . . .
   Greenpeace was leaked information by an outraged
French scientist at the site along with pictures of
penguins killed in the explosions.
                                    (*The Guardian*, 7 January 1989)

Safety 'in doubt' as N-power gauges fail: Engineer
criticises 'string and sticky tape' repair
VITAL temperature gauges designed to prevent catastrophic failure of a pressure vessel at the Trawsfynydd
nuclear reactor have failed and been given replacements
which have led to serious safety fears. A confidential
paper from J. T. Williams, resources manager of the
Mid-Wales station, to the manager, J. S. Fricker, express-
ing concern has been leaked to the Guardian via
Greenpeace.
                                    (*The Guardian*, 16 August 1990)

$10-a-barrel oil tax under discussion
. . . The measures, to cut fossil fuel emissions and
promote greater energy efficiency by keeping fuel prices
artificially inflated, are revealed in a confidential discussion document prepared jointly by the EC Energy and
Environment Commissioners. The paper was leaked to
the environmental group Greenpeace and released yesterday.
                                    (*The Guardian*, 5 February 1991)

More often though Greenpeace attaches itself to – and, more
importantly, frames – developments in other institutional fora by
producing evidence or information which carefully targets a particular aspect of such developments. The evidence generally takes the
form of opinion polls, surveys, scientific analyses or studies commissioned by Greenpeace, but as Eyerman and Jamison (1989, see above)
point out this is not principally a question of producing knowledge or
science for the people or for the sake of knowing, but a question of
producing knowledge and information which can be used strategi-
cally in public arena debates:

Hinkley inquiry: Residents near PWR site oppose
more nuclear power
NEARLY 70 per cent of people living near the Hinkley
power station site in Somerset oppose the expansion of

nuclear power, a poll commissioned by Greenpeace discloses today. The results of the pressure group's survey were published to coincide with the final week of the Hinkley C public inquiry.

(*The Guardian*, 25 September 1989)

80pc in poll fault energy effort

FOUR in five people questioned in a survey whose results were published yesterday believed the Government was doing too little to promote energy conservation and combat the 'greenhouse effect'.

. . . Friends of the Earth, Greenpeace, and the Association for the Conservation of Energy, who commissioned the poll, are urging Mrs Thatcher to agree to accept a minimum 20 per cent cut in carbon dioxide emissions over the next 10 years.

(*The Guardian*, 14 July 1989)

50 nuclear weapons lost on ocean floor: Study reveals one serious naval accident a week

The US and Soviet navies have lost 50 nuclear weapons and eight nuclear reactors on the ocean floor, according to a new study of naval accidents. The study, commissioned by Greenpeace and the Institute for Policy Studies, documents 2,000 incidents since 1945, including 345 involving the Royal Navy, and suggests that many more may have been concealed by the Soviet and French navies in particular.

(*The Guardian*, 7 June 1989)

Poll shows Cunningham's seat at risk over Sellafield dump

LABOUR'S campaign co-ordinator, Dr John Cunningham, risks losing his seat at the election if he supports an underground nuclear waste repository at Sellafield in his Copeland constituency, according to an opinion poll commissioned by the environment group Greenpeace.

(*The Guardian*, 7 October 1991)

Traffic fumes 'asthma risk for children'

ROAD transport is the biggest contributor to air pollution that puts children at risk of developing chest infections and asthma, a study commissioned by the environmental group Greenpeace UK has found.

(*The Guardian*, 29 July 1991)

Cheaper Sellafield wins nuclear dump: Nirex accused of headlong rush as consultant's report for Greenpeace attacks geological case

SELLAFIELD in Cumbria was confirmed yesterday as the preferred site for an underground dump for Britain's nuclear waste. The decision brought fresh criticism that too little is known about the safety of deep disposal and the local geology to go ahead. . . .

At a press conference in London Dr Alan Hooper,

Nirex's safety and technology manager, said preliminary results from four test boreholes revealed rock at a suitable depth which was stronger than had been expected. . . .

But an independent report, by a consulting geologist, Philip Richardson, said the company's plans were the result of political expediency and not based on sound science. He said: "Nirex have rushed headlong into an announcement decision and the geological case doesn't stand up." His report, commissioned by Greenpeace, said: "The very limited scale of the site investigation carried out to date by Nirex at Sellafield is simply not sufficient to address adequately the uncertainties which exist concerning deep disposal."

(*The Guardian*, 24 July 1991)

Firm's car perk costs us all £150
TAX subsidies on company cars cost each household in Britain £150 a year. The perk also adds to pollution by encouraging people to use large-engined firm's cars for private travel, a report reveals today. Greenpeace, which commissioned the survey, now wants a shake-up of the company car system, saying it forces ordinary people to pay so others can have the "privilege to pollute".

(*Today*, 4 March 1991)

As journalists themselves have observed (see for example Chapter 3) Greenpeace has increasingly allied itself with science and built its claims-making around 'fact-finding' studies and publications. Not only does it commission research, but it also sponsors a university science fellowship. While the alliance with science is not a new phenomenon for environmental pressure groups in general or for Greenpeace more specifically – indeed both Greenberg (1985) and Lowe and Goyder (1983) refer to this – the emphasis on this does seem to have increased in the period analysed here. Thus, 'science' and related synonyms (scientist, scientists, scientific) appeared[3] 139 times in the coverage of 1987 and 1988, but 249 times in the coverage of 1990 and 1991. More specifically, 'science', 'research', and related synonyms appeared within ten words of 'Greenpeace' in forty-five cases in 1987/8 compared with seventy-three cases for 1990/91. While the number of articles was considerably higher in 1990/91 than in 1987/8 (368 to 269), this finding points to an increased association between Greenpeace and 'science' in the coverage.

Conclusion

I have attempted to show in this analysis of press coverage of Greenpeace during the five-year period 1987–91 that while Greenpeace does indeed enjoy a comparatively (compared with more traditional 'conservation' groups) remarkable degree of coverage (although not quite as much as the other major modern environmental pressure group, Friends of the Earth), it would be a mistake to 'read' the amount of coverage as a sign in itself of successful claims-making activity.

Greenpeace succeeds quite differentially in getting coverage on different issues; in particular, it would appear that the more saturated the media arena is with a particular issue, the smaller the claims-making power of Greenpeace on that particular issue. Thus, the dominance of nuclear and radiation-related issues in the Greenpeace coverage is itself just a function of the overall prominence (although rapidly declining over the five-year period) of anything nuclear in the press coverage. The more detailed analysis of the ups and downs of issues coverage also indicated that Greenpeace's ability to gain coverage is closely related to major campaign initiatives. This observation may seem self-evident, but it does nevertheless indicate that Greenpeace, despite its increasing alliance with science, has not yet become an 'automatic' routine news forum.

The examination of 'Greenpeace coverage' relative to overall coverage on selected issues also indicated that while Greenpeace claims-making or action is the primary catalyst of coverage in a significant proportion of the coverage in which Greenpeace is mentioned, the extent to which Greenpeace can be seen as a major factor in increasing the visibility of selected issues shows a less than straightforward picture. Thus on some key issues, the overall amount of coverage seems to rise and fall relatively independently of Greenpeace-related claims-making. Despite the obvious complexity of the relationship between Greenpeace activity and extent of press coverage, one particular finding points to the extraordinary agenda-setting power of Greenpeace, and that is the relative uniformity across different newspapers in the trends – although not in terms of the absolute amount – of Greenpeace-related coverage.

Despite the above qualifications concerning the 'success' of Greenpeace as a claims-maker and agenda-builder on environmental issues, it is also clear, however, from the more detailed examination of *how* Greenpeace is portrayed that Greenpeace is shown as a highly legitimate and credible source. There is little overt criticism of Greenpeace – in fact, one of the most remarkable aspects (and an aspect that distinguishes it from many other pressure groups) of its career as a pressure group is the way in which it has succeeded in deflecting negative scrutiny and attention away from itself onto the issues on which it campaigns. Greenpeace representatives are quoted directly in a large proportion of the coverage (and increasingly so as we move through the five-year period); its legitimacy is further reinforced by the way in which Greenpeace is frequently used as a shorthand signifier, signifying not just the pressure group itself, but the entire environmental movement and anything 'environmentally conscious or friendly'. The increasing alliance with science, as a way of reinforcing legitimacy and authority, is evident in the five-year period of coverage. The analysis of the alliance with science in Greenpeace coverage confirms Eyerman and Jamison's important point that science is used by Greenpeace as a strategic weapon for engaging established news fora.

While the meteoric rise of Greenpeace during the late 1980s is amply evident both in terms of membership figures and in terms of media coverage, it is also clear that the amount of coverage is declining toward the end of the period analysed. The real test of Greenpeace's success then may reside in the extent to which Greenpeace can keep up its media momentum in the face of what would appear to be the beginning of the end of the late 1980s (cyclical) boom in media and public concern about the environment.

Notes

I am grateful to the Leicester University Research Board for awarding the grant which made this study possible. I would also like to thank Kealie Duncalf for her contribution to the coding of newspaper coverage.

1 The broadsheet 'quality' paper *The Guardian* has a long and established reputation for its commitment to environmental coverage – it is the only national daily paper with a weekly 'environment' section. The 'middle brow' tabloid *Today*, launched in 1986, straddles the divide between the serious sober reporting of the quality papers and the popular sensationalist reporting of the mass circulation popular press. The two papers cannot be taken as representative (politically) of the spectrum of British national daily newspapers, but they are reasonably representative of some of the defining characteristics underlying the division of the national press into a quality press and a popular press. While these defining characteristics are themselves an interesting dimension of the reporting of Greenpeace and environmental issues, the differences between the two papers are not a central focus in this chapter.

2 The rise in *Today*'s coverage also significantly coincides with the paper's creation of an environmental reporter post. The first time an article in *Today* was bylined 'environment editor/reporter' was on the 5 November 1988.

3 This keyword analysis was done with the text-analysis/text-retrieval program *Sonar Professional.*

References

Eyerman, R., Jamison, A. (1989), 'Environmental knowledge as an organisational weapon: the case of Greenpeace', *Social Science Information,* 28 (1), pp. 99–119.

Gitlin, T. (1980), *The whole world is watching: mass media in the making and unmaking of the new left*, Berkeley: University of California Press.

Grant, W. (1989), *Pressure groups, politics and democracy in Britain.* London: Philip Allan.

Greenberg, D. W. (1985), 'Staging media events to achieve legitimacy: a case study of Britain's Friends of the Earth', *Political Communication and Persuasion*, 2 (4).

Hansen, A. (1990), 'The news construction of the environment', in O. Linné and A. Hansen, *News coverage of the environment*, Copenhagen: Danmarks Radio Forlaget, pp. 4–63.

Kielbowicz, R. B., Scherer, C. (1986), 'The role of the press in the dynamics of social movements', in G. Lang and K. Lang (eds), *Research in social movements, conflicts and change*, Greenwich, CT: JAI Press Inc, pp. 71–96.

Lowe, P. D., Goyder, J. (1983), *Environmental groups in politics*, London: George Allen & Unwin.

Lowe, P., Morrison, D. (1984), 'Bad news or good news: environmental politics and the mass media', *The Sociological Review*, 32 (1), pp. 75–90.

McCormick, J. (1991), *British politics and the environment*, London: Earthscan.

Molotch, H., Lester, M. (1975), 'Accidental news: the great oil spill', *American Journal of Sociology*, 81 (2), pp. 235–60.

Yearley, S. (1991), *The green case: a sociology of environmental issues, arguments and politics*, London: HarperCollins Academic.

Part 3:

Making sense of mediated environmental meanings

9
Television and the cultivation of environmental concern: 1988–92

James Shanahan

Since the abnormally hot US summer of 1988 and the accompanying panic over global warming, the environment and the threats to its overall health have gradually but consistently crept into the news and into the national consciousness. In that summer there was an enormous amount of coverage in the popular press of the environmental threat, including a cover story in *Time,* the US national news magazine. About two years later, the twentieth anniversary of Earth Day was celebrated, providing yet another focus for environmental news coverage and a way perhaps to galvanize national consciousness on the issue.

Since that time, the environmental issue has remained in the public consciousness, although it is by no means clear that the public's appetite for environmental information will remain as voracious as it once was. As the US economy has declined, the potential costs of environmentalism have become more obvious, especially through very visible and divisive issues such as the pitting of the spotted owl against Oregon loggers.

At the same time, the meaning of environmentalism has begun to change as business and industry have sought to incorporate 'green' consciousness into marketing and advertising plans, seeking to associate 'green' with their products, while assuaging consumers' incipient environmental concern. Peggy Filis, an expert on 'green marketing', writing in *Electronic Media* (Filis, 1992) notes that '[n]ew products, new packaging, repositioning, seal-of-approval certifications and green advertising are all elements of the marketing quest for what is expected to be a $10 billion pot of gold within a very few years' (p. 36). Obviously, the ideological content of the broad movement of public opinion toward 'environmentalism' is up for grabs.

While a 'light-green' environmentalism is becoming rather commonplace in the mainstream media and among many consumers, opposition to the more radical forms of environmental concern is making itself manifest. The Bush 'environmental' presidency has panned out, and the electoral politics of 1992 have made 'regulation' a devil term in the rhetoric of politicians seeking to stimulate a failing national economy. The issue has been practically absent from the presidential campaign at this writing. Because scientists have predictably failed to reach a consensus on the benchmark issue of global warming, the global environmental campaign has not proceeded much farther than where it was in 1988, and the issue risks subsiding in the public consciousness much as it did after reaching a peak in the 1970s. Indeed, at this writing, Bush administration memoranda in preparation for the Rio environmental summit show that the Bush administration will continue to adopt a 'wait and see' attitude toward real environmental change.

Because we have seen about five years of the resurgence in environmental issues, now is a convenient time to assess aspects of public opinion on the issue of environmentalism. This chapter focuses on the contribution of US television programming to environmental concern over this period (1988–92).

The environmental function of media

Looking at today's environmental situation, it seems clear that the responsibility for our problems rests not solely with particular actors, but with an overall system of consciousness trained largely to ignore the environmental impacts of our everyday behavior. Surely nobody has been trained *specifically* to damage the environment, and so environmental damage is principally a consequence of the fact that we were concerned with other issues. What were these issues? Economic growth, technological progress, material comfort and fun probably lead the list.

In order to overcome our environmental problems, it will probably not be enough to simply acquire an environmental consciousness in addition to our other mental predispositions: we will also have to restructure our current goals and especially our everyday awareness which leads us ('us' meaning anything from individuals to nations) to commit environmentally insensitive acts. Even individuals who are nominally environmentally concerned (many people think of themselves this way; see Gillroy and Shapiro, 1986) find it difficult to escape the prevailing paradigm of economic growth and material comfort because the economy is structured in such a way that material survival often depends upon environmentally insensitive acts. The problem is one of ideology and consciousness. The dangers threatening our environment have not acquired sufficient material force to threaten the overall mental picture in the industrialized world, which acts quickest when economic welfare is threatened and only reacts to the environment as resources and global attitudinal energy permit. So it is no surprise that individuals, by and large, while willing to proclaim themselves 'environmentalists', have not adopted radically new behaviors as steps toward benefitting the environment.

What is the role of mass media in this process, and what could it be? Clearly, at least part of the environmental role of mass media is to make us aware of problems. Media should report on environmental harms and should tell us about progress being made in the environmental struggle. In short, environmental news must find a regular and prominent place in the flow of the world's news, and the presentation of this news would hopefully avoid much of the inequity that has been observed in the general flow of news worldwide. But does this exhaust the roles that the media should play in the environmental struggle?

The answer is that it was not a lack of environmental news which prevented us from acting in a 'concerned' way in the past; rather we simply failed to even consider that environmental resources should be evaluated as part of the overall economic equation. Even if there had been more environmental news, it would have likely produced little reaction in a world bent on mastery over nature rather than cooperation with it. So merely increasing the flow of environmental news, while a necessary step, does not attack the ideological base of the problem, which is a fundamental mental tendency to ignore the environment when making everyday life decisions.

From a communication perspective, then, it becomes necessary to address media in their ideological fullness, so to speak, rather than just examining the important though limited issue of news coverage. This chapter's focus therefore includes the entertainment aspect of mass media, and attempts to look at the broader ideological effects of mass media, instead of the specific informational problem that is more often presented by news coverage.

As Lippmann (1922) and countless others have pointed out, our actions in the world are strongly conditioned just as much by our picture of the world as it is by the real world itself. Clearly, if we are presented and we internalize a counterproductive picture of the world, we will not be properly prepared to act responsibly in that world.

In the environmental case, the role of pictures is particularly important. Because of technology, our physical actions have much broader consequences than was the case before, say, the industrial revolution. The byproducts and effluents of everyday existence are, theoretically, transmissible throughout the entire biosphere. Waste products are flushed, thrown out or disappear into thin air, no sooner than which they have exited the sphere of our immediate consciousness. This gives us the paradoxical situation where we can be living environmentally destructive lives within an otherwise clean environment.

And what of our symbolic environment? Obviously, the technological capacity of our symbolic environment has developed perhaps even faster than the physical technologies which have produced the present situation. Indeed, the possibility exists for these information technologies to serve a function similar to that served by simple 'awareness' in preindustrial days. That is, one of the things we might expect our symbolic environment to do for us is to monitor our physical environment so that we become more realistically aware of the true consequences of our actions. In order for the symbolic environment to legitimately perform this function the scope at which it informs about environmental problems would have to match the scope at which our own actions contribute to those problems.

Clearly this is not happening. Though we continue to increase the rate at which we transmit pollution of all kinds throughout the biosphere, the symbolic environment has not kept up with the rate of this transmission, and indeed has continued to serve largely the same social function as it has served throughout this century: entertainment.

Though some news attention is being given to the environment, most of our symbolic environment, and especially television, is still devoted to the same ends which have always been our goals: material growth, progress, fun, etc. If television will remain our primary source of information about environmental health there are several reasons for concern. First, until recently there has been relatively little information about the environment on television, and to this point the televideo 'environment' has been limited to news coverage. And this coverage has itself been confined primarily to environmental catastrophes, such as oil spills, forest fires, etc. The environmental story has been told in ways which emphasize simplistic themes and has not adequately covered significant environmental topics which are less 'visual', such as radon gas, long-range environmental effects of pollution, etc. (Diamond and Mead, 1989). Also, environmental stories covered on the news are routinely covered the way all news is, in small quantities, for short amounts of times, and cyclically (McGeachy, 1989). Television's principal sources for environmental news have been limited to relatively few individuals or organizations, and television news usually presents environmental issues utilizing oppositional views from citizen groups or bystanders and government or corporate officials in a simplistic, diametrical manner (Greenberg et al., 1989).

So, while we argue that any increase in news coverage is probably a good thing, we should observe that well over half of the US television environment is devoted to pursuits that require far less attention to the environment. Television is a key part of what Meadows (1991) terms the 'informationsphere'. The informationsphere is an area of the global ecology where humans can have immediate and measurable impact, by changing our informational goals and making sure that information-gathering technologies deliver environmental information with fidelity. Meadows argues that the informationsphere is a key contributor to the development of the anti-environmental paradigm under which we currently subsist.

A paradigm is upheld by the constant repetition of ideas that fit within it. It is affirmed by every information exchange, in families, churches, literature, music, workplaces, shopping places, daily chats on the street. The key to paradigm stability and coherence is repetition. Therefore when people learned how to repeat information on a mass basis – to make printing presses and send messages over electronic waves – they not only created tools with the potential to improve vastly the information flows in systems, they also inadvertently invented potent techniques for paradigm affirmation and, theoretically, for paradigm change. (Meadows, 1991, p. 74)

Pirages and Ehrlich (1974) suggested that the 'dominant social paradigm' (or DSP) embedded in the media stresses traditional beliefs and values emphasizing progress, technology, production and materialism. Dunlap and Van Liere (1984) found a negative correlation between measures of attachment to the DSP and degree of environmental concern. Television, of course, tends to reflect the DSP since as the primary cultural arm of the existing social and economic order (Gerbner and Gross, 1976) it must be commercially and socially acceptable to the largest number of people possible.

Most television is devoid of explicit environmental messages, although all television implicitly says something about the environment. One of the most typical messages of television entertainment is that there is, in fact, no environment as we know it, since much of television programming is set in sanitized studio settings. Prime-time TV has been set for the most part indoors. Outdoor scenes exist mostly as background for otherwise environmentally apathetic dramatic or comedic action. This mimics our general inattention to the environment in everyday life, and appears to reproduce the paradigmatic depiction of the environment to which we have become accustomed.

Of course, some television programs have begun to incorporate explicitly pro-environmental messages, a trend which should be applauded, even if the messages represent a tiny fraction of the average viewer's symbolic experience. There are the passing public service announcements (which are becoming slightly more frequent as Hollywood entertainers jump on and off the environmental bandwagon) but the solution is given in a fifteen or thirty second spot. Although there are at present groups such as the Earth Communications Office and the Environmental Media Association, which attempt to get environmental messages into TV shows, movies and pop music (Cox, 1989; Hickey, 1990), several new series devoted to environmental themes (for instance, *Captain Planet and the Planeteers* of the Turner Broadcasting Service) and occasional mentions of recycling or global warming, the world of prime-time television has always been one in which even the most complex problems are resolved in twenty-two or fifty-two minutes.

At this time, a preliminary analysis of content data from US television in 1991 shows that, while the environment does pop up as a news item with greater regularity, it is still practically absent from the world of television entertainment, at least in prime time (Shanahan, 1992). Indeed, common sense and a perusal of almost any evening of prime-time television shows that the focus is squarely on consumption rather than conservation and technological progress rather than environmental stability.

Given that television, as a whole, can be considered moderately unfriendly with respect to the environment, we should investigate the notion that this plays some role in the maintenance of both attitudes and behaviors that are part and parcel of the general environmental problem. Of course, the environmental problems began long before media came onto the scene, and so there is no doubt that media images do not 'cause' environmental deterioration. Also, it is increasingly difficult to argue that media have direct 'effects' in the sense in which specific situations are produced by programs regardless of their social context (Hansen, 1991). At the same time, it would be hard to argue that a system of communication so pervasive as electronic media, especially television, has no role in the maintenance of values and norms which undergird the basic social understandings that have contributed for so long to the problem of the environment.

Thus, this study will examine the effect of the medium of US television upon the general system of beliefs having to do with environmental issues: the notion of environmental 'concern'. If the environment is going to become more of an issue in people's minds, it ought to be possible to identify statements and issues with which they would be likely to agree. Also, if television is playing a role in the formation or non-formation of these beliefs, then it ought to be possible, at some level, to identify the nature of the relationship. It should be possible to specify, broadly speaking, how heavy television viewers in fact differ on environmental issues from the lighter viewers. Although many will disagree with the hypothesis that the effect of television viewing on viewers' attitudes and behaviors can be assessed solely as a function of viewing time, even more people may disagree with the hypothesis which we advance here, which suggests that as viewing time increases, environmental concern will decrease. That is, television is an anti-environmental force.

Cultivation analysis

The hypothesis which has just been advanced is a hypothesis that can be tested using the methodology of 'cultivation analysis'. Cultivation analysis is part of the overall research program that has been headed by George Gerbner at the University of Pennsylvania. At base, cultivation is a theory of story-telling, which assumes that repeated exposure to a set of messages is likely to produce agreement in an audience with opinions expressed in (or attitudes consonant with) those messages. The term 'cultivation' is used to indicate that the process is conceived as a cumulative one; there is really no question of immediate effects or impact.

Gerbner (1990) writes that:

Cultivation is what a culture does. That is not simple causation, though culture is the basic medium in which humans live and learn. Cultivation rarely brings change except between generations and regions or among styles of life of which it is more or less a part. Cultivation is not the sole (or even frequent) determinant of specific actions, although it may tip a delicate balance, mark the mainstream of common consciousness, and signal a sea-change in the cultural environment. Strictly speaking, cultivation means the specific independent (though not isolated) contribution that a particularly consistent and compelling symbolic stream makes to the complex process of socialization and enculturation. (p. 249)

The primary use of cultivation theory has been to assess the impact of television viewing on violence in society, a historically frequent concern of governmental and social authorities in the United States. Generally, cultivation theory measures television exposure in individuals, and attempts to associate that measurement with attitudes about any dependent variable of concern. In the case of violence, for instance, it has been found that exposure to television is associated with more violent appraisals of the state of society: heavier viewers are more likely to think the world is a violent place.

This hypothesis has been tested not only for violence (Gerbner and Gross, 1976), but for sex-role attitudes (Morgan, 1982), aging (Gerbner et al., 1980), racial stereotypes (Gross, 1984), intellectual skills (Morgan and Gross, 1980), socialization and peer-groups affiliations (Rothschild and Morgan, 1987), and a variety of other dependent variables. In most of these cases, the argument has been that television, by virtue of portraying various stereotypes and issues, *actively* suggests mental constructs to its audiences, which are then presumably adopted more frequently by heavy viewers.

The environmental case is somewhat different. Here we are arguing that cultivation may be possible because of a *lack* of images, or even as a result of having one's attention directed somewhere else. This is not completely new. For instance, cultivation analysis research on the elderly is another case of 'cultivation in reverse'. In any case, the basic hypothesis is the same; we are saying that the thrust of television is anti-environmental, and so we would expect heavy viewers to manifest this anti-environmentalism more so than light viewers. The effect might be subtle, as cultivation would predict, but should be measurable. Thus, this study, using samples from four years beginning in 1988, seeks to track the impact of television upon viewers' conceptions of environmental reality.

Methods

The samples for this study were taken from four undergraduate communication classes at two large northeastern universities. One sample was gathered in 1988 ($N = 105$), one in early 1990 ($N = 165$), one in late 1990 ($N = 523$), and one in 1992 ($N = 230$). None of the three samples reflects a probability design, and all are skewed in some ways (in 1988 the sample was 61 per cent female, in early 1990 it was 67 per cent female, in late 1990 it was 66.2 per cent female, and in 1992 it was 62.1 per cent female). Also, compared to the general population, college students as a group would be expected to be lighter television viewers and to be more concerned about the environment. Despite these limitations, the main concern was to explore relationships among variables rather than to make population projections about baselines, and college students are frequently used in exploratory cultivation studies (see for example, Carveth and Alexander, 1985; Perse, 1990). Also, the fact that college students watch television less than most people and are more environmentally concerned is something that would tend to work against finding the patterns we are searching for. Any evidence we find may in fact be underestimates of the true extent of cultivation of environmental concern.

In all years, a survey was administered in the classroom setting prior to a normal lecture period. In order to avoid the possibility of sensitization, no prior mention was made of either television or the environment (and media measures came at the end of the instrument); students were only informed that they were being asked to answer some questions about their opinions about social trends. The first wave of data, collected in spring 1988, was done before the heavy barrage of environmental issues in the news in the summer of 1988 and in the fall presidential campaign. The second wave of data was collected in spring 1990, after the environment had become a major news issue, but before the publicity of Earth Day of April in that year. The third wave of data was gathered in October 1990, some six months after Earth Day, deep in the middle of the Kuwaiti oil crisis and in the midst of a contentious political campaign in which the environment was an important issue. The final wave of data was collected in early winter 1992, with the environment on the back burner due to presidential politics (amazingly, the issue has barely dented the public agenda, while tales of Bill Clinton's personal life have received reams of coverage), although Albert Gore's volume on environmental policy was released during the sampling period, creating a few media events in the process. In all years, respondents answered nearly identical survey instruments. Although these are not the same students (i.e., this is not a panel study), having four waves allows at least for a general analysis of trends over time.

The survey instrument was composed of several parts. First, respondents were asked about the level of importance they assign to eighteen social issues, both environmental and non-environmental, ranging from reducing nuclear weapons to assuring economic growth to finding a way to stop acid rain. A five-point scale ranging from 'very concerned' to 'not at all concerned' was used for each issue. One item in the list was simply 'the environment', which is referred to in this chapter as the general 'one-item' measure of environmental concern. This was intended to provide a simple, overall measure of concern about the environment, with the methodological advantage of being embedded in a series of other issues, thus avoiding sensitization problems. The question also provides a way to assess whether people 'think of themselves' as environmentalists, in a way that could be differentiated from whether they actually held environmentally concerned beliefs.

Respondents then answered a battery of questions comprising a 'concern inventory', loosely based upon an environmental inventory created by Weigel and Weigel (1978), but updated to measure more contemporary issues. Finally, media use was reported by each respondent. In addition to amount of television viewing, frequency of viewing of television news and newspaper reading were also measured. Television viewing was measured on a five-point scale, ranging from 'less than half an hour a day' to 'more than three hours a day'. News reading and news viewing were also measured on five-point scales, ranging from 'almost never' to 'almost daily'. Additionally, the third and fourth sample added measurements for frequency of radio news listening and news magazine reading. The final sample included some demographic measures not present in the other samples to allow for more sensitive statistical control.

Reliability analysis for the entire inventory produced a high Cronbach's alpha of .85 in 1988, .85 in early 1990, .85 in late 1990, and .83 in 1992. Four sub-scales were created, based both upon conceptual decisions and exploratory factor analyses. The specific scales were:

- 'Environmental optimism', six items which asked respondents to state their agreement with statements that predicted the future environmental health of the planet (for example, 'We shouldn't be too concerned about things like acid rain and the ozone layer, because they will take care of themselves in time'); 1988 alpha = .77, early 1990 alpha = .70, late 1990 alpha = .72, 1992 alpha = .71;
- Four items addressing the 'Relative importance' of environmental issues compared to economic and technological progress (for example, 'The good things that we get from modern technology are more important than the bad things like pollution that may result'); 1988 alpha = .63, early 1990 alpha = .62, late 1990 alpha = .63, 1992 alpha = .65;
- Four items composing an index of attitudes towards 'Specific issues' which are the focus of much contemporary activism and concern (for example, 'Companies should stop using plastic for

food packaging, even if it costs consumers more at the grocery store'); 1988 alpha = .65, early 1990 alpha = .72, late 1990 alpha = .69, 1992 alpha = .68; and
* Three items assessing the perceived potential 'Personal impact' respondents feel they have in affecting the environmental situation (for example, 'It doesn't matter what I do, the environmental problem is too big for any one person to have any impact'); 1988 alpha = .41, early 1990 alpha = .40, late 1990 alpha = .51, 1992 alpha =.53. The Personal Impact measure reveals quite low internal homogeneity. Data for this measure will be reported but should be interpreted with caution.

Findings

In the first two samples, all media exposure levels remained statistically constant. Between early and late 1990, however, our surveys registered a decline in TV viewing, which we provisionally attribute to the change of sample sites from a public to a private university. Thus, the results from the first two samples are not completely comparable to the latter two samples. However, despite these differences, it will be seen that the relationships were remarkably similar across the first three samples, with only the fourth sample suggesting the possibility of change.

As we might expect, there was an increase in baseline levels of environmental concern between 1988 and 1990. Table 9.1 shows that in all categories of concern measured there were monotonic increases in environmental concern between 1988 and late 1990, particularly for concern about specific issues and for the general inventory itself. Compared to 1988, respondents in early and late 1990 felt less optimistic about the future of the environment, and ascribed greater relative importance to environmental matters. Thus, as measured by these samples and as would be hypothesized, environmental concern increased between 1988 and 1990.

Table 9.1 *Changes in environmental concern, 1988–92*

Scale	Scale values: 1988	early 1990	late 1990	1992	F ratio	sig.
Scale items						
Overall inventory	63.71	67.38	69.68	66.93	17.46	p<.001
Optimism	22.27	23.25	23.58	22.78	6.71	p<.001
Relative importance	14.63	15.47	15.74	14.99	8.62	p<.001
Issue concern	12.88	14.20	15.62	14.94	37.73	p<.001
Personal impact	10.65	11.39	11.70	11.23	10.65	p<.001

Note Scale ranges: Overall inventory:18–90; Optimism: 6–30; Relative importance and Issue concern: 4–20; Personal impact: 3–15. High values signify greater concern.

However, this level of concern dropped between 1990 and 1992. The overall inventory registered a nearly three point drop, bringing the measure back to below where it was in the late 1990 sample. This is due to the fact that economic issues had replaced environmental ones in the minds of most Americans, and perhaps especially the college students in this last sample. While people were still calling themselves environmentalists, they were objectively less concerned when measured on a variety of important environmental issues. Although these data can not be the last word on the subject, the cyclical and fragile nature of public opinion, particularly with regard to the environment, is demonstrated.

To what can we attribute these fluctuations in concern? While the overall level of concern did increase notably over the first three samples, these samples nevertheless showed significant negative associations between overall television exposure and environmental concern. The tests with the detailed inventory of environmental concern show that heavier viewers, as a rule, were less environmentally concerned than their lighter-viewing counterparts. Correlations between media usage and the environmental attitude scales are shown in Tables 9.2 and 9.3. For the overall inventory in the 1988 and 1990 samples there is a moderate, negative and significant association between amount of viewing and environmental concern that stands up under controls in the first three samples. Moreover, the same pattern holds for each of the inventory's sub-scales, again in the first three samples. In the case of the 'Optimism' measure, we see a relationship between heavy viewing and the tendency to believe that the future of our environment is secure. Heavy viewers were also less concerned about the 'Specific issues' which threaten the environment. With respect to the 'Relative importance' index, the negative relationship indicates that heavy viewers tended to assign less importance to the environment than to other issues. Heavy viewers also tended to see themselves as having less 'Personal impact' on the environment (though, recall the low alpha for this measure).

Table 9.2 *Partial correlations of television viewing with environmental attitude scales, 1988, 1990 and 1992*

Index	1988 n = 105	early 1990 n = 165	late 1990 n = 523	1992 n = 230	All samples
Overall inventory	−.22*	−.18*	−.18***	−.05	−.19***
Optimism	−.19*	−.12	−.14***	.00	−.13***
Relative importance	−.19*	−.14*	−.13**	−.05	−.14***
Specific issues	−.19*	−.16*	−.16***	−.01	−.19***
Personal impact	.16*	.15*	.11**	−.07	−.14***

Note Controlling for age, sex, political affiliation and political activism.
*** p < .001; ** p < .01; * p < .05

Table 9.3 *Partial correlations of news viewing and newspaper reading with environmental attitude scales, 1988, 1990 and 1992*

Index	1988 $n = 105$	early 1990 $n = 165$	late 1990 $n = 523$	1992 n = 230	All samples
TV news viewing					
Overall inventory	−.06	−.12	−.12**	.06	−.09**
Optimism	−.10	−.16*	−.08*	.06	−.06*
Relative importance	−.02	−.10	−.10*	.03	−.07*
Specific issues	−.11	−.09	−.04	.14*	−.04
Personal impact	.04	−.04	−.08*	−.05	−.06*
Newspaper reading					
Overall inventory	−.05	.04	.00	−.03	.05
Optimism	−.04	−.04	.01	.03	.03
Relative importance	−.16*	.00	−.09*	.06	−.02
Specific issues	.03	.10	.02	−.11*	.09**
Personal impact	−.02	.02	.01	−.07	.02

Note Controlling for age, sex, political affiliation and political activism.
*** p < .001; ** p < .01, * p < .05

Thus, most correlations with amount of television viewing were negative and significant, indicating that heavier viewers consistently express lower levels of environmental concern. The patterns were remarkably consistent between the three samples, despite significant overall increases in environmental concern in those years.

This suggests that for those in our first three samples, television viewing was not contributing to environmental concern, and did in fact seem to be retarding it. However, in the final and most recent sample, the negative relationships we saw with television viewing and environmental concern were not present. In fact, the partial correlation coefficients were all close to zero and were non-significant. The relationships did not become positive, but the data suggest that some years of marginally increasing concern in television programming is having some impact, at least in the types of samples we have measured. However, the fact that the negative relationships disappeared in years when absolute levels of concern decreased should point out that television is not a monolithic factor in the formation and maintenance of public opinion. We also measured negative relationships in years when concern was increasing, suggesting that there were other sources of communication contributing to the increase. Now, as we have measured a decrease in concern, we do not observe the negative television–concern relation.

Of course, it may be that television viewing is too broad a construct and that it would be necessary to measure more specific kinds of viewing to observe relationships with environmental concern. While we feel the overall exposure measure provides needed and over-looked information about this problem, we also measured news viewing and newspaper reading to compare any possible relationships. As Table 9.3 shows, and in contrast to overall television exposure, exposure to news media (electronic and print) was less related to environmental attitudes. Typically, we would assume that television news viewing would actually add to environmental concern, by virtue of its increasing portrayals of these important issues (see LaMay and Dennis, 1991, for essays on this issue). In fact, our studies showed that amount of television news viewing showed generally negative but weak and sometimes non-significant associations with environmental attitudes, especially in the first three samples. However, the final sample showed a non-significant but positive relationship, reversing the trend of the three previous samples. This reversal was especially notable on 'issue' environmental concern, where respondents expressed opinions on specific environmental issues, many of which receive more play in the press than other, less tangible, environmental problems. In general, though, heavier news viewers were not more environmentally concerned.

Frequency of newspaper reading was not significantly associated with environmental concern for the most part in any sample year. Again, only on specific issues was there any hint of a positive relationship, although the patterns have varied without stability across the samples and do not warrant much conclusion.

Thus, level of news media usage does not appear to be responsible for increased environmental concern in our respondents, when objectively measured with a variety of attitudinal questions. We should note however, that respondents in our sample have increasingly come to term themselves 'environmentalists'. When we began these studies, heavy viewing respondents were less likely to *say* they were concerned about the environment, when that concern was measured with the 'one-item' measure. This was remarkable because environmental concern was one of the few issues (among all the various issues in which environmentalism was embedded) where we could even observe a significant relationship. The fact that it was negative was somewhat disturbing. Over the years, that negative relationship has decreased and is now in fact a small positive relationship, although not significant. It may be that television viewing is related as much to how people *perceive* themselves environmentally as to how people actually think about environmental issues.

It may also be argued that television viewing would be likely to be associated with an overall lack of concern for all kinds of issues, because television in general cultivates alienation and stifles activism. This was not observed in these data. We divided the various issues which were presented to respondents into two categories: environmental and non-environmental. For the most part, viewing was positively associated with concern about non-environmental issues while negatively associated with environmental issues. This suggests that television does not uniformly cultivate 'non-concern'.

Additionally, we looked at associations with environmental concern and television in various sub-groups to examine whether there were important or amplified patterns in these various groups. Figure 9.1 presents one of these analyses, using political activism as a control. We wanted to see whether the respondent's perception of his or her own political activism was an important factor in relation to environmental concern across different levels of viewing. This analysis is presented for the entire combined data set.

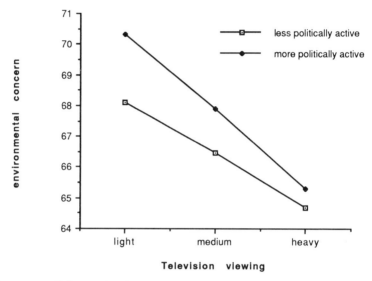

Figure 9.1 Relationship between viewing and environmental concern, by political activism

Figure 9.1 shows that environmental concern decreases as viewing increases, both for people who were less and more politically active. However, the decrease was steeper among politically active respondents, producing an overall pattern termed 'mainstreaming' in the cultivation literature. Mainstreaming suggests that one of the impacts of television is to produce agreement in groups of heavy viewers who would otherwise disagree based upon other demographic characteristics. In this case, political activism differentiates high from low concern to an extent, but the difference in concern is narrowed significantly among heavy viewers. The suggestion is that television's consistent stream of messages is associated not only with simple changes in attitude, but can also draw groups closer to the cultural mainstream which television represents. According to these data, the television mainstream is closer to the lower end of the concern scale.

Discussion

The results of this study contradict the common sense notion that media are the main forces by which environmental concern will be increased, since increases in environmental concern were registered while negative relationships were being observed. Even with regard to press coverage, the extent of a relationship is extremely small.

In relation to television viewing and environmental concern, the data suggest that the overall ideological message of television is either contradictory to the newly emerging environmental ideology, or (if the last sample is indicative of an upcoming trend) perhaps catching up with some of the tenets of this ideology. Of course, there are other factors which could play a role in the relationships we observe. For instance, heavy television viewers are probably simply less likely to go outside, and so they have less personal investment in and understanding of environmental problems. In any case, we are not suggesting that television viewing *causes* lack of environmental concern. We are suggesting, however, that television is a key player in the way the culture receives and interprets messages, and messages about the environment are no exception to this rule. Thus, television's role, if not directly causal, is as a systemic factor which can work against environmental improvement in a cyclical fashion.

How would this cycle work at the individual level? Assume that we start with an individual who is, as many people are on the average, uninformed about environmental problems and not very likely to do much about them. If this person is a heavy viewer of television, most entertainment programming will not suggest that the person change his or her ways; after all, this kind of person is ideal as a television consumer. Television might not have caused the lack of environmental concern (it was hardly caused; it was a mental feature of twentieth century existence) but it certainly reinforced it.

Now if we assume that this person is a lighter viewer of television the force of one of the main cultural story-tellers is lessened, and there is greater chance for exposure to environmentally concerned messages: in the alternative press, in interpersonal communication, and even just in communication between the individual and the environment.

Indeed, it would seem that the less we mediate our communication with the environment the more we are likely to see it as a real problem. Media should serve an environmental function as much as they can, especially by extending the reach of our awareness. However, the actual awareness must begin from an objectively real basis. Mass media, in so far as they can provide only a simulacrum of a real environmental experience, are not the only or best solution.

Indeed, we might wonder whether the media can produce a situation where people believe they are saving the environment if they adopt media-endorsed strategies: recycling and purchasing 'environmentally friendly' products are examples of things that can be done without challenging the dominant paradigm. More and more companies are claiming to be friendly to the environment, and the symbolic environment has been flooded with blue and green images whose general message is that the environmentally friendly future is a corporate one. Oftentimes these messages seek to interpret environmentalism within the context of the current paradigm, preserving the general notion that consumption is a valid social goal.

It is worth noting that these messages are increasingly being directed at children. For instance, 'Jaws', a character in Burger King's 'kid's club' advertisements announces his environmental policy: 'Jaws is my name and my number 1 favorite thing is protecting the environment. That means I make sure my food comes in bio-degradable packages . . . And I throw my trash away!' Jaws then asks: 'What are some ways you can protect the environment *and* do your "fave" things?' Clearly, the emphasis is on accommodation between environment and fast-food fun; no potential danger to the anti-environmental paradigm is posed.

The future of communication research about the environment will have to address this process, continuing to monitor the success with which we communicate to ourselves about this most grave problem. The evidence of this chapter is that there is a considerable distance to travel down this road.

Acknowledgements

As data were collected for this study, versions of this chapter were presented at the meeting of the Eastern Communication Association in 1989 and at the American Psychological Association in 1990. I would like to thank Michael Morgan and Julie Dobrow, who were co-authors of these earlier versions, for their excellent contributions to this work. I would also like to thank Anniken Naess who has provided invaluable assistance in the collection and analysis of these data.

References

Carveth, R., Alexander, A. (1985), 'Soap opera viewing and the cultivation process', *Journal of Broadcasting and Electronic Media*, 29, pp. 259–73.
Cox, M. (1989), 'TV is giving star status to environment', *Wall Street Journal*, 3 October, p. B1.
Diamond, E., Mead, R. (1989), 'Is TV news getting all the dirt?' *TV Guide*, 24–30 June, pp. 20–22.
Dunlap, R.E., Van Liere, K. (1984), 'Commitment to the dominant social paradigm and concern for environmental quality', *Social Science Quarterly*, 65, pp. 1013–28.
Filis, P. (1992), 'TV: The greenest ad medium', *Electronic Media*, 6 January, p. 86.

Gerbner, G. (1990), 'Advancing on the path to righteousness, maybe', in N. Signorielli and M. Morgan (eds), *Cultivation analysis: new directions in research*, Beverly Hills, CA: Sage, pp. 249–62.

Gerbner, G., Gross, L. (1976), 'Living with television: The violence profile', *Journal of Communication*, 26, pp. 173–99.

Gerbner, G., Gross, L., Morgan, M., Signorielli, N. (1980), 'Aging with television: Images on television drama and conceptions of social reality', *Journal of Communication*, 30 (1), pp. 37–47.

Gillroy, J., Shapiro, R. (1986), 'The polls: Environmental protection', *Public Opinion Quarterly*, 50, pp. 270–79.

Greenberg, M.R., Sandman, P.M., Sachsman, D.B., Salomone, K.L. (1989), 'Network television news coverage of environmental risks', *Environment*, 31 (2), pp. 16–20, 40–43.

Gross, L. (1984), 'The cultivation of intolerance: Television, blacks, and gays', in G. Melischek, K. E. Rosengren and J. Stappers (eds), *Cultural indicators: an international symposium*, Vienna: Verlag der Osterreichischen Akademie der Wissenschaften, pp. 345–63.

Hansen, A. (1991), 'The media and the social construction of the environment', *Media, Culture, and Society*, 13, pp. 443–58.

Hickey, N. (1990), 'TV's campaign to clean up the planet'. *TV Guide*, 21 April, pp. 20–26.

LaMay, C., Dennis, E. (eds) (1991), *Media and the Environment*. Washington, DC: Island Press.

Lippmann, W. (1922), *Public Opinion*. New York: Harcourt Brace.

McGeachy, L. (1989), 'Trends in magazine coverage of environmental issues', *Journal of Environmental Education*, 20, pp. 6–13.

Meadows, D. (1991), 'Changing the world through the informationsphere', in C. La May and E. Dennis (eds), *Media and the Environment*, Washington, DC: Island Press, pp. 67–79.

Morgan, M. (1982), 'Television and adolescents' sex-role stereotypes: A longitudinal study', *Journal of Personality and Social Psychology*, 43 (5), pp. 947–55.

Morgan, M., Gross, L. (1980), 'Television viewing and reading: Does more equal better?', *Journal of Communication*, 30 (1), pp. 159–65.

Perse, E. M. (1990), 'Cultivation and involvement with local television news', in N. Signorielli and M. Morgan (eds), *Cultivation Analysis*, Newbury Park, CA: Sage.

Pirages, D.C. Ehrlich, P.R. (1974), *Ark II: social response to environmental imperatives*, San Francisco, CA: Freeman.

Rothschild, N., Morgan, M. (1987), 'Cohesion and control: Relationships with parents as mediators of television', *Journal of Early Adolescence*, 7 (3), pp. 299–314.

Shanahan, J. (1992), 'Green but unseen: Marginalizing the environment on television', Paper presented to Mainstream(s) and Margins conference, Amherst, MA.

Weigel, R., Weigel, J. (1978), 'Environmental concern: The development of a measure', *Environment and Behavior*, 10, pp. 3–15.

10
The circulation of claims in the cultural politics of environmental change

Jacquelin Burgess and Carolyn M. Harrison

In 1989, a development consortium led by a subsidiary of the Music Corporation of America (MCA) announced plans to build a 2.4 billion theme park, film studios, housing and commercial development on a site legally designated for nature conservation at Rainham, Essex. Information about the project entered the public domain in June 1989 after several months of secret negotiations between the developers, national and local politicians, land owners, and statutory agencies. The history of the project was complex, involving political activity at international, national and local levels. The scale of the proposal meant that the scheme had implications for the national economy of the UK, as well as that of the London region as a whole, and the local economies of the London Borough of Havering (LBH) and south Essex. The case had all the elements of a classic conservation struggle: inadequately financed and marginalized environmental groups or non-governmental organizations (NGOs) fighting the might of multinational corporate power, supported by a national government anxious to attract inward investment regardless of the consequences. Not surprisingly, the conflict was reported widely in the national, regional and local media.

Our research has focused on the material and symbolic processes involved in both the production and consumption of media discourses about the scheme. Here we explore the circulation of claims about the economic and environmental implications of the proposed development by tracking how actions and rhetorical claims made by the developers and the voluntary organizations were encoded in national and local media, and then taken into local discourses. We shall show how the development consortium was able to establish 'green credentials' and thereby gain ascendancy over the conservationists opposing the scheme. Finally, we will demonstrate how different audiences evaluated and appraised these competing claims in the contexts of their lived-cultures and daily lives.

Re-integrating producers, texts, consumers and contexts

Sociologists have highlighted the importance of claims-making in the social construction of environmental problems but their researches have been concerned primarily with the production and representation of claims in the mass media rather than with questions of audience reception. To complete the circuit (Johnson, 1986; Burgess, 1990), field research methods drawn from cultural studies and ethnography offer the best means of understanding the ways in which different audiences make sense of media products within the contexts of everyday life. We shall review briefly both strands of work before introducing our case study.

Claims-making and the social constructions of environmental problems

It is widely acknowledged that environmental events do not map easily within traditional news values and representational practices. Apart from spectacular natural disasters like earthquakes or hurricanes, environmental changes are complex, long term and slow acting. In recognition of this fact, a number of authors (Schoenfeld, Meier and Griffin, 1979; Hilgartner and Bosk, 1988; Hansen, 1990; Yearley, 1991) have argued that the environment has been constructed as a social problem through the claims-making activities of a variety of institutions and agencies. Claims-making thus encompasses the tactics of organizations seeking coverage, the definition and launch of campaigns, staged events and other media management strategies (Greenberg, 1985). It also requires the analysis of the ways in which claims are represented in different rhetorical forms (Best, 1987). Through increased media coverage of these claims which are mapped into the pre-existing hierarchy of news values, specific environmental problems gain political and social saliency. Thus, Hansen argues, the current importance of environmental problems such as ozone depletion and global warming:

indicates that, rather than focusing on the time scales of individual environmental problems in relation to a conventional notion of news value, it is necessary to focus on claims-making activity in relation to environmental issues, and, crucially, to focus on the ways that mass media interlink with the societal fora in which such claims-making activity takes place. (Hansen, 1991, p. 449)

The MCA case study contained several traditional newsworthy elements which ensured coverage in a wider range of media than normal. First, the connection with Universal Studios meant show-business celebrities and Hollywood provided a number of hooks for stories in the popular press. Second, the case involved competition tinged with elements of chauvinism and prejudice because MCA had options on two sites – Rainham and another in Paris near EuroDisney. What was required to secure the development against the French option became a major issue for journalists in the national and local media. Third, the consortium consisted of an American multinational, entertainments conglomerate and British Urban Development (BUD) – a consortium of UK construction/development companies – who were 'politically correct'. The director Hartley Booth was a close personal friend of Mrs Thatcher (then Prime Minister). The partnership with BUD ensured that the economic and political claims made for the development would mesh well with the dominant thinking of the day and therefore, the political agendas of national newspapers supportive of Conservative Party ideology.

The processes of determining plans for development projects are a particular form of claims-making in which different media play a central role. From initial sketches and physical models through to articles and debates in the mass media, proposals about alternative futures for a site involve different claims which need to be evaluated. Relatively little is known about the choice of communicative strategies used to promote or contest a planning proposal (Appleyard, 1979). It is important to understand how the mass media represent the meanings of dominant and subordinate groups caught up in the cultural politics of environmental change, and how these meanings are transformed by audiences in different public and private contexts. The cultural studies literature and, especially, the new qualitative work on audience reception provides some helpful guidance.

Cultural studies perspectives

The move towards qualitative research methodologies in media and cultural studies over the last decade has come from recognition of the need to naturalize audiences within their everyday settings, to find ways of 'combining interpretative studies of people's "lifeworlds" with attempts to map the contours of the wider formations that envelop and organise them' (Morley, 1991, p. 1). This refusal to separate texts from contexts marks the development of studies which are often grouped generically under the title 'audience reception studies' (Morley, 1989; Jensen 1990; Moores, 1990). They are characterized by a fundamental shift from the privileged readings of media texts by theoretically informed academics to field research in which different audiences are consulted about their own readings and interpretations. There are many reasons why this shift should have occurred, not least the widespread recognition of the central role played by media in articulating national and local cultures. The media are an integral part of everyday life, contributing to collective processes of 'making sense' in different social contexts, localities, class and cultural formations. What characterizes the new developments in audience research is the attempt to capture the richness and diversity of 'readings from below' (Seiter et al., 1989, p. 10) in empirical research.

Interest is growing in empirical studies of consumption of media, both as texts and as technology, at the household/family level (Lull, 1990; Silverstone, 1991). Silverstone describes an 'intermittent audience', arguing that people are not only constituted as audiences but they are 'firmly embedded in the social and cultural environment of both public and private spheres. Their involvement with media . . . is both an expression and a constitution of the relationship between these spheres' (Silverstone, 1991, p. 143). Silverstone and his colleagues (Silverstone, Hirsch and Morley, 1991) argue that the family and household constitute the primary communicative environment in which decisions about media consumption are made. But other communicative environments such as work-places and leisure venues are also influential in terms of understanding how meanings are made and how audiences are constituted. 'Talking about television programmes and what has happened in them is essential to making a programme popular and part of the cultural capital of general discourse' (Hobson, 1989, p. 167). Our own research focuses on the significance of the lived-culture of localities in understanding the ways in which audiences transform media communications (see also Smith, 1985).

Developing an ethnographic approach

Field research into audience reception usually involves the production, transcription and analysis of talk: informal, more or less unstructured conversation between people, often in the context of focus groups (Corner, Richardson and Fenton, 1990; Livingstone and Lunt, 1992). The term 'ethnography' is currently being used to describe a number of different methodological strategies in media research (see Jensen and Jankowski, 1991; Silverstone, Hirsch and Morley, 1991). However, many studies are not truly ethnographic because they do not establish any long-term involvement with the communities being studied. Ethnographic research should combine observational and participatory activities with the production of an analysis of oral-visual and written texts, everyday speech and communications to elucidate the bases of local knowledge and experience within a given locality. Further, ethnographic research requires a focus on the practical actions taken by members of the culture over time.

In developing an ethnography of the conflict over Rainham Marshes, we wished to track the ways in which different individuals, institutions and groups, construed both as 'producers' and 'consumers' of media communications, determined their courses of action and developed their discourses. We were particularly interested in discovering how the development consultants for MCA and the NGOs used the media to achieve their goals (Harrison and Burgess, 1992). At the same time, we wished to explore how members of the local community evaluated the two cases and the extent to which their beliefs and attitudes about environmental changes were reinforced or challenged by different media communications.

Briefly, the research strategy covered the period April 1989 to April 1991, by which time it was obvious that the parent company in America was no longer interested in the site. The continuous elements of the research programme included participant observation at all the staged media events and local public meetings; repeated, informal interviews with the key actors including the consultant for the developers, local authority planners, campaigners of the NGOs, and local journalists; and monitoring/transcription of national and local press and broadcast coverage of the Rainham marshes issue over two years. Discrete research activities were mapped onto this basic frame and were focused primarily on working with the local population in Rainham. We conducted a household survey in January 1990 to ascertain local opinion about the scheme. Following the household survey, we recruited two in-depth discussion groups: each met for six sessions of one and a half hours each during the spring and autumn of 1991 (Burgess, Harrison and Maiteny, 1991, p. 502–4). The first 'lay' group comprised ten local men and women who largely supported the MCA scheme; the second was also composed of ten men and women who lived in the locality but these were all paid-up members of nature conservation and environmental organizations. Finally, a series of semi-structured interviews were conducted with the environmental correspondents of national newspapers in the early part of 1991.

The rhetorical conflict: competing claims in context

A simple content analysis of the media texts produced about the MCA scheme would lead to a thin and ahistorical account of the events. Stories connected with MCA ran in the national press over the period 1989–91, Figure 10.1. Peaks of coverage signified a number of different events: press conferences in June 1989 to announce interest in the site and November 1989 to announce the submission of a planning application to LBH; a flurry of press releases from the NGOs between September and the decision by Christopher Patten (then Secretary of State at the Department of the Environment) in April 1990; the destruction by fire of Universal Studios in Hollywood and the takeover of MCA by Matushita which occurred in November 1990. A similar distribution of coverage occurred in the broadcast media. Coverage in the local press was much more intense. Stories, editorials and letters about the scheme were published almost every week in the local paper over the period May 1989 to April 1990.

A closer reading of the newspaper texts in conjunction with the press releases issued by MCA and the NGOs produces a more interesting account of the cultural politics underpinning the debate about the marshes. To summarize, the local press engaged with nature conservation issues from the day the story broke officially. It was clearly stated in reports that the site was designated as a site of special scientific interest (SSSI) for nature conservation and that conservation groups opposed the scheme. The conflict became one of the major newsworthy aspects of the story but the conservation arguments were always subordinated in the paper's discourses. This subordination was achieved in one or more of three ways; first, the nature conservation issue was mentioned at the end of articles and reports, indicating its lesser importance (van Dijk, 1988); second, when objections from NGOs constituted the main item of a report, a counter-story from MCA was always run with it on the same page; third, the editor wrote a series of strongly worded editorials in favour of the scheme over the period (see Burgess, 1992a).

At a national level, the coverage by broadsheet and popular papers was much more variable and the key elements of the story changed over the nine month period June 1989 to April 1990 (see Figure 10.1). When the story first broke, there was no mention of the nature conservation importance of the site in any of the national papers. The conservation case rose up the national press agenda relatively slowly. Three press releases from the NGOs issued in September finally triggered one story in *The Times* (9 October 1989) and a piece in the *Observer* colour magazine. After the November launch of the planning application, the majority of press reports failed to mention the status of the site, while those who did positioned it at the end of their reports. The only exception was *The Independent* which led on NGO opposition to the scheme. Two more overtly critical conservation-led features followed in the *Morning Star* (6 December 1989) and *Evening Standard* (2 January 1990).

Thereafter the conflict between the developers and the conservation groups came to dominate the reports in the national press until the Secretary of State announced that he would not call a public inquiry. This slow response of the national press highlights the problem media personnel have in categorizing environmental stories because, for several months Rainham was covered by financial, local government and media correspondents, as well as ordinary staff reporters. This meant that the political significance of the conservation case was lost on the majority of journalists dealing with the story (Burgess, 1992b). Second, the history of coverage supports Hansen's (1991) analysis of the importance of societal fora in framing

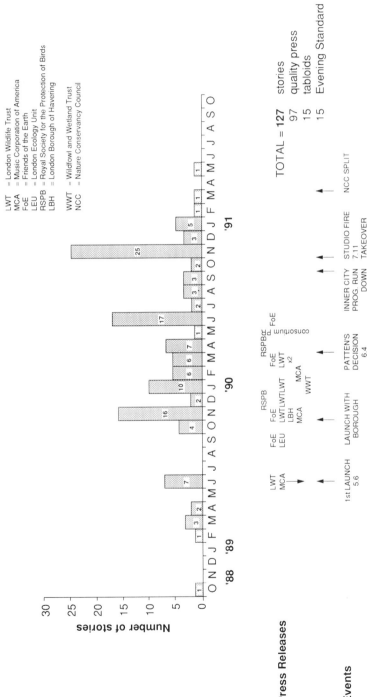

LWT = London Wildlife Trust
MCA = Music Corporation of America
FoE = Friends of the Earth
LEU = London Ecology Unit
RSPB = Royal Society for the Protection of Birds
LBH = London Borough of Havering

WWT = Wildfowl and Wetland Trust
NCC = Nature Conservancy Council

TOTAL = **127**   stories
            97   quality press
            15   tabloids
            15   Evening Standard

Figure 10.1 Rainham in the national press

environmental news. The critical breakthrough in terms of the coverage of Rainham came when connections could clearly be made between the local case and national politics. The then Prime Minister, Margaret Thatcher stood damned from her own mouth for a comment about the importance of SSSIs. She had said at an international conference on 6 September 1989: 'We have made great efforts to identify areas of special scientific interest because of their animal and plant life and others which are environmentally sensitive – and we have taken steps to protect them.' Yet here was her Government apparently actively colluding in the destruction of one such site. This statement was first brought to journalists' attention in a press release issued by Friends of the Earth (FoE) in September 1989. The quote was eventually used as the first paragraph of the *Morning Star*'s story (6 December 1989) and later, as we have shown elsewhere (Burgess, Harrison and Maiteny, 1991) formed a key element in the documentary produced by London Weekend Television (LWT). Further political elements made the story stronger and more attractive to the news desks. *The Independent on Sunday* ran a piece suggesting that the agreement to sell public land to MCA was in breach of government rules. Finally, Christopher Patten (then Secretary of State for the Environment) was apparently under considerable political pressure. On the one hand, he could satisfy the environmental groups and call a public inquiry, in which case MCA said they would choose Paris. On the other, he could decide to approve the application and keep the option open for MCA, in which case the Government's own stance on nature conservation and environmental protection would be cruelly exposed.

Developing and using claims

The economic case

The proposal by MCA was the latest in a series of options for the marshes all of which had been contested by the NGOs. This pre-existing oppositional context put pressure on MCA, at least in the crucial early stages of project development. The overall strategy of the developers was determined by the need to gain time and ascendancy in the debate about the SSSI. The reality was that the developers proposed to *destroy* approximately 890 acres of the 1,200-acre SSSI. How were they to achieve political and public acceptance for that destruction without being forced into a lengthy public inquiry about the costs and benefits of their application?

The parent company in the USA had an overall game plan based on competition between the London and Paris sites. By funding two separate development teams to take the proposals through to completion, the American company put intense pressures on the UK government, the local authorities, the development consortium and its contracted consultants, and the local community in Rainham. The threat was always present: if the UK government agreed it would be necessary to hold a public inquiry into the application, then MCA would choose the Paris option. But the major uncertainty for the UK development consortium was whether the Nature Conservancy Council (NCC) with statutory responsibility for SSSIs, and the NGOs would be able to mobilize public opinion sufficiently so as to compel the local authorities to turn down the application, or to force central government to concede an inquiry.

MCA never deviated from the position that it was still considering the two sites while working hard to justify that the economic benefits of their scheme outweighed the environmental costs. In all its public statements, economic claims for the development were based on 'big numbers': the scale of the investment (2.4 billion pounds), the number of jobs (14,000), the number of tourists (5 million a year), the range of attractions (better than Florida). The reputation of the companies involved and their different expertises were lauded; the support of major commercial and media institutions, including the BBC and British film industry, and widespread political support for the scheme at national level were cited; the importance of the development for the locality, the London region and the country as a whole was stressed. The competition between London and Paris was blended with Hollywood celebrities in the national media. Locally, the press was exultant: *MEGA STARS MEGA JOBS* the banner headline shouted on 9 June 1989.

In public, there was little dispute about the economic benefits of the proposal. National NGO campaigners found it difficult to argue against the economic case. To say publicly that such a development was not needed would have been foolhardy politically, and so the NGOs were forced into a defensive stance of accepting the economic case for the development but arguing about where it should be located. As an activist said at the public meeting between MCA and conservationists: 'It's not what you want to do but where you want to do it.' Similarly, the Royal Society for the Protection of Birds (RSPB) issued a press release on 11 December 1989 in which their campaigner said: 'It is insane to replace the last vestige of London grazing marsh with a development which could just as easily be sited on derelict land or surplus farmland.' The press release provided the main elements of a story in the *Evening Standard* under the headline 'Park plan could sink marshland sanctuary' (2 January 1990). The above quote was used in the report and functioned to give legitimacy to the economic claims. And yet, as the MCA consultant admitted many months after the scheme died, the economic claims were 'theoretical' as they were based on projections of future economic trends. He commented that it would have been difficult to substantiate some of the figures had he been challenged.

The nature conservation case

While the power to define economic benefits resided with MCA, the authority of claims over the environmental and nature conservation case resided with the NGOs and NCC. Despite this, MCA had several advantages: surprise, exceptionally strong contacts throughout central government, a local authority anxious to see a development on the site, a large budget, and the NCC reeling from the shock announcement in July 1989 that it was to be split into three. The strength of the scientific claims for the marshes were never fully explored, in public at least, because the upper levels of NCC refused to enter any public debate. One of the London regional officers of NCC did play an important role, however, by attending NGO meetings and providing scientific material for press briefings. Only after the matter was decided did NCC representatives appear on television to object that the development would destroy the scientific interest of 66 per cent of the Inner Thames Marshes SSSI. The acute observation made by a journalist writing in the specialist journal *Planning* suggests either an amazing ability to read the future – or a mole. '*Planning* understand that the Nature Conservancy Council may not ultimately object as long as a number of key safeguards are incorporated into the project' (9 June 1989, p. 1). These 'safeguards' ultimately became enshrined in a mitigation package negotiated between MCA and NCC which was worth 16 million pounds and retained 428 acres of the SSSI.

The main elements of the NGOs' case were established in a series of press releases over the period. These were backed up by an authoritative briefing paper on the flora and fauna of the marshes produced by the NCC officer who had done the work which led to site designation in 1986. The case combined scientific evidence with assertions about the significance and value of the site. In the way MCA used big numbers, so did the NGOs. Much was made of the size of the site (1,200 acres); the number of species of birds recorded (170), the number of rare and threatened species of invertebrates (30) and wetland plants (20). A number of claims are to be found in the press releases: the Marshes are described as 'the last substantial area of a now rare habitat', possessing 'a very rich population of birds and plants'. The reduction in size of the SSSI is described as being 'catastrophic for the capacity of marshes to support its rich variety of wildlife'. In the June and September press releases, Rainham was described as 'one of the best wildlife sites in Greater London'; 'the most important wildlife site in London'; and 'one of the largest SSSIs in London'. The scale of destruction was said to be 'unprecedented' and 'catastrophic for nature conservation', while MCA's expressed concern for nature conservation was described by the NGOs as 'cosmetic'.

MCA establish their green credentials

It could be argued that the NGOs did have one advantage in the crucial early stages of the proposal. The lead consultant of MCA responsible for finding the site and achieving planning permission did not have any environmental experience and was on a rapid learning curve while also trying to hire consultants with the appropriate expertise. On the other hand, the NGOs and the NCC regional officers were already mobilized to fight a separate public inquiry about the marshes. They had good local intelligence and the scientific field evidence to substantiate the case for the SSSI. When the LWT campaigner first heard that MCA were announcing their interest at a restricted press conference in June 1989, he alerted regional television companies and was interviewed in a news item which foregrounded the conservation value of the site. The MCA consultant commented privately that he would not debate with the campaigner in the media because 'I'd lose hands down. He's an expert and I'm not.'

Aware of their vulnerability on conservation issues, MCA quickly appointed a specialist firm of ecologists to collect and evaluate the biological data on the SSSI, and to prepare a package of measures to ensure the overall acceptability of the scheme. But, while buying time, the developers also needed to reduce the possibility of local and national public opinion hardening against them. The tactic was to play down the conservation status of the site while somehow acquiring sufficient expertise to suggest they were sensitive to environmental concerns and competent to deal with them. First, MCA made no mention in their June press release that the site was an SSSI or had nature conservation value. Second, and more importantly, they manufactured a set of green credentials by claiming half way down the second page of the three page release: 'MCA, *which also manages Yosemite National Park* in the United States, and BUD are sensitive to the need for full consideration of local existing environments and amenities around the chosen site' (our emphasis).

The implication was that MCA had direct responsibility for managing nature in Yosemite, one of the prime wilderness parks in the USA. This was not strictly true. In fact, a subsidiary of MCA owned a concession for visitor services in the park which included hotels, restaurants and campgrounds, subsequently valued at 300 million dollars in the takeover of MCA by Matushita (*The Guardian*, 2 January 1991, p. 12). So, MCA did not 'manage Yosemite'. It was responsible for the commercial operations which included some environmental input in terms of visitor safety, for example, and preventing disturbance of animals but not the day-to-day ecological management of the park. This resided with the US National Park Service. This sleight of hand was never challenged by any of the NGOs or environmental correspondents. It served MCA well in the critical early stages of the development.

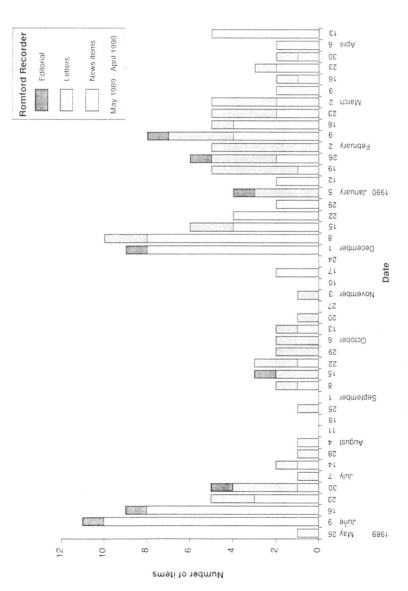

Figure 10.2 Rainham in the *Romford Recorder*

None of the national press in June 1989 even mentioned the environmental issue. By contrast, the local weekly paper (*Romford Recorder*) dealt very fully with environmental and conservation issues from the beginning (see Figure 10.2). Factual information about the status of the site as an SSSI and reasoned arguments from NGOs were published regularly, although as we have shown elsewhere (Burgess, 1992a) the discourses of the paper were biased in favour of the developers. 'Yosemite' was of major significance in the local campaign as it was fought out in the pages of the local paper. Specifically, it gave the company the green credentials they needed. On 9 June 1989 for example, the *Romford Recorder* ran a story about opposition to the scheme under the headline 'Group slams "barbarism"'. The second story on the same page had the headline 'Nature is safe say company' and substantiates the MCA assertion that the ecology of the marshes will be 'protected' by reference to the Yosemite claim.

The following week, the editor of the paper came out more strongly. Referring to 'emphatic opposition from local conservation bodies' he wrote: 'I feel their reaction is a typical "knee-jerk" one. The Hollywood organisation has vast experience of managing nature reserves, for which it has won awards' (*Romford Recorder*, 16 June 1989, p. 4). This 'fact' comes from an attributable briefing by the development consultant published as a separate story: 'Plan will boost marsh: award winners slam attackers'. The MCA consultant is quoted as saying that the environment will be enhanced by the development because: 'Our record in America shows MCA cares for the environment. We have managed the Yosemite National Park since the 1930s and have won numerous awards for our work there' (*Romford Recorder*, 16 June 1989, p. 7).

The transformation in MCA's case over the critical six months between the first public expression of interest in the site and the submission of a planning application at the beginning of December was revealed in their November press conference. The environment had moved up the agenda and was mentioned in the first paragraph of the MCA press release. The development 'will be the centre of a conserved landscape, given over to ecological and recreational use'. Nationally, this increased attention was politically expedient to reduce opposition in Parliament. Locally, it represented a response to the debate which had run throughout the summer and autumn in the weekly paper at a time when the plan was due to go to public consultation. Further, MCA had to demonstrate that the local authority were taking the conservation case seriously and were responding to the demand by the strategic planning agency for London (LPAC) that NCC should be consulted on how much land was needed to maintain a viable SSSI within the development. Based on detailed evidence from their ecological consultants, the main claim of the company for the project had expanded dramatically. Now the development apparently would offer a greatly improved quality of life for both people AND nature. The grounds of this claim were based on evidence that the site was currently used largely as an official and unofficial rubbish and silt tip and as a military firing range. The warrants for the claim were acceptance that: the development would be an improvement aesthetically; it would offer the controlled use of the land; and that MCA could deliver this improvement (another allusion to the Yosemite credentials).

The fact that the site is an SSSI was mentioned half way down page 5 of the release: 'a considerable area of the existing site is designated as a Site of Special Scientific Interest (SSSI) but there is substantial pollution and deterioration of the environment'. Speakers at the press conference iterated claims made in the press release which emphasized plans for the 'enhancement and restoration of natural landscapes and habitats together with plans for keeping 310 acres of Thames Grazing Marsh. This is to be kept in perpetuity and managed as a nature reserve in order to protect and enhance the existing habitats of the area. These are currently deteriorating.' The rhetorical purpose of these claims was to challenge the assertion of the NGOs that the whole site, as an SSSI, was important and valuable. The consultants managed to shift the grounds of the argument to consideration of the relative importance of different parts of the SSSI.

The press conference was very well attended. Journalists' questions, not surprisingly given that the majority were financial correspondents, concentrated on the London–Paris competition and precisely when, why and how MCA would choose one site in preference to the other. The conservation issue arose only towards the end of the conference and in muted terms. There were twelve reports in the national press with all but one emphasizing the Hollywood connection in their headlines and the competition with Paris in the body of the text. Only one paper (*The Independent*) framed the story in terms of the conservationist's fight: 'Marshland fight likely over 2bn theme park' (30 November 1989).

Over the next few months, there were hectic rounds of public meetings and many private negotiations between MCA, NCC and other interested parties to agree a mitigation package so the scheme could go ahead without formal objections from the NCC. Meanwhile the NGOs began a letter-writing campaign to senior MCA representatives in America, and to pressurize Patten to call a public inquiry. They staged an event on the steps of the Department of the Environment to submit a petition to the Minister. Individuals dressed up in costumes from Universal Studios films and although the event attracted little media coverage, the event brought the issue of an inquiry up the agenda and attracted more attention from environmental correspondents. Although the NGOs lost their case – LBH approved the application and Patten finally decided against a public inquiry they had the eventual satisfaction of seeing the case framed as an environmental conflict. Virtually all the national reports of events between February and April 1990 led with the wildlife designation of the site. Paul Brown, the environment correspondent of *The Guardian* for example, wrote in his report of 23 March 1990: 'The development would be on the biggest site of special scientific interest (SSSI) in the London area and is seen by wildlife groups as a fundamental test of principle on whether such statutory designations give real protection to the environment' (p. 4). The NGOs' case was finally made.

How local people made sense of competing claims

To interpret the ways in which different audiences made sense of the conflict, it is essential to understand the changing political, social and media contexts within which they were situated. Crucially, the MCA proposal was not produced in a geographical and cultural vacuum. Indeed the whole case history demonstrates the profound importance of understanding how the global – in this case, a multinational conglomerate with a huge amount of symbolic as well as material capital – is incorporated in, and transformed by the local. We want to illustrate how the claims identified above were articulated and refracted through the experiences and lived-cultures of local people in Rainham.

Claims about the benefits of the proposal and its impact on the environment were in the local public arena in a variety of different communicative forms throughout the period: plans, diagrams, pro-motional videos, an expensive glossy brochure, press releases and conferences, press reports, radio interviews, television broadcasts, magazine features, and public meetings. Camera crews visited local schools, helicopters filmed the marshes, people were asked to sign petitions, write to their MPs, talk to us. These different communica-tions permeated the locality and the lives of local residents who, in turn, gossiped and argued about them at home and in many different social contexts. People evaluated the cases of the developers and the environmentalists on the bases of their local culture, local knowledge and practical everyday experiences. For several months, the pros and cons of the MCA scheme were the most important item on the local agenda. Much of the argument and debate focused on the current value of the site for 'nature' when weighed against the economic, social, cultural and environmental benefits that would, apparently, accrue from the MCA scheme.

But these debates must also be understood within an historical context. There had been a history of struggle over the site which had a significant bearing on the ways in which local people and their political representatives responded to MCA and the conservationists. Briefly, the key moments of immediate relevance here are that the SSSI had been designated in 1986 after several years of dispute between the local authority (who wished to develop part of the site they owned) and the NCC/NGOs. Additionally, the Department of Transport proposed to reroute a major trunk road over the marshes and away from the village of Rainham itself. The A13 has a damaging effect on the quality of life of local residents. The great majority had welcomed the road proposals despite an intensive campaign by conservation groups to save the marshes from the road. These events had all received extensive coverage in the weekly paid and free local press.

This recent history was highly influential in determining the strategies of MCA and the NGOs, and the ways in which local people made sense of media coverage of the scheme. Most importantly, the NGOs were already positioned by local people as being more concerned to save the wildlife and habitats of the marshes than improving the quality of life of local people. As a woman said at the start of the first public meeting: 'What about the people who live here? What about us? Talking about conservation, don't forget, we need to be conserved, too!' Although there was considerable antipathy towards the local authority for allowing part of the riverside site to be used as a refuse dump for Westminster, and doing nothing to control illicit motorbike scrambling on Rainham marshes itself, the desire by the authority to attract inward investment to improve local prospects was largely welcomed.

Our household survey of 251 Rainham residents conducted in January 1990 showed that public awareness of the MCA proposal was high and that most people (61 per cent) had first heard about the proposal through the local press. By contrast only 8 per cent of respondents had attended any of the public meetings. The two in-depth group discussions held through the summer and autumn of 1990 revealed a pattern of media consumption in which the local press was unself-consciously incorporated into discourse on an equal footing with other forms of social interaction and exchange. 'They say' and 'people say' were phrases used routinely in discussions when group members were in fact drawing on information given in the local press. But there was much more often an acknowledgement of national media sources which 'distanced' them from everyday life in the locality. Often, this would surface in critical reaction to the ways in which the place itself was being represented. Referring to the proposed LWT documentary, for example, Kate said:

It will be interesting to see how they portray Rainham because I know the back page of *The Guardian* about 6 weeks ago, had a picture and it said: 'Rainham Marshes, where they might be building this theme park'. And it was awful because they'd taken it through a horrible wooden box that's all broken or something. And it just looked like a dump. . . . Although it's not entirely misleading, it is somewhat misleading because it isn't ALL that dumpy and it could be quite nice. It was a deliberate ploy.

This comment articulates a more general mistrust of the national media which was evident in the discussions of both our groups and supports observations from other audience reception studies (Corner,

Richardson and Fenton, 1990; Wren-Lewis, 1985). Individuals rely on the media for much of their information about the world but do not trust them, and tend always to privilege their own practical everyday experiences and knowledge over the 'public' comments of national media.

Evaluating the economic case

At one of the public meetings, a local resident commented that 'this development will secure the future of the area. It won't be chemicals and industries. It's a nice development. It will secure the future for ever.' His views were widely shared. The members of our lay discussion group were also prepared to accept the developers' arguments about the anticipated economic benefits the theme park would bring, not least because they resonated with their own perceptions of the economic needs in the locality. Reflecting widely held views, members were angry and anxious about the lack of existing employment opportunities available locally for both themselves and their children. The new jobs associated with the development were construed as tangible and realizable benefits that would otherwise not be available. They were prepared to believe that the scheme was soundly based, would work and would improve the image of the area. But they also remained resolutely sceptical about the real motives of the developers. Further, the group members, again reflecting comments made often in the community, were well aware of the futuristic nature of the claims being made, and indulged in humorous fantasies about filmstars talking to local people 'over the garden fence'. The group based its assessment of the economic claims primarily on accounts of members' personal experiences of visiting Disneyland and Universal Studios in the US. In all these discussions, the media provided a pervasive background of information and impression-formation but only very rarely would people refer directly to an item in the media, unless to establish a common ground for debate.

By contrast the group of environmentalists were not prepared to accept the economic claims advanced by the developers. Much of their discussion was devoted to demonstrating why the vision of society advanced by the developers conflicted with the world envisioned by environmentalists. Group members challenged the assumptions, underlying motives and goals associated with promoting economic growth rather than sustainable development. For these members of the public, the MCA scheme represented the height of 'consumerism' which in turn was identified as the problem underpinning MCA's case. At the same time, these committed conservationists were much more willing privately to question the basis of MCA's economic claims. For example, members agreed with Sarah's view when she said:

I read . . . that jobs would be created but they would be on a short-term basis. While the thing was being built. Once it WAS built, we're then looking to specialist people coming in from outside. So the actual job creation would be very short-lived. And I thought that was pulling the wool over the eyes of the local population.

In this sense, environmentalists contested the economic claims of the developers from a standpoint of conviction. But they were also drawing on their own considerable competence in contesting the validity of media reports through their cumulative lived experiences as active campaigners.

What to believe about conservation

Members of both discussion groups shared a healthy scepticism about the environmental claims made by MCA. Neither group were prepared to accept uncritically the claim that 'nature would be safe with MCA' as the local headlines had professed. For example, members of the lay group were dubious about MCA's ability to 'create nature' out of the huge rubbish tip covering part of the site. The company had promised to turn this into a new ecology park by creating a variety of different habitats. That was almost as fantastic as having Steven Spielberg walk down Rainham High Street.

Tom	This is the area they're going to make their Ecology Park, isn't it?
William	That's right.
Tom	(laughing) Well they've got a job there haven't they?!
Vicky	They'll have to import the insects!
Tom	If they can make an Ecology Park out of that, then I think it's worthwhile doing it to get rid of that tip.

Similarly there was scepticism about MCA's general expertise in the field of conservation and, interestingly, no one in either group ever made explicit reference to the 'Yosemite' claim. Kate, for example, said:

I'm not convinced about this ecology bit. Because I know somebody that's seen the proposal plans and HE says – I mean he was talking to some conservationist fella. And he says, on the plans the lake appears to be half way up a hill. Which doesn't seem very practical to me. Which tells me that maybe their heart's not in it.

The group of committed environmentalists, too, were completely dismissive of the developer's mitigation package. Using sophisticated arguments which exposed the limitations of attempts to put a price on what was to be lost, the notion that one unique site could be substituted by other sites and that creative conservation could provide equivalent opportunities to those which would be lost, this group gave no credence to MCA's environmental claims. Pippa expressed the central concern of the group when she said:

I think the thing that makes me MORE angry – I mean, obviously the fact that these things are disappearing – but the fact that future generations aren't going to know they were there in the first place. So they're never going to have the benefit that we've got now. And I think that's sad.

True to beliefs and concerns of the nature conservation movement in this country, the group of committed conservationists did not contest the claims made by environmentalists about the threat to species and habitat the development posed. Familiar with the justification for the SSSI designation by the NCC, there was consensus within the group about the need to conserve the site in its entirety. By contrast, members of the lay group were much less ready to accept the environmental claims made by the NGOs, especially those arguments associated with the site's designation as an SSSI. We have argued elsewhere that the conservationists were remiss in not committing more time and effort to working with the local community and sharing what is widely perceived to be their 'secret knowledge' about nature (Burgess, Harrison and Maiteny, 1991; Harrison, 1992). The local paper, with its in-built bias against the conservation case, was in fact primarily responsible for conveying information about the site. As Gillian said; 'I never knew that this was err, umm – is it SI? – until all this started up about MCA . . . I had no idea that I had that on the doorstep.' Most of the lay group rejected the conservationists' arguments, widely reported in the local paper and rehearsed in the LWT documentary, that there was wildlife on the site worth preserving. Further, they refused to accept the claim that species would be lost if the development were to go ahead. As Lucy remarked: 'How do they really know that these birds and insects and everything are just going to disappear? How do they know?'

During the life of the lay group, each member had watched the LWT documentary in their own home. The film had illustrated the range of plants and animals living on the marshes and after watching it all the members of the group were prepared to admit that there was more wildlife on the marsh than they had previously believed. Similar comments were made by some of the committed conservationists, too. But on its own this information and the arguments advanced by the environmentalists did not persuade the group that the development should be opposed. Drawing on their local knowledge of the site as a rubbish dump populated only by rats, mice and mosquitoes, and taking a lead from arguments advanced in the local press by environmentalists which took little account of the concerns of local people, the lay group marginalized both the scientific claims and the general veracity of the conservationists. As Vicky put it:

That's why I can't understand the big fuss that people are making – about how wonderful these marshes are. Because most of them have never been here. They've never seen what a mess it is. . . . So at least, if they build this and they build the ecology bit, you'll be able to walk around that and at least see the wildlife which is more than you can do now!

But more than this, we can show a specific instance in which the representational practices used routinely in television documentaries seriously undermined the credibility of the conservationist's case. The LWT documentary contained stock library footage of bird species that could be found on the marshes. There was no indication on screen that these were library shots, the material was simply edited into a number of interview segments. The lay group slowly realized what had happened:

Tom	. . . even if it was part of Rainham. IF it was. I mean, you saw some birds. Were those birds actually THERE or were those birds photographed somewhere else?
Kate	But you got the impression that . . .
Vicky	You're kidding! They weren't all there, them birds. (agreement)
Nick	But I suppose this is legitimate film practice, isn't it?
Vicky	Naw, they weren't there when they filmed 'em. If they were there for a whole week, they wouldn't have seen that many birds. (agreement)
Tom	It was deception really. Because you're turning round to the public and saying "this is what you're going to lose", you know?
Vicky	Yeah. "All these millions of birds. We've only been here a couple of hours and look what we've seen.". . . But I suppose that's television full stop. You watch it and most of it is a load of rubbish. I mean, you see what they want you to see.
Tom	They can tell you whatever they want.

The nature conservation argument about the 'richness' and 'variety' of birds, insects and plants on the marshes ran counter to local people's experience and understanding of the marshes. Rainham marshes is coded as 'a dump' in the local culture, without any 'nature'. It became necessary to find ways of resisting the conservationist case which had been put strongly in the LWT documentary. As the extract of discussion reveals, this audience was able effectively to do so through its rejection of standard wildlife film practice as 'a deception'. Further, the deception itself was mapped into a stronger resistance to being 'duped' by the agents of television. In this instance rather than helping people to understand the nature conservation case, the LWT documentary reinforced the local belief that the conservationists were outsiders without any real knowledge of the marshes, and that their case was indeed based on a lie (Burgess, 1991; Burgess, Harrison and Maiteny, 1991).

Conclusions

Our case study demonstrates the value of an ethnographic approach for revealing the cultural circuit of claims-making about environmental change. In particular, the research has shown the fundamental importance of situated knowledge in the production and consumption of media texts. Without an understanding or appreciation of these contexts, it would not be possible to make more than a superficial reading of the media coverage of the Rainham story. The study reveals how individuals and agencies involved in the production of texts about the conflict were also consumers of those texts, adjusting their claims and their tactics in response to their own readings of the effectiveness of media coverage on their opponents and 'public opinion' at large. There can be little doubt that the media played a significant role in the evolution of the environmental claims associated with the Rainham case.

But our ethnography also reveals how deeply embedded in people's lives the media have become and how seldom are media claims instrumental in opinion formation. Whether broadcast or text media, national or local, this study demonstrates that audiences rarely discriminate among different media in terms of veracity; people are awash with communications, rarely paying direct attention to them and adopting a sceptical attitude towards both the content and the agencies who produce them. Confirming other studies, our research suggests that it is practical life lived locally which determines the sense that people make of media texts. This is especially true when the issue is one which affects the landscapes and settings within which people live their lives. People actively evaluate media claims using their own cultural values, experiences and local knowledge.

In the Rainham case, the single-mindedness with which the developers used the local paper to advance their environmental claims was matched only by the paper's willingness to engage in a stereotypical debate by marginalizing the conservationists. Local activists were framed as well-meaning but unworldly cranks; national activists as individuals interfering in something which was really none of their business. Had the conservationists chosen to challenge the economic claims advanced by the developer with this same single-mindedness in the local paper, they may well have been able to reframe this set-piece debate into wider societal and political fora. Without these counter-claims, the developer and the local paper, over the life of the debate, 'appropriated' the environmental arguments used by conservationists to the point where local audiences distrusted any environmental claims whether these were made by the developer or the NGOs.

In the national media, the NGOs were, eventually, able to position their environmental claims in a political forum precisely because 'the environment' had been placed on the political agenda after the Prime Minister's 'conversion' to sustainable development in 1988 (Anderson, 1991). In 1984, Lowe and Morrison suggested that environmental issues would continue to be covered in the national press for as long as 'the environment is taken to be a politically neutral area relating to the quality of life rather than its organisation' (Lowe and Morrison, 1984, p. 88). It is increasingly clear that the environment in the last ten years has been reframed as a political issue. Paul Brown, of *The Guardian* for example, discussed the problem of writing nature conservation stories with us. Dismissively commenting that any journalist on any newspaper could write a 'cuddly animal story', he then said, 'but you need an environmental correspondent to understand the political issues and what lies behind it' (Brown, 1991). But the Rainham case also shows that the political forum within which the story was mapped at national level was still one determined by traditional news values of political personalities and wrangles over national party politics rather than any broader critique of advanced capitalism as represented in the MCA project.

Acknowledgements

This research was funded by the ESRC and the NCC (grant no. W110251001) under the People, Economies and Nature Conservation programme. The interviews with national environmental correspondents were conducted by the Research Assistant for the project, Mr Paul Maiteny.

References

Anderson, A. (1991), 'Source strategies and the communication of environmental affairs', *Media, Culture and Society*, 13, pp. 459–76.
Appleyard, D. (1979), 'Understanding professional media: issues, theory, and a research agenda', in I. Altman and J.F. Wohlwill (eds), *Human behaviour and environment: advances in theory and research*, Vol. 2, London: Plenum Press, pp. 47–176.
Best, J. (1987), 'Rhetoric in claims-making: constructing the missing children problem', *Social Problems*, 34, pp. 101–21.
Brown, P. (1990), '£2bn theme park decision postponed', *The Guardian*, 23 March, p. 4.
Brown, P. (1991), Interviewed by Paul Maiteny, 15 February.
Burgess, J. (1990), 'The production and consumption of environmental meanings in the mass media: a research agenda for the 1990s', *Transactions, Institute of British Geographers*, NS15, pp. 139–61.

Burgess, J. (1991), 'Images and realities: the views of wildlife film audiences', *Image Technology*, 73 (12), pp. 472–5.

Burgess, J. (1992a), 'The cultural politics of economic development and nature conservation', in K. Anderson and F. Gale (eds), *Inventing places: studies in cultural geography*, Melbourne: Longman Cheshire, pp. 235–51.

Burgess, J. (1992b), 'Representing nature: conservation and the mass media', in A. Warren and B. Goldsmith (eds), *Conservation in progress*, Chichester: John Wiley, pp. 51–64.

Burgess, J., Harrison, C.M., Maiteny, P. (1991), 'Contested meanings; the consumption of news about nature conservation', *Media, Culture and Society*, 13, pp. 499–520.

Corner, J., Richardson, K., Fenton, N. (1990), *Nuclear reactions: form and response in public issue television*, London: John Libbey.

Greenberg, D.W. (1985), 'Staging media events to achieve legitimacy: a case study of British Friends of the Earth', *Political Communication and Persuasion*, 2, pp. 347–62.

Hansen, A. (1990), *The news construction of the environment: a comparison of British and Danish television news*, Leicester: Leicester University, Centre for Mass Communication Research.

Hansen, A. (1991), 'The media and the social construction of the environment', *Media, Culture and Society*, 13, pp. 443–58.

Harrison, C.M. (1992), 'Nature conservation, science and popular values', in A. Warren and B. Goldsmith, (eds), *Conservation in progress* Chichester: John Wiley, pp. 35–49.

Harrison, C.M., Burgess, J. (1992), 'Rainham marshes in the media', *Ecos*, 13, pp. 20–26.

Hilgartner, S., Bosk, C.L. (1988), 'The rise and fall of social problems: a public arenas model', *American Journal of Sociology*, 94, pp. 53–78.

Hobson, D. (1989), 'Soap operas at work', in E. Seiter, H. Borcher, G. Kreutzner and E.M. Warth (eds), *Remote control: television, audiences and cultural power*. London: Routledge, pp. 150–67.

Jensen, K.B. (1990), 'The politics of polysemy: television news, everyday consciousness and political action', *Media, Culture and Society*, 12, pp. 57–77.

Jensen, K.B., Jankowski, N.W. (eds) (1991), *A handbook of qualitative methodologies for mass communication research*, London: Routledge.

Johnson, R. (1986), 'The story so far: and further transformations?' in D. Punter (ed.), *Introduction to contemporary cultural studies*, London: Longman, pp. 277–313.

Livingstone, S., Lunt, P. (1992), 'Expert and lay participation in television debates: an analysis of audience discussion programmes', *European Journal of Communication*, 7, pp. 9–35.

Lowe, P., Morrison, D. (1984), 'Bad news or good news: environmental politics and the mass media', *Sociological Review*, 32, pp. 75–90.

Lull, J. (ed.) (1990), *World families watch television*, London: Sage.

Moores, S. (1990), 'Texts, readers and contexts of reading: developments in the study of media audiences', *Media, Culture and Society*, 12, pp. 9–29.

Morley, D. (1989), 'Changing paradigms in audience studies', in E. Seiter, H. Borcher, G. Kreutzner and E.M. Warth (eds), *Remote control: television, audiences and cultural power*, London: Routledge, pp. 16–43.

Morley, D. (1991), 'Where the global meets the local: notes from the sitting room', *Screen*, 32 (1), pp. 1–15.

Schoenfeld, A.C., Meier, R.F., Griffin, R.J. (1979), 'Constructing a social problem: the press and the environment', *Social Problems*, 27, pp. 38–61.

Seiter, E., Borcherz, M., Kreutzner, G., Warth, E.M. (eds) (1989), *Remote control: television, audiences and cultural power*, London: Routledge.

Silverstone, R. (1991), 'From audiences to consumers; the household and the consumption of communication and information technologies.' *European Journal of Communication*, 6, pp. 135–54.

Silverstone, R., Hirsch, E., Morley, D. (1991), 'Listening to a long conversation: an ethnographic approach to the study of information and communication in the home', *Cultural Studies*, 5 (2), pp. 204–27.

Smith, S. (1985), 'News and the dissemination of fear', in J. Burgess and J. Gold (eds), *Geography, the media and popular culture*, London: Croom Helm, pp. 229–53.

Wren-Lewis, J. (1985), 'Decoding television news', in P. Drummond and R. Paterson (eds), *Television in transition*, London: BFI, pp. 205–34.

van Dijk, T. (1988), *News as discourse*, Brighton: Lawrence Erlbaum Associates.

Yearley, S. (1991), *The green case: a sociology of environmental issues, arguments and policies*, London: HarperCollins.

11
Environmental communication and the contingency of meaning: a research note

John Corner and Kay Richardson

The influence of television news and current affairs reporting upon public understanding and opinion has to work through the meanings which its particular images, words and sounds help to generate in the viewer's mind. This is so, no matter how that irredeemably awkward term 'influence' is defined for the purposes of research. For there to be any chance of assessing what these meanings are, inquiry has to be made into the practices of audience interpretation, since television programmes do not contain meaning but act as dense and complex cues for its production. Given that audiences are differentiated, sometimes radically so, in the nature and use of the knowledge they draw upon when making sense of television, it is likely that interpreted meanings and values will show variation too.

In the context of current media theory, all the above propositions are relatively unexceptionable in basic form given a decade of research since the publication of David Morley's pioneering study of audience interpretation (Morley, 1980). However, the further hypotheses which might follow from them and their implications for research design and method continue to provide the field with its most intensive area of debate (see, for instance, Lewis, 1983; Dahlgren, 1988; Morley, 1989; Höijer, 1990; Jensen, 1990; and Corner, 1991). Given acceptance of them, inquiry into public communication as a process whereby form/content is translated into attitude/action becomes a good deal more slippery a business than might once have seemed the case. The propositions are central to what we can describe as a new emphasis on *contingency* in contemporary media research. By placing a more thoroughly theorized notion of meaning as social action at the centre of the analysis of public communication, research has been routed away from both the functionalist linearity of 'message flow' and structuralist fascination with a semiotically imperial 'text'. A concern with the *pragmatics* of mediation has thus begun to appear, alert to the disjunctions and variables of the public communication process but still wishing to pursue substantive, empirical research and to work with hypotheses which accord the media effectiveness and power.

How does inquiry into mediations of the environment fit into this broad picture of a rapidly developing research field? And within the mediating process (a process involving, first of all, a transformation into signs and symbols, then a transformation into meaning-for-the-viewer) what distinguishes environmental themes from other topics of public concern? Drawing on our own recent work on television portrayals and audience understandings of nuclear energy (Corner, Richardson and Fenton, 1990a, 1990b) we want to highlight some issues which seem to us to have broad implications for how the public meaning of the environment is sustained through the media. We also want to provide a few pointers for future research.

A brief summary of our research design and our findings is a necessary preliminary to this discussion, but before offering such a summary we will note here three general dimensions of the environment as a public issue which we sought to take account of and explore in devising our particular study of energy policy. As a recent overview suggests (Hansen, 1991), the environment is a news realm with distinctive features.

First of all, mediations of the environment are often characterized by a strong element of threat and risk, ranging from ill health to planetary death. This element is often central to the narrative structure of reporting and to the explicit or implied system of values behind the 'facts'. Second, following from this, many images and phrases used in coverage acquire a highly charged symbolic resonance, drawing on the central iconography of the culture (for example, those concerning 'nature' and 'death') and re-charged by frequent media usage. Third, given the scientific nature both of many perceived threats to the environment (for example, in our case, nuclear engineering) and the detection and assessment of such threats (for example, monitoring of radiation and the setting of 'safe dosage' levels) there is often a core of esoteric, 'expert' knowledge at issue in many environmental stories. The interplay between discourses of knowledge and the more directly symbolic discourse seemed to us to be of importance.

Television and nuclear power

In 1988 we began a study designed to explore how viewers made sense and significance of the nuclear power debate from its televisual or video representation. During the late 1980s nuclear power was high on the agenda of environmental issues (recent publications concerned with this topic include Cutler and Edwards, 1988; Mackay and Thompson, 1988). After Chernobyl, nuclear power was widely seen as a global threat, not to be confined within national boundaries, while the local dimension was given resonance in the worrying health statistics relating to communities close to nuclear plants. The industry itself made considerable efforts to counteract the bad news through positive promotion, including the production of video cassettes.

Thus it was not only in the domain of broadcast television that the topic received audio-visual representation. In addition to broadcast documentaries, our study looked at the industry's promotional tapes, and at materials from the independent video sector which were critical of nuclear policy. The programmes in question differed widely, and not just in being either supportive of the industry or critical of it. The interest of the comparison lay as much in the differences of formal and rhetorical organization.

This became very significant when looking at the responses of the audience groups who discussed selected items with us after video viewing. Most respondents participated as 'interested parties', thus one set were all Friends of the Earth members, another consisted of employees at Heysham nuclear power plant. Other groups came from political parties or from particular occupational categories. Interestingly, respondents in all groups criticized programmes for lack of fairness, if for different reasons. They did this even when their own sympathies lined up with the perceived bias. The programmes elicited from pro-nuclear groups anxieties which they shared with anti-nuclear ones. All group talk showed evidence of, and sometimes acknowledged, the *affective* powers of audio-visual representation – potent images, dramatic simulations, eloquent personal narratives. However, where it was acknowledged, there were different reactions to this affective dimension. Some groups objected that it inappropriately bypassed rationality. Others believed that emotional appeals would win viewers from indifference and ignorance.

In the next section we discuss three themes which emerged as important in the course of our research. Undoubtedly salient in relation to the topic of nuclear energy, the themes can readily be extended to the mediation of other environmental issues. Our treatment of them here varies in the extent to which we concentrate upon specific instances or the more general implications.

'Expert' and 'ordinary' discourse

As noted above, the coverage of many environmental topics requires the testimony of experts, the voice of science (and technology) to explain the complexity of cause–effect relationships, both those designed to be under human control and those which, like the greenhouse effect, are happening as an unplanned consequence of human activity.

But in reading expert testimony, different kinds of response are possible, as our study was able to show in some detail. It is true that in our culture, science is one form of authority that we are taught to respect, even when (and sometimes, perhaps, because) we cannot understand it. But it is not an unchallenged authority, particularly from the perspective of the new environmentalism. At one, apocalyptic, extreme this can produce a generalized sense of Western technological rationalism as the effective cause of the planet's material and moral crisis.

The voice of science can still, nevertheless, call up a deferential response from its audience. Experts on television purport to offer evidence and argument to support their claims, perhaps suitably translated into lay terms. The cogency of argumentation may then help convince viewers of the case being made. Yet in our research we also found viewers who accorded respect to argumentative *form* without having the capacity or desire to engage very deeply with its *content.* The former permitted viewers to infer that 'these experts know what they are talking about'.

The inability to judge scientific testimony is compounded when, as is now regularly the case in environmental matters, each side in the argument can produce its own independent experts. Where experts disagree, it is hollow to invite viewers to judge between them in terms of attributed expertise. Indeed, one possible reaction to such scientific controversy is a retreat into scepticism: 'If the experts can't agree, what price their expertise?' (a question currently not restricted to scientific topics, as debate about the economy clearly demonstrates). It is increasingly common for the voice of science to be sceptically received by lay publics. Science itself can be perceived as an interested party, interested at least in freedom to pursue its goals without challenge from outside the scientific community. Scepticism can also base itself upon the links between science and industry, for example where experts are industry employees. Even the spokespersons of government watchdog bodies (for example, the Nuclear Installations Inspectorate) are not categorically above suspicion, for the government is an interested party too.

Thus, in our material, one profoundly mistrusted expert was the then Chairman of the Central Electricity Generating Board (CEGB) and nuclear power advocate Lord Walter Marshall. His testimony was sympathetically framed in a CEGB promotional tape in which he was 'interviewed' by Brian Walden (all questions and answers having been discussed in advance of shooting). Even in this favourable context it proved impossible for most of our respondents to hear that ('interested') testimony as reassuring, to take his word that a Chernobyl-scale disaster was impossible in Britain, or that radiation was a minimal risk to health.

Scientific evidence typically takes a generalized, statistical form, remote from the level of personal experience. It is not uncommon for viewers to resist the former on the strength of the latter (see the variant viewer understandings of 'nature conservation' discussed in Burgess, Harrison and Maiteny, 1991, another recent audience study). And experiential evidence does not have to be at first hand to support such resistance. Mediated personal testimony can have a powerful effect upon viewers, against the grain of scientific discourse. The role of the ordinary person, particularly in programmes dealing with the consequences of specific events (Bhopal, Three-Mile Island, Chernobyl) is extremely important. Lay accounts can offer a density that scientific abstraction cannot match, as viewers hear about, and also see, the crops that failed, the animals that starved, the children who fell sick and lost their hair.

Both experts and ordinary people are seen on television as they are mediated through specific programme contexts. The viewing orientations of respect, scepticism and trust that we have discussed are orientations that can be prefigured in the texts themselves. But it would be wrong to assume that viewers invariably take the prefigured stance. What becomes interesting in relation to the mediation of accessed voices, expert and lay, is the extent to which purposive framings are perceived by viewers, and how they evaluate those purposes. When a BBC documentary is seen as setting out to cast doubt upon the testimony of an expert, as happened during our research, such perceptions feed into another, broader set of concerns to do with the assessment of programmes in relation to their civic integrity and/or persuasive intent. These concerns we address below, in the section on 'Framing'.

Symbolic resonance

The second broad theme which our work engaged with in an illuminating way, and which is worthy of more intensive research, is that of symbolic resonance. The idea of the symbolic is an awkward one in communications analysis, having a number of different literary and linguistic definitions which threaten clarity of usage. However, our use of symbolic here is meant to indicate the way in which, both in analysing the programmes and talking to viewers about them, we identified a powerfully associative, often metaphoric, level of meaning to be operative. This level ran alongside, and sometimes interconnected with, the explicit, rational processing of information and evaluation undertaken both by the programmes and the viewer/respondents. As noted earlier, the topic of nuclear energy, and more broadly, the realm of environmental news, resonate strongly within the terms of primary cultural classifications, such as 'nature', 'growth', 'dirt' and 'death'. This is because news about the environment is often articulated within the narrative dynamics of 'deep threat', however measured and technical the terms of specific description and assessment. Reporting of nuclear energy combines this factor with the awesome character (and profound non-naturalness) of the particular technology, whose key terms ('nuclear', 'fission', 'radioactivity') have popular connotations inextricably linked to the global nightmare of mass destruction. (Silverstone (1986) usefully explores the complexity and ambiguity of science/technology/nature imagery on television.)

Within the discourse of most of the material we examined, a symbolic contest was being carried on (mostly, if not always, with calculated strategic intent) in a way which was largely both irresolvable and unacknowledged at the explicit level of factual and evaluative debate. In our research report, we characterized this as the 'imagery of threat' since, first of all, it was largely through particular types of visualization (sometimes supported by music) that the symbolic level was mobilized and, second, a strong negative emphasis tended to set the terms for any positive counter.

Our examples included the opening scene of an ostensibly balanced, investigative documentary in the BBC2 series *Brass Tacks*. Here, a village close to a nuclear power station is depicted, through a sequence of shots underneath eerie electronic music, as already, 'on the brink of disaster'. This is achieved both through the juxtaposition of resonantly 'abnormal' objects (geiger counter, emergency plan leaflets, iodine tablets) with rural normality, and by the use of a film language drawing on those familiar cinematic devices by which the viewer is cued into recognition of the presence of the sinister.

Another scene which raised important questions came in a sequence from the same documentary where the symbolic resonance of 'radiation' was being contested both visually and verbally (for instance, a pro-nuclear participant asserted that radiation was everywhere in the world and was put there by God). The scene showed the lake adjacent to a nuclear power station, a lake whose surface steamed with the increased temperature caused by coolant outflow from the plant. The commentary noted 'the ghostly beauty' of this and then, as the camera slipped underwater, commented on what pollutants might be found in 'the lower depths'. The sheer strength of the figurative polarities mobilized here (surface/depth, visible/ invisible, beauty/menace) was enough to ensure that most of our respondents remembered and remarked on the scene, and that a number of them found it to be self-evidently damaging to the pro-nuclear case. After analysing respondent accounts, we concluded that a key element in this latter reading was the way in which the steam acted as an effective symbolic indicator of excessive radiation, working figuratively to close that which, at the explicit level of the programme's investigations, remained open to debate. Indeed, a few of our viewers performed a literal misreading here, taking the steam *to be* radiation.

Many other examples of a symbolic dimension – not debated but simply projected – could be drawn from our research on nuclear power (those concerning the depiction of waste and the problem of waste disposal being particularly strong in their projection). Moreover, the symbolic configuration within which the nuclear energy debate is set has altered steadily since the completion of our research (in 1989) as a result of the increasingly bad image of fossil fuels. A splendid example of pro-nuclear publicity, alert to the need to manage its discourse both at rational-scientific and symbolic levels, is provided by a recent British Nuclear Fuels advertisement in newspaper colour supplements (our example comes from the *Observer Magazine*, 10 November 1991). This features a large and detailed artist's depiction of a greenhouse bench, with its tools, pots and seed trays. One wooden tray contains, not seeds, but a perfect replica of a nuclear power plant, with its cooling towers steaming and cars and people in its open spaces. The main caption reads: 'There is one good plant in the Greenhouse'. While the detailed text below the picture discusses the problem of the 'greenhouse effect' and the consequent advantages of nuclear energy, this punning combination of image and caption attempts a deep reworking of that technology's cultural meaning.

Our work on this topic thus points to the need for research to avoid an over-rationalistic model of how mediations of the environment are organized and read. Earlier, we pointed to the way in which audience scepticism worked upon the reception of official rational-bureaucratic discourse; here we are talking about a mode of mediation which makes itself less detectable by those cognitive filters upon which scepticism depends. And far from the symbolic being a secondary feature of public discourse, the consequence of emotive 'overflow', it might be seen more productively as a principal organizing feature of discursive conflict. In particular, through the crystallizing capacities of visual depiction, it can connect the specific to the general with speed and effect, bypassing evidential reasoning and the proprieties of debate in the process.

Framing

In this section we want to focus upon the text–audience relation in such a way as to further develop the idea, central to modern media studies, that different viewers will approach the same programme with varying frameworks of interpretation. Such a 'frame' variation will produce not only different responses to the programme but also different readings of what it means – an awkward distinction which nevertheless needs to be made if audience research is to avoid a fundamental confusion between understanding and attitude (a point explored in recent critical commentaries, see Corner, 1991).

The first point to make is that both programmes and viewers use frameworks of interpretation. Therefore, audience research should be preceded by close textual analysis. We reject the notion that textual meaning is so radically indeterminate that analysts' readings of texts are illegitimate in principle (a point canvassed in Lewis, 1983). As well as inhabiting the same media-interpretative community as most 'ordinary viewers' at the most basic level of construing speech and imagery, analysts working on specific issues like the environment are often in a position consciously to contextualize media accounts within a range of other media and non-media treatments and thus to bring out the distinctive contours and features of any specific version.

Programmes are, of course, highly prepared texts and it may be that in understanding their discursive operations a greater coherence and consistency is to be expected of them than in the spontaneously produced talk of viewer/respondents. In an illuminating attempt at plotting frame variants in coverage of nuclear energy, Gamson and Modigliani (1989) concentrated upon the former, arguing that US media discourse on the topic has been organized into several distinctive interpretive packages, each with its own central propositional structure and its evaluative position on the issue. The authors' typology thereby usefully avoids a simplistic 'pro/con' approach to the analysis of mediated controversy; indeed its level of sensitivity to variables finally risks a reduced sharpness of differentiation between 'packages'.

The same difficulty of avoiding both a reductive pro/con schema and an over-elaborated one exists when the object of the exercise is to produce a typology sensitive to the frameworks of interpretation used by respondents rather than by programmes. The analytic difficulties are probably worse here, since respondent talk will move between frames in a more fluid way, given the unprepared nature of that talk, its nature as thought in process and the influences that group members can exert upon each other as the talk progresses. This was certainly true in our own case study.

For respondents, the task of interpreting a programme quite explicitly involves more than developing a position on the nuclear power issue. It can also involve such strategies as: relating programme material to their own personal experiences or temperamental predispositions (the personal frame, in our account); filtering what they see and hear through a grid of political, including environmental, concerns (the political frame); assessing arguments, narratives, images, statistics, people, etc. in terms of how these contributed to their knowledge about the issue (the evidential frame); judging the programmes according to criteria of balance and fairness (the civic frame).

The prevalence of the civic frame in our respondents' accounts we found particularly noteworthy. Balance and fairness are civic criteria premised on a model of the television audience in which viewers, as citizens in a democracy, are arbiters of public policy (Blumler, Dayan and Wolton, 1990, and Golding, 1990 offer recent arguments about the importance of making citizenship a more central issue in media research). Our viewers were reluctant to abandon the civic frame even for accounts originating outside the sphere of public service broadcasting, accounts that were under no legal obligation to be non-partisan. Such partisan versions were seen to assume, rather than to argue, their case (even when they pretended otherwise) and were thought unreliable for that reason – a piece of reasoning which, in our typology, provides a link between civic and evidential framings. No doubt the research context itself put respondents under some pressure to present themselves as both rational and, if not impartial, then at least fair-minded. Yet for that self-presentation to be successful, it requires respondents who know what to say (as ours did) when rationality and fair-mindedness are called for, in such specific terms that they could scarcely have been prepared in advance or entirely assumed for the occasion. Clearly, the capacity to produce civic readings is in potential conflict with the consequences of symbolic resonance, noted earlier.

Most recent audience research, ours included, has been conducted in the expectation of discovering interpretive variation and with the belief that variations may be explicable by reference to the socio-cultural location of viewers. But there is more than one way to conceptualize location (Brunt and Jordin, 1988, explore in some detail the problems this causes for reception study methodology). There is the macro-structural approach in which categories such as class and gender are taken to be primary variables and are, as it were, 'beamed down' on to the data to classify it. But, at best, without further sociological argument, this can yield no more than suggestive correlations. The more recent argument that understanding (and its variant framings) emerges according to the networks of discourse within which social identity and subjectivity are formed, requires one to hypothesize in advance the relevant 'discursive formations' (MacDonell, 1986, provides a useful theoretical starting point; for an attempt to rethink the issues and apply ideas regarding discursive formations in empirical research, see Frazer, 1987; also Davies, 1990). In our case this meant thinking about the kinds of occupations, interests and activities which might relate viewers differently to the topic being researched. Our project was partly successful in revealing how this relational variable worked, as interpretative action, across the different programmes viewed. However, we would have liked to have known far more about the precise sources (media and non-media) from which particular elements of understanding and response were fashioned. This clearly requires both a refined and more expansive research design.

Before concluding this note, there are two further, related aspects of method which we want to address briefly, since they have an important bearing on the primary conceptualization of reception inquiries. The first concerns how language and language analysis figure in such projects.

Audience research is commonly described as 'qualitative' if, among other things, it liberates respondents from the tyranny and limitation of yes/no and multiple choice answers to preformulated questions, and instead invites them to talk about their viewing. The worth of such data is largely lost if respondents' remarks are then just taken at face value, as straightforward 'evidence' of response. To avoid this, it is important to pay close attention to the language used in the articulation of responses. The interactional context – the play of discussion between group members who may have different reactions to viewed material – is relevant to the interpretation of individual comments. Moreover, citation and analysis of respondent comments should always be done in the light of the other things which that particular respondent said, which may suggest a complication or an uncertainty not evident in one extracted utterance, however self-contained it might appear. Finally, the significance of comments made may not always reside in overt propositional content, but in the implications that they carry. It is not necessary to declare 'I distrust these nuclear scientists' in order to convey an unmistakeable scepticism regarding a particular piece of expert testimony. All these points indicate methodological hazards for data analysis, but reception research cannot evade these except by limiting its explanatory potential.

The other issue concerns the degree to which audience studies should include study of 'single text' interpretation within their scope, that is to say the analysis of how particular items were read by viewers. Our assessment here is that however broad the research scheme may be in the materials and the themes it addresses, attention not only to how individual items were interpreted but also to how particular sequences in them were understood and reacted to is a vital component of media inquiry. Although there are dangers if 'micro-level' analysis of this kind is abstracted from the broader contexts both of programming and viewing, continued attention to this level is the only way in which we will get to know how, in detail, media representations interact generatively with viewer knowledge (Lewis, 1985; Richardson and Corner, 1986; and Burgess, Harrison, and Maiteny, 1991 demonstrate, in different ways, the value of continuing such work).

Environmental news-making and debate will continue to offer a challenge and an opportunity to media researchers, connecting with some of the primary concepts and theories (of news management, of representational convention, of influence) which constitute the field. At the same time, the realm of the environment is likely to grow even further in public significance, acting in many ways as an international test-case for assessing the flow and the form of public information and the creation and maintenance of fora for debate. Research on audiences has a role to play both in academic study and in the larger, public monitoring of environmental mediations. We think that our own study has been instructive in suggesting how this important work might best be developed.

References

Blumler, J. G., Dayan, D., Wolton, D. (1990), 'West European perspectives on political communication: structures and dynamics', *European Journal of Communication*, 5 (2–3), pp. 261–84.

Brunt, R., Jordin, M. (1988), 'Constituting the television audience: a problem of method', in P. Drummond and R. Paterson (eds), *Television and its audience*, London: BFI.

Burgess, J., Harrison, C., Maiteny, P. (1991), 'Contested meanings: the consumption of news about nature conservation', *Media, Culture and Society*, 13 (4), pp. 499–519.

Corner, J. (1991), 'Meaning, genre and context: the problematic of "public knowledge" in the new audience research', in J. Curran and M. Gurevitch (eds), *Mass media and society*, London: Edward Arnold.

Corner, J., Richardson, K., Fenton, N. (1990a), 'Textualizing risk: TV discourse and the issue of nuclear energy', *Media, Culture and Society*, 12 (1), pp. 105–124.

Corner, J., Richardson, K., Fenton, N. (1990b), *Nuclear reactions: form and response in 'public issue' television*, London: John Libbey.

Cutler, J., Edwards, R. (1988), *Britain's nuclear nightmare*, London: Sphere Books.

Dahlgren, P. (1988), 'What's the meaning of this?: viewers' plural sense-making of TV news', *Media, Culture and Society*, 10 (3), pp. 285–301.

Davies, B. (1990), *Frogs and snails and feminist tales*, London: Unwin Hyman.

Frazer, E. (1987), 'Teenage girls reading Jackie', *Media, Culture and Society*, 9 (4), pp. 407–25.

Gamson, W. A., Modigliani, A. (1989), 'Media discourse and public opinion on nuclear power: a constructionist approach', *American Journal of Sociology*, 95 (1), pp. 1–37.

Golding, P. (1990), 'Political communication and citizenship: the media and democracy in an inegalitarian social order', in M. Ferguson (ed.), *Public communication: the new imperative*, London: Sage.

Hansen, A. (1991), 'The media and the social construction of the environment', *Media, Culture and Society*, 13 (4), pp. 443–58.

Höijer, B. (1990), 'Studying viewers' reception of television programmes: theoretical and methodological considerations', *European Journal of Communication*, 5 (1), pp. 29–56.

Jensen, K. (1990), 'The politics of polysemy: television news, everyday con sciousness and political action', *Media, Culture and Society*, 12 (1), pp. 57–77.

Lewis, J. (1983), 'The encoding-decoding model: criticisms and redevelopments for research on decoding', *Media, Culture and Society*, 5 (2), pp. 179–97.

Lewis, J. (1985), 'Decoding television news', in P. Drummond and R. Paterson (eds), *Television in transition*, London: BFI.

MacDonell, D. (1986), *Theories of discourse: an introduction*, London: Blackwell.

Mackay, L., Thompson, M. (eds) (1988), *Something in the wind: politics after Chernobyl*, London: Pluto Press.

Morley, D., (1980), *The 'Nationwide' audience: structure and decoding*, London: BFI.

Morley, D. (1989), 'Changing paradigms in audience studies', in E. Seiter et al. (eds), *Remote control: television, audiences and cultural power*, London: Routledge.

Richardson, K., Corner, J. (1986), 'Reading reception: mediation and transparency in viewers' accounts of a TV programme', *Media, Culture and Society*, 8 (4), pp. 485–508.
Silverstone, R. (1986), 'The agonistic narratives of television science', in J. Corner (ed.), *Documentary and the mass media*, London: Edward Arnold.

Index